9/20/96

D0857859

Navalism and the Emergence of American Sea Power, 1882-1893

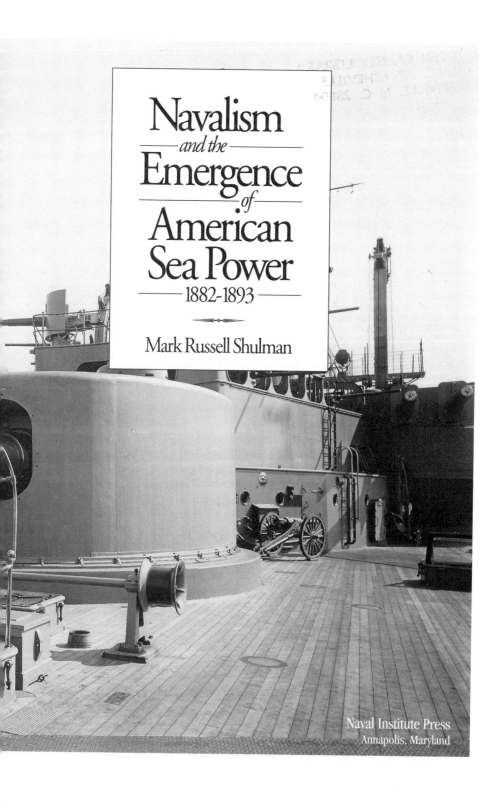

Navalism
—and the—
Emergence
—of—
American
Sea Power
—1882-1893—

Mark Russell Shulman

Naval Institute Press
Annapolis, Maryland

Library of Congress Cataloging-in-Publication Data

Shulman, Mark R.
    Navalism and the emergence of American sea power, 1882–1893 / Mark
Russell Shulman.
        p.   cm.
    Includes bibliographical references (p.   ) and index.
    ISBN 1-55750-766-X (alk. paper)
    1. United States. Navy—History—19th century. 2. Sea-power—
United States—History—19th century. 3. United States—History,
Naval—To 1900. 4. United States—Military policy. 5. United
States—Politics and government—1881–1885. 6. United States—
Politics and government—1885–1889. 7. United States—Politics and
government—1889–1893. I. Title.
VA58.S53   1995
359′.03′097309034—dc20   94-48539

Printed in the United States of America on acid-free paper ∞

02 01 00 99 98 97 96 95   9 8 7 6 5 4 3 2
First printing

Frontispiece: The forward 12-inch turret of the USS *Iowa.*
Unless otherwise noted, all illustrations are courtesy of the U.S. Naval
Institute collection.

To my family—
James, Katie, Joel, Stephanie, Bob, and Lee

Contents

Acknowledgments

This book, like the new navy, emerged from the efforts of many people on both American oceans. In their courses at Yale, Paul Kennedy and Robin Winks introduced to me the ideas of sea power and empire—daunting new views of the world. Then I was treated to the Oxford experience and further study of the British empire. Only upon my return to the United States did I begin in earnest my study of American culture, politics, and empire. At Berkeley, Richard Abrams, Diane Clemens, and Nelson Polsby taught me their own particular brands of American history. They encouraged and supported my interest and effort.

At Yale, Michael Howard and Paul Kennedy were extremely gracious, helpful, and supportive. My writing and rewriting has benefited greatly from suggestions from Kenneth Hagan at the Naval Academy, John Hattendorf at the Naval War College, Peter Karsten at the University of Pittsburgh, Ronald Spector at the George Washington University, and Jon Sumida at the University of Maryland, as well as John Beeler, Gaddis Smith, Bruce Russett, and Rebecca Ullrich at Yale.

This work has been supported financially by the history department of the University of California at Berkeley, the Eugene McCormac Fund, the Pittsburgh Center for Social History, the Naval War College Foundation, the John M. Olin Foundation, the John T. and Catherine D. MacArthur Foundation, and Yale's history department.

It benefited from comments on presentations to the University of Pittsburgh Department of History, the Society of Military History, the U.S. Commission on Military History, the American Historical Association, the Consortium for the Study of Intelligence, an SSRC/MacArthur workshop at the University of Texas, Austin, and Yale's Military and International History Colloquia.

I have also received invaluable assistance from and wish to thank numerous librarians, archivists, and curators, including those at the University of California at Berkeley (Doe and Bancroft), Yale (Beinecke, Mudd, and Sterling), Harvard (Houghton and Baker), the Naval War College (library and archives), the Naval Historical Center (library and archives), the Library of Congress (social sciences, music, and manuscripts), the Wisconsin State Historical Center (manuscripts), and the National Archives (Military Records Division).

Others who have helped me during the past several years include Roger Baldwin; Ron Yanosky; James Kettner; my Berkeley friends, especially Eric Friedman, Michelle Goman, Rie Takashima, and Tom Kerrihard; and my friends "back east," especially Susan, Howard, and Shirley Lamar, Jon Haidt, Diego Diaz, and Beth Knobel. As this book is dedicated to my family, I need not attempt to detail what they have meant to me.

Navalism and the Emergence of American Sea Power, 1882-1893

Introduction

The first major American peacetime military buildup (1882–93) created a new navy that inevitably and irreversibly reshaped the nation's role in world affairs. Since 1815, America had relied mostly upon Pax Britannica and the continent's natural defenses for the protection of national sovereignty. Most of the small regular army was scattered along the frontier while the militia remained on the books in case of mobilization to protect local order or to fight a major war. The small United States Navy provided a traditionally balanced defense that included commerce-raiding cruisers for an offensive defense, while boats, coastal batteries, and the local militia provided a defensive defense. In time of peace, the cruisers policed American trade and performed diplomatic functions, and the defensive systems remained on standby, costing little and threatening no one.

By 1893, an emerging internationalist agenda evoked a new strategy, with the United States independent of Britain's defensive umbrella and capable of undertaking its own offensive operations against the navies of other nations. Yet these changes reflected neither a split with the British agenda, nor a change in the importance of the natural land defenses. Rather, the new policies resulted from factors within America's political and strategic culture. Most sig-

1

nificant of these was the rise of navalism—the dedication to the creation of an imperial navy—among people in positions of power.

These navalists were part of a larger movement in late nineteenth-century American political culture—an elite rebellion against the longstanding commercial and agrarian national ethos. Taking up a century-old debate, they intended to replace the Jeffersonian democracy with a more Hamiltonian republic. Navalists, such as Theodore Roosevelt, James Russell Soley, and Alfred Thayer Mahan, saw America as the world's great hope, but only if its people could be made to understand the importance of its mission—a lesson apparently forgotten during the Civil War and Reconstruction. Navalists called for a navy to fulfill the nation's destiny, and by 1890 agreed that it should be a "blue-water navy"—a battle-oriented fleet of fighting ships. Taking advantage of a service aggressively rebuilding at every level—officers and men, ships and guns, public relations and even the nation's intellectual culture—navalists vastly accelerated America's emergence as a great power.

In one form or another, navalism had existed since the earliest days of the republic. Historian Craig Symonds noted of the early nineteenth century that

> navalists were men for whom the practical problems directly concerned with national defense were not the sole or even a primary consideration. Navalists were generally concerned with image, honor, prestige, and diplomatic clout. . . . Navalists yearned for empire, not only for purposes of economic exploitation, but also from a unique vision of what constituted national greatness. To them a naval fleet was physical evidence of national adulthood.[1]

But the navalists of the early nineteenth century focused their efforts too narrowly and, on the whole, were out of step with the increasingly democratic ways of the nation. Eventually they died off, and the drive to empire was subsumed in the conquest of North America. Resurgence of that impulse awaited the consolidation of that empire at the end of the Civil War and Reconstruction.

This book opens with the onset of the nation's first major peacetime military buildup in 1882 and concludes with the first of the new navy's overtly imperialist actions: decisive participation in the 1893 Hawaiian revolution by sailors and marines of the USS *Boston*. The approach is thematic rather than chronological. The first chapter, "The Influence of History upon Sea Power," examines how navalist historians paved the way for the buildup by generating new historical treatments of the War of 1812. The revised lessons emphasized the dangers of inadequate preparations for war, the inefficacy of land war, and the need to control the seas. Much like the siren call "Munich" several generations later, these historiographical changes directly supported the authors' political agendas, which advocated the creation of a large battlefleet to defend the nation's interests and to support increasing expansionism across the seas. Recasting a single historical interpretation, navalists reformulated the predominant intellectual rationale for the nation's geostrategic perspective.

The second chapter, "Cleaning Up the Act," examines how the Navy Department modernized its organization and facilities. Its administration abandoned obsolete management techniques to become competent and more cost-effective. Temporarily turning away from "pork-barrel" politics, the navy also reformed or reduced the administration at antiquated and corrupt eastern and southern yards, while opening new coaling stations and dry docks on the blossoming Pacific coast. Recruiting and educational practices also reflected the period's concern for rationalization and specialization. These changes typify the efforts to reorganize naval administration along the lines of efficiency and economy.

Selling the navy to the American people is analyzed in chapter 3. A broad range of venues for the popularization of the new navy included media campaigns in books and newspapers, as well as parades, exhibitions, and musical works. Among the most interesting texts are the boys' magazines, in which navalists conjured up romanticized visions of navy life: its ethos, heroics, and access to gee-whiz technology and travel. By 1893, the navy basked in a vast popular enthusiasm, based in part on the recasting of itself as the heroic representative of the nation.

The leaders of this new movement used technology to support an imperial agenda. Their desire for sensational machinery often undermined support for more practical tools of war. Martin van Creveld has labeled these pursuits "make-believe war" and "real war."[2] In general, contemporary naval construction plans in less-democratic powers tackled "real war" with greater enthusiasm: witness Britain's battle cruisers and Germany's U-boats.[3] Engrossed in "make-believe war," American navalists used technology to generate public appeal, frequently at the expense of "real war" military effectiveness. The navy also suited the changing worldview of the officers who designed it.

Chapters 4 and 5, on the navy's Pacific, present changing attitudes among naval officers regarding the Pacific Ocean based upon their diaries, letters, memoirs, and autobiographies. Midshipman David Dixon Porter joined his father's ship during the War of 1812 and eventually succeeded David G. Farragut as Admiral of the Navy, serving in that post from 1869 until his death in 1891. Porter's leadership provided a visible symbol of nostalgic and traditional service. Officers of Porter's navy viewed the Pacific as a place of physical challenge, where native peoples controlled their own destinies and where commerce was best based upon exporting fine goods to the United States. By the 1890s, these notions had been reversed for the officers of the new navy. The Pacific no longer represented a challenge to modern ships and men, while its peoples had become less individualistic and more like shadows: the region was valued more for its strategic position, as a field upon which the great powers would express a counterforce sea power rather than the countervalue warfare of the old navy. Mahan the officer represented this cultural shift, while Mahan the writer popularized and accelerated it.

Chapters 6 and 7 analyze the political debates over what type of naval construction and strategy the nation required. The subject is the traditional wartime strategy generally favored by the majority of the defense establishment, including many senior officers, congressional Naval Affairs Committee members, strategic writers in the press, and armaments manufacturers. Through the early 1880s, this strategy favored a coastal defense bolstered by the deterrent of cruisers, which would engage in *guerre de course,* or commerce raiding. During the mideighties, the navy altered its strategy, succumbing to pressures from navalists and a Congress that funded construction only of large ships. By 1886 the old strategy had been replaced by a forward maritime strategy in which the navy abandoned coastal defense. Chapter 7 discusses the formulation of this forward strategy, which by the early nineties had discontinued even commerce destroying in favor of battlefleets, or *guerre d'escadre*—the expressions of sea power popularized by Captain Mahan.

Chapter 8 analyzes efforts to oppose construction of a great navy. This opposition failed, in part, because of the effective popularization of the service, but also because the opponents of the new navy came from diverse backgrounds with often contradictory agendas; they could not agree upon what they *did* want. At various times, opponents included mugwumps, religious pacifists, and populists from the old Northwest and the Deep South: groups unlikely to coalesce into a strong political force. Never prone to understatement, Theodore Roosevelt characterized these people as "flapdoodle pacifists and mollycoddlers." In the end, Roosevelt had little to fear from the antinavalists.

Those opposed to the creation of an imperial navy failed to devote themselves to the education and political efforts their cause required. On the other hand, the navalists were intensely and personally devoted men with a great deal of institutional and political savvy. Although the attitudes and efforts of individuals will be discussed throughout this book, the major players should now be introduced. And while most of those discussed here were white, Protestant, male, upper-class graduates of either Harvard or Annapolis, the roster includes men from within the service's officer ranks as well as civilians. It encompasses Democrats and Republicans, some protariff and some opposed, southerners and Yankees, and men from a variety of social backgrounds.

Never members of a cabal nor even a society, navalists were united by the belief that a larger navy could only benefit the nation. Not until after the 1890 publication of Alfred Thayer Mahan's *Influence of Sea Power upon History, 1660–1783* did they even agree as to the shape of such expansion. Until then, their ranks included those, like Stephen Luce, who would have built cruisers and those, like Benjamin Franklin Tracy, who favored battleships. They encompassed Naval Academy professor James Russell Soley, who was interested in the education of sailors and officers, and former Harvard professor Henry Cabot Lodge, who had a much larger audience in mind. A navalist society could even have counted among its brothers former lieutenant colonel Hilary A. Herbert, who had led the Eighth Alabama Regiment during the Wilderness campaign against a Union army that included Col. Benjamin F. Tracy's 109th New York Volunteers. And yet such a society never existed.

Rather, American navalism reemerged during a historical moment in the 1880s when the nation seemed destined for greatness and sea power was the standard by which navalism would be judged as well as the tool with which it would be implemented. An examination of navalism's first dozen years affords insights into the dynamics of militarism, the degree to which politics, pork, and strategy are linked, and the interrelatedness of various social discourses in the early Progressive era. It also places the fame and impact of Mahan and his writings into a context from which his successors too quickly removed him. The cost of mounting him upon a pedestal has been paid many times over by the nation. In the past century, the Mahanian navy has proven to be the single most expensive organization ever, a status toward which it had been launched by 1893.

By the early 1890s, the United States had become a naval power. Certainly the impetus was provided by navalist elites, but at each stage, domestic politics and social constructs molded the shape and direction of American expansion. The complex negotiations between the leaders and the followers explains in part how a self-absorbed, inward-looking nation became an imperial power.

To understand larger trends in America's strategic evolution, one should examine the ways in which the nation faced the world absent of clearly defined threat. A Pearl Harbor, for instance, would diminish considerably the number of possible outcomes of a strategic reformulation. The 1880s, however, presented no such clear threat and thus allow a view into the process with few external factors. No specific enemy had to be met; no particular interest had to be satisfied; no institution needed a greater share of the appropriations.

A narrative of strategic change in the 1880s and early 1890s can follow any of several approaches. A bureaucratic model, such as that laid out in Graham Allison's *Essence of Decision,* would attempt to demonstrate where particular institutions prevailed. It would undoubtedly scrutinize the Navy Department and the officer corps, and indeed, these institutions did affect the outcome—although not always in favor of their perceived interests. The secretaries played important roles, but none were professionals with standing interests in building an imperial navy. And as for naval officers, while most supported improving the navy's efficiency, a surprising number opposed the blue-water doctrine.

A realist interpretation needs to show a threat, or at least a perceived threat, that forced strategic reconsideration. This approach has obvious value in explaining the changes of late 1941–42, but less value for 1882–93. While the scramble for Africa began in the eighties, this hardly affected American national security as it had traditionally been interpreted. Nor did the renewed interest in ports of extraterritoriality in China play any significant role in the debates over a naval buildup; the United States had long enjoyed some trade with these regions but had never seriously considered fighting to protect them. While the Royal Navy was facing invigorated threats from Continental rivals that explained its own buildup, the United States faced no analogous threats in the Western Hemisphere. Perhaps, then, the shift in the European balance of power itself triggered modification in the American defense posture. Similar changes had altered U.S. strategy during the wars of French revolution and empire, but not in the three-quarters of a century that followed. And yet these concerns were not reflected in congressional hearings and debates, contemporary accounts of geopolitics, lectures at the Naval War College, party platforms, or in the various other fora in which grand strategy was debated. Nor did the changes in the international threat-capability environment alter the U.S. Army in any significant way in this era. While navalism may have spawned the realist school, it did not itself succeed because of real or perceived foreign threats.

Alternatively, the narrative might be constructed to answer the question *cui bono,* or who gains? The creation of Germany's modern navy owed much to the domestic political capital the kaiser hoped to draw from it. And one is tempted also to explain strategic change in America in this way. One might look at such devoted party members as Theodore Roosevelt and Henry Cabot Lodge and wonder if their support for building a new navy were not truly designed to win votes for the Republicans. And yet these men worked with Democrats like Hilary Herbert on this project while constantly opposing them on politically charged issues such as the tariff, Civil War pensions, the Lodge Force Bill, and coastal or maritime improvements. If not before, the GOP certainly knew by the end of 1890 that an expensive new navy did not necessarily win votes.

If the interests were not political, could they have been material? Indeed, navalism found few supporters who would lose out on its success. Support frequently came from districts that gained directly from contracts, but these numbered closer to a dozen than to the hundreds of the post–World War II era. And the industrialists themselves frequently showed ambivalence about the creation of the new navy; witness Andrew Carnegie's strong support for the Anti-imperialist League and his reluctance even to accept navy armor contracts.

Political scientists struggle for parsimony in their explanations hoping that one methodological approach will explain as many outcomes as possible, and I have profited greatly from their labors. But historians have the luxury of inclusiveness. This book takes advantage of each of the above approaches to explain one phenomenon or another. If pressed for a single cause, however, I would point to the matching of an idea (navalism) to flexible, aggressive politics.[4] The idea of navalism resulted from many historical trends present in the late nineteenth century, feeding from Social Darwinism and the forces of free trade despite their fundamental disagreement about the world's finiteness; from messianic imperialism and Jeffersonian isolationism; as well as from personal profit and evangelical Protestantism. Each of these currents fed a geopolitical theory: a great navy makes a nation great.

None of this would have mattered if the ideas had not found their way through the political process. Through such remarkable men as Roosevelt, Soley, and Mahan, the idea became a political force that eventually changed the course of the nation.

CHAPTER ONE

The Influence
of
History upon Sea Power

The Navalist Reinterpretation of the War of 1812

Between 1882 and 1893, navalist historians resuscitated debates about the Anglo-American War of 1812–15 as an intellectual forum to support their political agenda. They argued that building a strong navy would fulfill the nation's strategic and political needs as well as the moral imperatives that guided righteous people and society. Newly revived lessons taught the danger of inadequate preparations for war, the futility of land war and consequently of an army, and the need to control the seas. By 1893, these navalists had successfully rewritten the history of the war, passing on their politically based judgments to the broader writings in American history. These revisions of the history of the War of 1812, germinated by the voluble navalists, had spread to the works of more general and well-established historians. Only one major historian, Henry Adams, resisted the trend but did so in a way that insured his failure. When Alfred Thayer Mahan set out at the end of the century to write his books on the naval war of 1812, he was entering a well-established debate already redefined in the eighties and early nineties.

The navalist historians of the 1880s included those well known for historical and political exertions: Theodore Roosevelt, Henry Cabot Lodge, and Alfred Thayer Mahan. Indeed, they and their now-obscure ally, James Russell Soley, launched the crusade, but were quickly joined by a legion of supporting historians. These others were not necessarily committed navalists, although they certainly found common ground. The wide acceptance of the navalists' interpretations must be attributed, in part, to a variety of revisionists, not just those with an overt navy-building agenda.

The histories written before the resurgence of naval enthusiasm in the early 1880s told a story of the Anglo-American War of 1812–15 very different from what most Americans now believe. While two extremely popular historians, James Fenimore Cooper and George Bancroft, thrilled readers with descriptions of heroic frigate battles, most studies portrayed the war as one fought primarily on land, with land-war lessons. The works of Cooper and Bancroft, like Oliver Wendell Holmes's endearing poem "Old Ironsides," established the hagiology of the naval war, but they were not widely read in the Reconstruction era. In this period's writings, maritime operations played a secondary role, with the navy even less important than privateers. With the navalist writings, Americans took up the story of Cooper and Bancroft in order to reconsider the importance of sea power and its role in the War of 1812.

Prenavalist Interpretations

When John Lewis Thomson's *History of the Second War between the United States and Great Britain* was reissued in 1848, America was just concluding its primarily land-based war against Mexico. Thomson had published the first edition soon after 1815 at the beginning of the phase of expansion that brought Americans to the Rio Grande by 1845. Since it was involved in continental expansion, the United States did not interest itself greatly with naval affairs, and Thomson's history reflected this lack of concern.[1]

Thomson's 1848 edition provided a history then considered worth reissuing—a conventional military history of land campaigns and heroics. In five hundred pages, he did not stray from the military narrative, opening with the first campaigns and closing with the Battle of New Orleans. Only on page 504 did he add a concluding paragraph of commentary on how slowly the nation had geared up for war and how well the final outcome reflected on the honor of the people. Thomson's focus on the land war was typical for his day. Of his twenty-three chapters, only five mentioned naval campaigns or the navy. Eighteen discussed the army.[2] Only twenty-two of the ninety-five etchings illustrated naval themes. Thomson's book, in its several editions, focused overwhelmingly on the land war events of 1812–15.

General histories of the United States from the era before the new navalists also concentrated on politics and the futility of land operations of the war. J. H. Patton's *History of the United States of America* was released in 1862 but had been written (in 1859) before the first monumental land battles of the Civil War. Completed three years earlier, Patton's *History* reflected the compromise political agenda of the 1850s. With the Union moving precipitously close to civil war, Patton wrote of a nation that had been divided on whether to go to war in 1812, observing, "The people were far from being unanimous in their approbation of the declaration of war." Much of Patton's *History* concentrated on the various compromises that the American people had been making to preserve the Union. Considering the War of 1812, he found fault in some people's inability to sacrifice their own goals for the good of the nation. Many had been willing to accommodate the British, he noted, as "it was unreasonable to expect full recognition of neutrals' rights while the desperate conflict in Europe was in progress."[3]

The war could have and should have been avoided, Patton claimed. "It was remarkable that one of the causes for the war, was removed within four days of its declaration," he noted of the repealed orders in council. The British had been willing to accommodate, and had even given American vessels in British ports six weeks to unload and guaranteed safe passage home.[4] For Patton, 1812 provided an object lesson on how government should attend to the call of the people for peace.

For Patton to point out the folly of war in 1812, he had to downplay the issues that had excited the War Hawks in 1812, foremost of which were sailors' rights. Patton noted how politely the British treated the American merchant marine. Moreover, he consistently portrayed the role of the navy as minimally decisive in the actual conflict. He did this in two ways: by giving the navy less attention than the army, and by finding the privateers as important as the navy. In his discussion of the actual war, Patton mentioned the army and militia (the land forces) more than twice as often as the navy and in a positive light. To play down the role of the navy, he wrote, "The American privateers maintained the honor of the nation as much as the regular navy."[5] While holding some validity, this statement contrasts markedly with statements made by historians after the navalist rewriting of history.

Among the other authors to depict the war in prenavalist style was John Clark Ridpath, professor at Indiana Ashbury University and author of many books on American history. *A Popular History of the United States of America from the Original Times to the Present Day,* published in 1881, was "intended for the average American . . . [and] dedicated to the household and the library of the poor."[6] Ridpath viewed the 1812 war favorably, and, like Patton, emphasized land operations and politics.

Ridpath stressed the drive toward war, commenting "the elections, held between 1808 and 1811, showed conclusively the drift of public opinion; the sentiment of the country was that war was preferable to further humiliation and disgrace." After the orders in council, "it was only a matter of time when such insolence would lead to retaliation and war." Despite postulating its inevitability, he agreed with earlier historians that the war was probably imprudent, basing his assessment upon its costs. "At the close of the conflict the country was burdened with a debt of a hundred million dollars. The monetary affairs of the nation were in a deplorable condition. . . . Domestic commerce was paralyzed by want of money."[7] Ridpath disagreed with the pre–Civil War historians on the degree of genuine popular enthusiasm, but he agreed that the 1812 war was not exactly what the nation had needed.

Ridpath concurred with his predecessors on the role the navy played in the conflict, but unlike his successors, he credited the government with a certain amount of preparation. For although "the President himself had not disposition and little capacity for war, . . . vigorous preparations for the impending crisis were made by Congress." For Ridpath, the land forces were more important than Congress in the prosecution of the war. He devoted three times as many paragraphs to their operations as he did to those of the navy.[8] His conclusions on the war did not go beyond a summary of the economic havoc it had wrought. He did not mention "glory" or use the other words that characterized the more enthusiastic conclusions drawn by the post-1882 historians.

Among the last of the prenavalist histories, Ridpath's work fits the consensus regarding the War of 1812. Twenty years after the fall of Fort Sumter, his view of war was very different from that of Thomson or Patton, yet he still regarded the nation's enthusiasm for the Anglo-American war as a mixed legacy. Perhaps with an eye to the unreconstructed South or to the dearth of American-flagged shipping in 1881, Ridpath bemoaned the costs of the War of 1812, rather than discussing the valor that the nation's heroes had earned. Like his predecessors, Ridpath did not view sea power or the navy as particularly relevant to the War of 1812.

Another important litmus test of the degree to which new navalism affected historiography is the treatment of the surrender of Gen. William Hull, governor of the Michigan territory in 1812. Prenavalist historians generally viewed Hull with measured charity; this was rapidly disappearing, however. General histories, such as Elia Peattie's *Story of America*. . . . (1889), were relatively slow to be influenced by navalist revisions. Peattie's interpretation of Hull was fairly typical. Hull's first campaigns were minor but extremely unsuccessful; when faced with the forces of Gen. Isaac Brock on 16 August 1812, he surrendered Detroit and all of Michigan. Peattie treated Hull charitably, noting the mollifying factors in his ignominious decision.[9]

> When Brock demanded surrender he had said that he could not restrain his allies, the Indians, from rapine and murder in case the place should be carried by assault. Hull dared not rely upon his insubordinate militia for any desperate fighting, and as he had learned that the officers had formed a conspiracy to take away his command, he decided to surrender. He knew that if he defended the place and his enemies succeeded in defeating him, the fate of the women and children would be terrible.

This version makes the decision appear reasonable and the subsequent court-martial death sentence too harsh. The president's pardon, according to Peattie, was based on Hull's Revolutionary War service and a "feeling that the neglect of the government had much to do with the case."[10] This historical assessment lost favor once the practice of denigrating the army had been established within revised history.

Peattie did not engage in maligning the army; but by 1889, he was among a rapidly diminishing minority. This exception can be explained by the bibliography for his chapter on the war in 1812. His suggested reading list includes only two pieces of "fiction" and three of "poetry," and does not include any post-1882 writing. By then, almost everyone else was reading the new history.

——— New Historical Interpretations: Navalists ———

The new historical image of the 1812 war that historians created shared three common features, or lessons, which will be discussed below. First, they felt unpreparedness had crippled the war effort. Second, despite this hurdle, Americans struggled heroically and won essentially all that was important in the war—the glory and the control of the sea. Third, they attained a draw with the British on the less-significant field of politics. The historical questions of honor, command of the sea, and politics remain debated today, but it is worth noting that these writers consistently chose the one set of truths that fit their own contemporary political agenda. Far from being deceitful, the several authors openly acknowledged their political goals in the text.

The first of the three lessons taught by the new scholarship was that a nation's unpreparedness was sinful and dangerous. The new writers blamed this unpreparedness on three distinct groups—the people, the politicians, and the military. According to historians of the late nineteenth century, the citizens of 1812 were divided and weak willed about the defense of their national rights. This weakness and division made them unnecessarily vulnerable. The alleged weakness of the people resounds as a motif throughout the entire revision of the history of the war. It was not the loudest theme, but it was audible from the first new interpretation through the last.

First and best of the new navalist historians, Theodore Roosevelt published his *Naval War of 1812* when fresh out of Harvard College in 1882. This was not the work of a feckless undergraduate.[11] Rather, this intense young scholar observed the highest standards of historical scholarship, and the book ranks among the most authoritative works in the field. Military history was, in the late nineteenth century, a narrowly technical branch of study, generally confined to operations and the most basic political sketches. As far as it goes, Roosevelt's work remains today a definitive text on the operational side of the naval war.

Roosevelt's contribution was among the best for its multiarchival research, its fairness to both sides (although not claiming impartiality), and its historiographical texture. *The Naval War of 1812* outlined the new agenda, the biases of the navalist historians. The theme of a weak-willed people emerged in the preface; he wrote this book to warn the allegedly flabby citizens of the 1880s of the deadly mistakes of their grandfathers.

> The subject merits a closer scrutiny than it has received. At present people are beginning to realize that it is folly for the great English-speaking Republic to rely for defense upon a navy composed partly of antiquated hulks, and partly of new vessels rather more worthless than the old. It is worth our while to study with some care that period of our history during which our navy stood at its highest pitch of fame, and to learn anything from the past it is necessary to know, as near as may be, the exact truth.[12]

Roosevelt was concerned with the mistakes of irresolute people who could not have peace because of their unwillingness to prepare for a fight. He argued that "intelligent foresight in preparation and known capacity to stand well in battle are the surest safeguards against war."[13] He did not pretend that he was writing a history for any other age than his own, and consequently made quite explicit what he expected his readers to learn.

Roosevelt believed the people of the "great English-speaking Republic" were destined to overcome their temporary weak will; their race's destiny had greater things in store for them. Convinced of an Anglo-Saxon common destiny, Roosevelt emphasized that the New Englanders and the British were "men of the same race, differing but little from one another, and destined to share the rule of the globe." As he would later write in another history, coauthored with his close friend Henry Cabot Lodge, these were a people "who [had] joined to the stern and manly qualities which are essential to the well-being of a masterful race, the virtues of gentleness, of patriotism, and of lofty adherence to an ideal."[14] As it was for most navalists and imperialists, Anglo-Americanism symbolized a great ethnic destiny.

For Roosevelt, the failures of the early nineteenth century and the 1870s were not those of an inherent flaw of the people, but rather the fault of the leaders who had failed to lead. This theme, too, would follow the new navalists' interpretations throughout the following two decades. The greatest villains in this story were Presidents Thomas Jefferson and James Madison. Roosevelt attacked the father of the Democrats for having left the nation so poorly prepared for war. He scoffed at the little gunboats that comprised Jefferson's navy: "Their operations throughout the war offer a painfully ludicrous commentary on Jefferson's remarkable project of having a navy composed solely of such craft."[15] Concluding, Roosevelt decried his long-dead enemy,

> Jefferson, though a man whose views and theories had a profound influence upon our national life, was perhaps the most incapable Executive that ever filled the presidential chair: being almost purely a visionary, he was utterly unable to grapple with the slightest danger, and, not even excepting his successor, Madison, it would be difficult to imagine a man less fit to guide the state with honor and safety through the stormy times that marked the opening of the present century.

Uncharitable to Madison and vicious toward Jefferson, Roosevelt judged the latter purely on his ability to wage the war that he had actually managed to avoid.[16]

Another navalist historian, James Barnes, picked up on this condemnation of Jefferson. Barnes left the navy after graduating from Annapolis, yet he continued to serve with his patriotic pen. Barnes's "Naval Actions of the War of 1812" appeared in serial form through much of the 1890s in *Harper's Weekly*. Printed in 1896 with a new preface, these essays echoed the themes discussed by Roosevelt: "Under the 'gunboat system' of Mr. Jefferson, who believed in harbor protection, and trusted [it] to escape war, an act had been passed in 1805 which almost threatened the annihilation of a practical navy." This, Barnes claimed, would have left the nation without honor or heroes. For Barnes, as for Roosevelt, this shame would destroy a nation. He wrote, "The country that has not national heroes whose deeds should be found emblazoned on her annals, that can boast no men whose lives and conducting can be held up as examples of what loyalty, *valor,* and courage should be, that country has not patriotism, no heart, no soul."[17]

Barnes called on his readers to take pride in their nation, because of the heroes of 1812 who gave it such character. He believed in peace, in Roosevelt's peace "honorably" held, for "as a civilized people we desire peace, but the only peace worth having is obtained by instant readiness to fight when wronged—not by the unwillingness or inability to fight at all."[18] This, too, was a new distinction in American political discourse. For both authors, war gave the nation its soul and tested the mettle of its leaders. The test of a leader was how he behaved under the threat of war, and Jefferson fell short of this mark.

Roosevelt and Barnes had few kind words for the man who had actually led the nation in war. Rossiter Johnson, the next historian who approached the question of Democratic leadership, was no kinder to James Madison. He brought out his *History of the War of 1812–1815* in 1882, the same year that Roosevelt published his.[19] Johnson, an established nonacademic historian, wrote popular and widely respected history quickly proving himself a powerful ally for the navalist historians.

Johnson saw Madison in a decidedly unfriendly light. He depicted Madison as so innocent of strategic sense that he shied from using his own navy. "So blind was President Madison's administration to the country's main strength and advantage, that he actually proposed to lay up all the naval vessels, as the only means of saving them from capture."[20] Johnson could not appreciate the wisdom of harboring the gunboats and small frigates instead of leaving them prey to the seventy-fours of the Royal Navy, the world's greatest.[21] America's shipping had already suffered a disastrous decline as a result of the 1807 and 1809 embargoes. Perhaps there was some logic in saving the remainder. Faced with the reality of war, Madison actually did direct a variety of seaborne forces against British men-of-war and commercial ships on the oceans and the lakes.

The people and the leaders of the nation, according to these writers, had failed to fulfill their obligations to prepare for war. On these points, all the new navalist historians agreed. This failure, they maintained, was bad policy, and one that the armed forces had inadequately protested. The navy and army were both caught understrength, and these historians assigned some of the blame to their commanders, although considerably less than to the nation's political leaders.

The military commanders, the argument continued, must have known that war was in the offing, yet they criminally ignored preparations. By 1807, a war was inevitable. After Roosevelt discussed the insulting British orders in council and Congress's reactive embargo, he declared, "there could be but one result to such a succession of incidents, and that was war." In hindsight, Roosevelt saw the inevitability of war by 1807; so, he reckoned, must have the military leaders of the nation. Instead, the navy was training but not building ships. This training, mostly under the leadership of Edward Preble, gleaned considerable applause, but the lack of a building program left Roosevelt unimpressed.

Each major history of the naval war of 1812 introduced its subject with a thumbnail sketch of the political background and a statement on the readiness of the U.S. Navy, emphasizing various components. Johnson emphasized the potential of privateering without slighting the navy's own ability. He exculpated the navy's officers for lack of preparation, instead, as we have seen, blaming Madison for his craven strategy.[22]

Roosevelt emphasized a distinguished yet malnourished navy, treating men, officers, and ships with vigorous respect. He commented, "There was no better seaman in the world than American Jack; he had been bred to his work from infancy." Americans had improved upon the seamanship inherited from the British. Roosevelt's view was seminal as popular journals picked up on his interpretations. For example, an anonymous review in *Atlantic Monthly* echoed Roosevelt: "The American sailors proved themselves quite the equal, if not more, of the English seamen, who had learned to consider themselves invincible." In the navalist view, these men were destined for naval greatness not only because of their race, but also by their breeding.[23] Add to that their intense concern for natural rights (i.e., freedom of the seas) and excellent training, and "American Jack" could only win.

Roosevelt praised training and preparation of the men, which, he believed, won Oliver Hazard Perry a great victory at Put-in-Bay. Much of the preparation was moral; Roosevelt credited the valorous fighting of Perry and his men to their familiarity with the "just causes" for which they fought. These men were fighting for the freedom and honor that Jefferson had forsaken. Further to their credit, they had prepared well for such an honorable fight: "it must always be remembered that a victory, honorably won, if even over a weaker force [i.e., one less well-prepared] does reflect credit on the nation by whom it is gained."[24] Victory and glory were the rewards for hard training.

The ships and arms were another matter, as Roosevelt found their preparation inadequate. The nation's poor showing in the war demonstrated "evils produced by the original short-sightedness and parsimony" and left the nation vulnerable to all sorts of insults.[25]

The worst of these evils was the poorly equipped and trained army. Although Roosevelt found the army inadequate to its task, he believed this fault did not present a clear lesson for his own day. Although the army of 1812 failed to defend the nation's honor and failed to invade Britain's Canada, for Roosevelt these disappointments did not matter much. Originally, *The Naval War of 1812* was to have been followed by a companion volume on the land war. In the 1882 edition, he had claimed that the war deserved study both as it played out on land and at sea.[26] In the 1889 volume, he withdrew the promise to write on the land operations, and in so doing reflected a political-strategic agenda for the 1890s. For "these [land] operations were hardly worth serious study. They teach us nothing new; it is the old, old lesson, that a miserly economy of preparation may in the end involve a lavish outlay of men and money, which after all, comes too late."[27] It took seven years to acknowledge that he had little interest in the land operations. In doing so, he followed some of his contemporaries, such as James Russell Soley.

Soley taught history at the Naval Academy and was a widely published author. Indeed, just as Roosevelt sent his first edition of *1812* to press, he was chagrined to discover that Soley had recently published his own *Naval Campaign of 1812* in the United States Naval Institute *Proceedings*.[28] Fortunately for Roosevelt, they differed on interpretations of the particulars of the campaign. But Soley and Roosevelt independently agreed on the larger lessons of preparedness and the virtuosity of American efforts. Several years later, Soley came out with a contribution to the *Narrative and Critical History of America* entitled "The Wars of the United States 1789–1850," which treated more thoroughly the entire military history of the nation of that period. In this essay, Soley expounded his views of the War of 1812 from much the same perspective as Roosevelt and Johnson.[29]

Foremost, he agreed that history should be written for one's contemporaries. He wrote of the original congressional authorization of a navy, "no event in the history of the navy is of greater importance than the [1798] construction of these six frigates."[30] Soley was correct only if construction is considered the most important act of a navy; in time of war or pseudowar, one might consider fighting more important. But Soley wrote this in the 1880s when his navy was trying to secure congressional authorization. Soley's criteria suited his political agenda for the 1880s.

Soley also agreed with the other navalist historians that the government failed to prepare the nation for war or to provide an adequate deterrent. He noted that the navy "had never been regarded by the government with favor." Yet he found the navy to have compensated for this minimal cooperation with

> the three essential measures [that] had been adopted to secure its efficiency,—the ships built for it were the best of their class in the world. The officers had been carefully selected, . . . and they had received—at least a large number of them—in Preble's squadron at Tripoli a training such as has fallen to the lot of few navies, either before or since.

Like Roosevelt, Soley lauded Preble, for "although Commodore Preble died in 1807, the credit of the later war belongs more to him than to any other one man." Not only did he train the great officers during his daring war against the Barbary pirates, but also "he created in the navy a professional spirit or idea, which was the main quality that distinguished it from the army in the war with Great Britain."[31]

Here Soley introduced another theme that ran through most of these works, belittling the importance or effectiveness of the army. In a world of political compromises, the navy of the 1880s found itself in a great rivalry with the army of the 1880s. Congress and the people restricted defense appropriations, so navalists took every opportunity to obtain the larger portion for the navy. This involved deprecating the army while boosting the navy. Each navalist historian contributed to the effort: Soley's greatest contribution was the portion of an argument that denied the army a role in any intercontinental warfare; Johnson's contribution, which was soon adopted by Alfred Thayer Mahan, proclaimed the necessity of projecting power across the sea; Roosevelt proposed the notion that a nation's honor could best be proven on the seas.

The army, according to the navalist historians, served no positive function in 1812 and was apparently equally redundant three generations later. The army had two primary roles in the second Anglo-American war. In the first, the defense of the homeland, it proved painfully inadequate. In the second, the invasion of Canada, it also failed. When, in his third edition, Roosevelt stated that the army's actions were not worth study, he did append one chapter on a land battle. He did not add a chapter on an ignoble defeat, such as Bladensburg, which led to the burning of Washington. Instead he wrote on the Battle of New Orleans, which, coming after the Peace of Ghent had been signed, showed that even the army's most glorious battle had no strategic significance.[32]

Soley addressed the alleged uselessness of the army more directly. Its story sounds pitiful.

> The army entered upon the war with few officers of professional training or traditions. The general officers . . . were not even competent to discipline their own men, and much less to conduct strategic operations against the enemy. . . . there were only a few general officers worthy of the name and it required only the simplest strategic movement to demonstrate their incompetency.

And if the generals were not bad enough, they took their orders from "the War Department [which] did not have at its command either the men or the machinery to draw up a strategic plan or to put it into operation." Fortunately for the United States, the navy was able to save from complete loss the army's major front, the Canadian border. Due to the heroics of Oliver Hazard Perry and his sailor-warriors, "the supremacy of [the United States] thus established on Lake Erie and throughout the Northwest continued unbroken to the close of the war."[33]

Disparagement of the army took several forms and almost always preceded adulation for the navy. The army was bad at what it did, according to these navalists, but worse, its efforts were pointless. The projection of power across the sea, each historian agreed, was the best hope in war. For "a nation that is strong enough to carry war into its enemy's country, and keep it there, will certainly prove strong enough to win in the end." The poorly financed navy could not carry on all alone, so it turned to privateers to help out: "As England claimed to be mistress of the seas, and practically the claim was almost true, the determination to send our little navy and a fleet of privateers against her was essentially carrying the war into English territory."[34]

Johnson was an almost unwitting navalist because he did not overtly plead the navy's argument, as had Roosevelt and Soley. Rather, his ideas supported the navy-building movement by being one more voice claiming the importance of the projection of sea power. Where the others voiced a contemporary political agenda, Johnson merely echoed support of their historical perspectives.

The unsuccessful land war argued the uselessness of an army and reinforced the strategic imperative of controlling the seas. Navalist historians found proof of the futility of land warfare in the 1812–15 conflict and, consequently, support for their argument favoring the navy over the army in time of preparation for future war. To them, land war provided neither strategic, political, nor heroic boon to a nation, whether win, lose, or draw.

These three lessons, the importance of preparedness and sea power and of the futility of land war, comprise the navalist argument. Together, these three lessons support a political agenda and changing general historical interpretations.

New Historical Interpretations: Generalists

In addition to the navalists, who had come to dominate the writing of military history, mainstream historians picked up on the new historiography, adopting the same issues and language as the navalist historians. The third volume of the American history series, *The Making of the Nation 1783–1817*, by Francis A. Walker, then president of Massachusetts Institute of Technology and formerly professor of political economy and history at the Sheffield Scientific School at Yale, represents the complete triumph of the navalist historiography. Although his career started with remarkably successful service in the Civil War Union Army, Walker extended great praise to the navy throughout his *Making of the Nation*.[35] The effects of the navalists upon his work can be seen in the brief bibliography at the volume's close. It cites Roosevelt, Winsor, and Soley as well as Maclay.[36] He wrote sarcastically of Jefferson's embargo:

> The customs of oriental nations were not so well known as at the present; and Mr. Jefferson was not able to strengthen his convictions by a reference to the usage in certain provinces in India, by which a person who has been wronged sits down before the door of the evil-doer and there rips open his abdomen to bring a curse down on his enemy. Had Mr. Jefferson known this, it might have been of great comfort to him [and given him the strength to maintain his embargo].[37]

Walker echoed the navalists' vicious anti-Jeffersonian rhetoric. And like the navalists, Walker portrayed a war reflecting most gloriously on the small navy. His chapter "The War of 1812–1815" opened:

> If those are in the right who charge that the administration of Mr. Madison provoked war, not to redress our wrongs upon the ocean, but to gain glory and territory by the conquest of Canada, then the general results of the war would

seem to show the most remarkable discrimination upon the part of Providence in apportioning honor and shame, success and failure, according to the direction in which our efforts were put forth. Upon the ocean, our little navy of eight or ten frigates and as many sloops and brigs, was, in anything like equal combat, completely victorious.

Walker assigned great honor and credit to the navy.

In contrast, the army became an object of scorn. Indicting it for disgracefully failing to take Canada, Walker launched a merciless assault: "our ambitious enterprises against Canada were in the main characterized by blundering incompetence on the part of our own generals, and too often misconduct and seeming incompetence on the part of the troops." While the army could do no right, the navy could do no wrong, even though "it was true that these brilliant successes did not give us the command of even our own waters."

Working completely from recent secondary works, Walker placed himself in the hands of the new navalist interpretations. Publishing in 1895, Walker devoted as much page space to the navy as he did to the army, highlighting the navy's glory and the army's ignominy.[38] The navy received all the glory because the author owed his conclusions to navalist histories.

Grade school histories underwent the same revisions as did those of the university. Two examples suffice here. In 1884, Horace Scudder's *History* still emphasized the role of the army and the ambivalence of the nation to war. Twice as much space was devoted to land operations as was given to naval activities. Schools were receiving the standard and prevalent interpretations of the period. But by 1893, the pupils were learning of a different War of 1812. Allen Thomas's *History of the United States* noted that the nation was "ill-prepared for war." Then he mentioned the navy in as many paragraphs and as favorably as he did the army or militia.[39]

Denigrating the army, boosting the navy, explicating the causes of weakness among the people and leaders, and demonstrating the need for preparedness were all items in the contemporary political agenda of navalists who rewrote the history of the War of 1812. Within a dozen brief years, they succeeded in writing not only their histories, but rewriting the nation's perspectives of a previously obscure war. Part of this effort involved belittling the army for its meager, ill-conceived, and poorly executed role in the war. It followed that America's battles could only be successfully waged at sea. The navy, according to this new history, carried out its tasks with zeal and efficiency, and eventually deserved credit for the successes of the war.

——————————— The Feeble Voice of Dissent ———————————

While most historians were swept up in the abrupt historiographical changes, one writer resisted the tide. A mugwump and dissenter, Henry Adams did not become a navalist. In the dozen years covered by this study (1882–93), Adams was his most productive as a writer of history. In 1880, he had published *The Life of Albert Gallatin* on Jefferson's treasury secretary and through the following decade produced eight lengthy volumes in the series *History of the United States of America,* covering the administrations of Jefferson and Madison.[40] These works reflect an enduring antinavalist discourse.

Adams, in concurrence with his heroic Gallatin, opposed construction of a large navy by the Jefferson administration on the basis of economy. Adams agreed with his subject that construction of such a navy would have been at the expense of American credibility. He quoted Gallatin: "If the sum to be expended to build and maintain the frigates were applied to paying a part of our national debt, the payment would make us much more respectable in the eyes of foreign nations than all the frigates we can build."[41]

Adams represented these opinions as facts. He further noted, "government has to deal with being ruled not only by reason but by feeling." He claimed that emotions called for these ships when the rational grand strategy would not have.

Adams agreed with Gallatin in opposing the construction of the ships that great-grandfather John Adams had actually ordered built in 1798. Yet the historian noted Gallatin's continued dissonance with an American society that "would have seen the national debt and no small part of national life expunged rather than have parted with the glories of these ships." Adams could not have made his sympathies in this case more clear: "the cool and candid decision of history should be that Mr. Gallatin was essentially in the right."[42]

Adams would have preferred to continue that policy in the 1880s. Like the navalists whose works followed his by only two years, Adams was willing to jeopardize the integrity of his history with policy recommendations: "There could be no more instructive thesis proposed to future Secretaries of Treasury than to ask themselves on entering into office, 'What would Mr. Gallatin wish to do with the navy, were he now in my place?'" This *obiter dictum* was perhaps Adams's most overt effort to take part in contemporary political debate—a practice he relinquished in the 1880s, a period of severe personal disappointment.[43]

In the long decade that followed, Adams's intellectual perspective became more firmly set, and he refused to bend to popular trends. Indeed, he refused most of the rationalization of the period including scientific racism, Gilded Age politics, and navalism. Even to the cult of modern technological power, he would concede defeat only in 1893 after visiting the Columbian Exposition. It was during this period of intransigence that Adams compiled his multivolume history of the only early national years in which an Adams predecessor had not played a major role in a presidential administration.[44]

Henry Adams's *History of the United States of America* is the only major post-1884 history that successfully resisted the navalist interpretations of the role of the navy in the war period. Even so, Adams's *History* was more moderate in its mercantilist antinavalism than had been his *Gallatin*. In the first volume, published in 1889, Adams defended Jefferson and Gallatin's program for a low level of naval preparedness: while "the navy . . . was believed to be superfluous," it was not disproportionately hurt by cutbacks. "The navy was not a great sufferer."[45] Of the tense years of 1807 to 1812, Adams would evidently have preferred the navy to have been a greater sufferer at the hands of a tight economy.

When war finally erupted, according to Adams, its day had already passed and its passion "could not seem genuine to men who did not share it." Adams was the last of the nineteenth-century historians to defend the New Englanders plotting secession at the Hartford Convention. He scolded the navalist idea of the war having been fought for national pride. "What honor was to be hoped from a war which required continued submission to one robber [i.e., Napoleonic France] as the price of resistance to another? [Georgian Britain]"[46] Adams did not share the navalists' appreciation of the inherent nobility of war.

Adams neither exculpated the navy for its lack of preparedness at the brink of war, nor held the army completely responsible for the military failures. While America's "military condition could hardly have been worse . . . the Department [of Navy] perhaps shared the blame for want of readiness when war was declared." In the discussion of the war itself, Adams's interpretation even went so far as to defend General Hull who "would naturally have welcomed a chance of dying in battle" but had surrendered for the sake of the women and children.[47] Thus, Adams, perhaps tongue in cheek, would not even acquiesce to vilifying the army.

While not mentioning them by name, Henry Adams confronted the navalists' arguments at each point. His refutations, however, went no farther than the covers of his book. He had abandoned the direct political polemic that had marked his earlier works. By 1889, he was Henry Adams the reclusive scholar of his autobiography, *The Education of Henry Adams*. His histories were nearly as asocial—being eight volumes of approximately six hundred pages each, they were virtually inaccessible. Adams remarked on the books' popularity, characteristically in the third person, "As far as Adams knew, he had but three readers. . . . He was amply satisfied with their consideration and could dispense with that of the other fifty-nine million, nine hundred and ninety-nine thousand, nine hundred and ninety-seven" Americans.[48]

Adams's work failed to have the influence that its scholarship and strategic insights deserved; his small-navy ethos was ridiculed and rejected out of hand. Navalist historiographical revision continued unchecked by his cautious brand of research. Henry Adams abdicated the role of thoughtful leader that his progenitors had played. In an age when historians exerted unprecedentedly strong and overt political influence, Adams chose to avoid policy debates. Instead, those willing to make the effort and to expose their works to more of those sixty million were, in the end, successful.

The triumphant new history had originated in the works of avowed navalists Theodore Roosevelt and James Russell Soley. With precious little to hinder them and starting from such a broad range of works, their ideas spread quickly into general school histories and into more widely accepted political mythology. The new lessons of the War of 1812, in many cases constructed with an overt political agenda for the late nineteenth century, soon began to teach the American people the necessity of a strong navy able to protect the nation at a distance from its vulnerable cities as well as to project American power abroad. Navalists were redrawing the essential characteristics of the nation's military and strategic history in order to lay the intellectual guidelines for an unprecedented, vigorous, and sweeping peacetime buildup.

CHAPTER TWO

Cleaning Up
—*the*—
Act

Reorganizing and Rebuilding the Navy

> There is a homely adage which runs, "speak softly and carry a big stick; you will go far." If the American nation will speak softly and yet build and keep at a pitch of the highest training a thoroughly efficient navy, the Monroe Doctrine will go far.
>
> — ***Theodore Roosevelt***

As historians paved the way, professionals within the navy's administration strove to create a modern, efficient, and professional service. Throughout the course of the military buildup, 1882 to 1893, the United States Navy professionalized its officers and sailors, while reorganizing the bureaus and educational facilities to promote efficiency, economy, and integrity. Along with the technical changes that made the new ships more seaworthy and battleworthy, reforms from within the navy modernized and professionalized every facet of the service: the officers and men were cultivated, their education expanded, and their organization streamlined. By 1893, the infrastructure of a modern fighting navy was established.

—————— Naval Administration ——————

Rationalization of the management structure and personnel was necessary to build an efficient system. The first important change within the Navy Department was the appointment of relatively honest secretaries, beginning in 1881. The secretaries of the new navy proved, to varying degrees, politically well connected and competent, exploiting opportunities for changes not taken in the administrations of Andrew Johnson and Ulysses S. Grant. These secretaries included Garfield's William Hunt, Arthur's William E. Chandler, Cleveland's William C. Whitney, Harrison's Benjamin F. Tracy, Cleveland's Hilary A. Herbert, and McKinley's John D. Long. They followed in stark contrast to the Gilded Age secretaries; Grant's George Robeson had faced nearly continuous charges of corruption and incompetence, and Hayes's Richard Thompson was reported to have been surprised, upon first boarding a man-of-war, to find that it was hollow.

William Hunt (1823–84) was the first secretary after Lincoln's Gideon Welles to demonstrate honesty and political savvy. Although Yale educated and a lawyer, Hunt had not led the sheltered life of boardrooms and salons. His widowed mother's waning fortunes had forced him to leave Yale without graduating, to learn and practice law in New Orleans. Drafted as a lieutenant colonel in the Confederate army, Hunt was a Republican who had entertained David Farragut after the admiral had taken New Orleans. After the war, Hunt returned to his practice in New Orleans and then was appointed to sit on the U.S. Court of Claims. In an effort to avoid partisan rancor, President Garfield selected Judge Hunt as a noncontroversial appointment for navy secretary. Before an assassin's bullet brought down Garfield later in 1881 and ended Hunt's brief tenure, the secretary was able to bring together many of the officers who would soon build the new navy. Contrary to precedent, he organized a meeting of members of Congress's naval affairs committees, Rear Adm. John Rodgers's Advisory Board, and several leading officers to hammer out a compromise strategy for construction of the new navy. Bringing together key representatives of the executive and legislative branches broke tradition but also elicited the first bills of the new navy. This informal conference, held in Hunt's offices on 15 February 1882 marked the new "high-water mark" of Congress-navy relations.[1] Within two weeks, the navy was the beneficiary of authorizations for new ships and of some major administrative reforms. Hunt's biographer claimed for him the title "father of the New Navy" for these efforts.

William Eaton Chandler (1835–1917) was an even more adroit politician, succeeding Hunt when the liberal "half-breed" faction of the Republicans came to power. Known variously as a great patriot and as a political hack, Chandler had a flair for publicity and good marriages. A Harvard-trained lawyer from Concord, Chandler had by 1882 served as speaker of the New Hampshire Assembly, the first naval solicitor and judge advocate, assistant secretary of treasury (1865–67), and secretary of the Republican National Committee (1868–80). As Garfield's nominee for U.S. solicitor-general, he was rejected by the Senate; a year later steady pressure earned him Chester Arthur's appointment as navy secretary.

Chandler held generally conservative views of the navy's strategic needs along with progressive notions of management and of the place that the service should hold in the hearts of the people. On the former, he believed that the navy should rebuild along the traditional lines of balanced offensive and defensive capabilities, increasing its effectiveness but not altering its overall strategy. This effort to avoid an overreliance on offensive warfare ultimately failed. His greatest successes came from his progressive efforts in reforming the department's bureaucracy and especially in selling the new navy to the American people. From 1887 to 1901, Chandler (as a U.S. Senator) served on the Naval Affairs Committee and provided a persuasive voice against the battleship programs that had come to dominate the navy.

William Collins Whitney (1841–1904) was the first Democratic navy secretary after Buchanan's Isaac Toucey. A graduate of Yale College and Harvard Law School, Whitney had two careers. As a Democratic lawyer, he helped bring down Boss Tweed's corrupt political organization and made a name as a reformer. As the husband of Standard Oil heiress Flora Payne, he increased her millions greatly, mostly through the practice of corporate law and ownership of the New York trolleys. Appointed by Cleveland in 1885, Whitney put his knowledge of politics and finance to good use.

After a quarter century of one-party rule, the navy's acquisition and support apparatus was in dire need of reform. By cutting sinecures, streamlining supply processes, and disentangling the bureau system, Whitney financed the fleet's modernization without considerably increasingly costs. With these savings and better congressional relations, Whitney secured funds for approximately thirty ships, which formed the core of the new navy. Yet, for all his reforms and authorizations, Whitney has traditionally been reviled as the navy's enemy for opposing the battlefleet-oriented philosophy then emerging in Newport.

When Benjamin Franklin Tracy (1830–1915) became secretary in 1889, he built upon his predecessors' reforms while warmly embracing the battlefleet philosophy. The son of Oswego farmers, Tracy read law in an attorney's office, moving up through local political circles and taking a seat in the New York Assembly by the age of thirty. After meritorious service in the Civil War, General Tracy moved to Brooklyn to establish his legal practice and his political career.

In close alliance with his boyhood friend, New York's Republican boss Thomas Platt, Tracy was appointed navy secretary by President Harrison. Although he had no naval experience, Tracy became an extraordinarily influential leader, based on his political skills, his close ties to Harrison, and the fortune of good timing.

In opposition to Chandler's traditional vision of a balanced fleet, Tracy's offensive-defense agenda manifested itself from the start; it was a position he shared with much of Congress. After three small-ship secretaries, many members expressed new enthusiasm about Tracy's aggressive construction policy. Tracy's administration brought the naval revolution to fruition, seeing the first steam fleet maneuvers, the publication of Mahan's *Influence of Sea Power upon History*, the authorization of America's first battleship, and intervention in the Hawaiian revolution. Tracy's successes were unprecedented in time of peace, as he set a pace of construction that continued until 1922 and a strategy that endured into the early hours of 7 December 1941. His tenure saw the emergence of the battleship, which was to form the navy's backbone for nearly half a century.

Tracy's Democratic successor, Hilary Herbert (1834–1919), was more tightly coupled to Congress than any previous secretary. Like Tracy, he was a former army officer, lawyer, and career politician. He had chaired the House Naval Affairs Committee 1885–89 and 1891–93—supporting the construction of cruisers but not battleships—before being appointed by Cleveland. Defying his president and the majority of his party, he supported the first large peacetime naval buildup as well as an increasingly aggressive foreign policy. Converted in office by the navalists to the blue-water philosophy soon after taking office in 1893, Herbert continued the aggressive construction of his Republican predecessor and encouraged Secretary of State Richard Olney's blustering adventurism during the Venezuelan crisis of 1895.[2] As a southern Democrat in favor of the G.O.P.-originated, battle-oriented navy, Herbert represents the apogee of navalism.

While the secretaries were increasing their political activities, the rest of the department's management could concentrate on operations.[3] The reinstatement of the civilian post of assistant secretary of the navy allowed a division of the departmental responsibilities. The secretary led the political process that effectively left to the assistant secretary the daily management of the navy. This shift of responsibility came about through the seemingly unrelated kindness of President Harrison to a tragically distraught friend.

When Benjamin Tracy's house burned down in 1890, his wife and a daughter perished, leaving him temporarily unable to perform his duties. Harrison took him into the Executive Mansion to recuperate. The president, with the support of a sympathetic Congress, revived the post of assistant secretary to relieve Tracy of some of the daily burdens of the office. In the years since the previous assistant secretary, Lincoln's Gustavus Fox, the office had lapsed because there was so little to do in the secretary's office. But Tracy's personal tragedy offered Harrison the opportunity to appoint James Russell Soley as assistant secretary to administer daily affairs.

Soley, the naval historian who would later join Tracy in legal practice, proved to be an extremely competent administrator, using his excellent relations with the officers and the other naval enthusiasts to rebuild the navy.[4] As the author of several historical and legal texts on the navy, Soley provided the department with a sense of mission and tradition—a continuity sometimes lacking in institutions directed by political appointees. As noted above, Soley's writings on the War of 1812 had emphasized the importance of congressional and civilian relations for the navy. Soley's successor, William McAdoo, also provided this type of leadership while at the navy department and later as chair of the House Naval Affairs Committee. Following McAdoo as assistant secretary, Theodore Roosevelt brought the operational and figurative leadership to new heights, acting with decisiveness and characteristic vigor. Still, while the second tier of the department was frequently occupied by someone with a longstanding interest in the service, his superior remained in command.

The office of the secretary directed the service through the chiefs of the various bureaus. Despite periodic reorganizations, the bureaus of the navy remained the basic organizational units with the bureau chiefs retaining near feudal rights.[5] Throughout the 1880s, the premier bureau, that of navigation, was directed by Comdr. John Grimes Walker, an officer of great power. From 1881 to 1889, Walker, who served as acting secretary in his superior's absence, assigned officers to ships and ships to stations. He ordered ships to missions and fleets to action. Although the civilian head, or even the Admiral of the Navy, might occasionally offer recommendations, Walker directed naval operations until he was assigned to command the Squadron of Evolution (the White Squadron of new ships) in 1889. Additionally, the chief of the Office of Naval Intelligence (ONI) reported to Walker, from ONI's inception in 1882 until Walker went to sea and ONI was transferred to the office of the assistant secretary.

The Bureau of Navigation relinquished some authority to the new office of the assistant secretary, but generally increased in power as did the ships it commanded. In 1884, Secretary Chandler, in an effort to break up the feudal system, established an advisory board on the state of the ships with the authority to detail them to squadrons. Chandler's changes asserted his goal to move detailing, or ship assignments, out of the realm of the personal politics of navy officers. He partially succeeded, with help from the politically strong board he had appointed. Yet, Walker himself lost little real influence due to his central place on the board composed of Rear Adm. Edward T. Nichols and Comdrs. Montgomery Sicard, Winfield Scott Schley, and Walker. This well-known board was politically well connected, effectively combining its members' own political influence with Chandler's.[6]

In another effort to spread responsibility and increase the department's effectiveness, Chandler had created the Office of Naval Intelligence, the first such permanent organization in America.[7] The ONI fell initially under the aegis of the Bureau of Navigation. With its establishment in 1882, ONI gave the department an autonomous source of information, enhanced strategic planning capability, and provided a fast track for certain officers to influence policy before they had served decades as subalterns. But its greatest successes lay in its role as a promoter of the blue-water navy.

The status of the Office of Naval Intelligence waxed and waned in the late nineteenth century, but some themes remained constant. Paralleling the establishment of the Naval War College and Office of Naval Records and Library, the modernizing navy finally had opportunities and locations in which to think and the intellectual resources upon which to base this contemplation. The ONI provided the navy with an independent source of information concerning other nations' political climates as well as naval assets. This intelligence was frequently far superior to that provided by State Department representatives or even that available to foreign governments, for that matter. The ONI assigned attachés to the great powers to seek out practical information on naval and industrial construction, as well as to determine general levels of battle readiness and the political climate. Preceding the army's Bureau of Military Intelligence (later Military Information Division) by three years, ONI guarded its intelligence jealously—an astute political decision but one difficult to justify in terms of overall national intelligence or strategy.

Among its primary tasks, the ONI suggested the types of ships the navy should build, based on its understanding of the ships, fleets, and plans of the other nations. Its first success in this area came in 1889 when its officers convinced Congress to use new nickel-plated armor on battleships. For these specifications, the ONI had some tangible influence, but the independent naval advisory boards, the secretaries, and especially Congress had the final word on the construction programs, with ONI only advising them. The role of ONI in construction was useful but limited.

Initially the ONI functioned with some independent success as an intelligence-gathering organization. But after 1890, its work was politicized by the assistant secretary of the navy. For instance, while the ONI was charged with uncovering as much detail as possible about the war plans of the other powers, it was not asked for the political intelligence that might have permitted objective threat assessment. After falling under the direction of the politically appointed assistant secretary, ONI intelligence gathering became increasingly subject to a policy-driven methodology—which discourages creative or insightful officers. In fact, by 1893 the attachés' intelligence-gathering skills had deteriorated to the level of bean counting (i.e., tabulating the number and type of foreign ships on a station at any particular moment). All independent analysis was reduced to the level of attempting to demonstrate the need for a blue-water navy—a political goal. Still, before the politicization, it experienced several successes in intelligence gathering, communication, and public relations.

In 1888 ONI developed the first practical navy code to relay attaché reports and more urgent information. This code proved especially valuable in the Americas as the cable traversed the continents. The Navy Department in Washington had near-constant communication with the Pacific Station (which covered the west coast of the Americas) but frequently found itself attempting to convey confidential information along unsecured lines. During the U.S. intervention in Panama in 1885, American commanders communicated with Washington for orders and intelligence; only Panamanian indifference to signal interception saved a dangerously out-manned American force.[8]

The Office of Naval Intelligence was most competent in its promotion of the navy. The well-informed ONI pleaded the case of the new navy before the nation. An early coup for ONI came in 1884 when its attachés in Britain acquired the exploration ships *Thetis* and *Bear* for use on the highly lauded Greely Relief Expedition. Several years later, the secretary gave ONI the responsibility of putting on the department's greatest concerted public relations shows, the Naval Maneuvers of 1892 and the International Columbian Naval Rendez-Vous and Review of 1893.[9] Each of these high-profile events allowed ONI to sing the praises of the new navy. By 1893, in fact, propaganda for the battleship navy had become ONI's primary role.

The ONI was also intended to provide an avenue for ambitious and intelligent young officers to advance to power—a goal that the politicization of the

1890s quashed. Secretary Chandler's first directive regarding the ONI had declared, "The younger officers of the service will be encouraged in collecting and reporting intelligence and writing original articles on naval subjects."

With the further encouragement of Commodore Walker, the young officers did report and write. Two-thirds of the essays that were awarded first prize by the Naval Institute between 1882 and 1900 were by ONI staffers. Unfortunately, after its first few good years, ONI failed as a fast track. Still, the most brilliant and famous of its "Young Turks," William Sowden Sims, did rise in the naval aristocracy through his grasp of foreign intelligence as much as for his talent for improving the accuracy of gunfire.[10]

Despite losing ONI to the new assistant secretary, the Bureau of Navigation remained a formidable power, staving off the creation of a navy board or general staff. Before 1898, ONI and the Naval War College shared responsibility for war planning, in place of a general board that would have eclipsed the bureau's power. A strategy board was not founded until the outbreak of the Spanish war, at which time it was staffed by alumni of the Naval War College and the ONI. A proliferation of offices—the assistant secretary, Office of Naval Intelligence, and the Naval War College—threatened but did not seriously degrade the Bureau of Navigation's longstanding place of pride within the department.

Facilities

As with the Bureau of Navigation, other bureaus cultivated the fruits of modernization and efficiency. The Bureau of Medicine and Surgery enjoyed considerable success in the late nineteenth century; the conditions of the men aboard ship improved considerably due to the bureau's efforts to cooperate on the construction of the new, larger, and better-equipped ships. In each *Annual Report of the Secretary of the Navy,* the medical director, the surgeon general of the navy, would include his tallies and recommendations.[11] The statistics showed a general decrease in diseases over time, a trend opposite to many American cities of the day—a worthwhile comparison considering the crowded conditions and similar non-native populations. The recommendations generally called for healthier quarters for the crew—including forced air ventilation, electric lighting, and protected sanitary facilities. The bureau spearheaded the drive for hammocks instead of forcing the men to sleep on the planks. Disappointingly the medical corps had little success in the war against sexually transmitted diseases.

The navy's hospitals and asylum also demonstrated the newfound interest in taking care of the men, even after they had left the service. The old navy hospital in Chelsea, Massachusetts, was supplemented by others in the new navy. The department had established a hospital at Yokohama in 1870 to attend to the sailors of the *Benicia* stricken with smallpox. Fifteen years later, the navy opened a hospital and sanitarium at Widow Island, Maine. The next year, Newport opened its first permanent naval medical facility. Navy medicine was building the infrastructure that eventually provided the first-rate care given the wounded in the twentieth century.

Other land stations were cleaned up, at considerable expense. In fact, in the old navy, yards and docks cost more than anything but the payroll because of pork included in their budgets. Consequently, they received proportionate attention in the new navy. An increase in the number and extent of the navy yards, bases, and other shore establishments enabled the navy to increase friendly relations (and patronage) on domestic shores, while providing some desperately needed berths for the top grades, providing room for senior officer advancement.

Renovation of yards and bases, as well as the establishment of a new one on the Northwest coast, was traditionally decided after strategic, financial, and political considerations. Yards and bases also provided the navy with local showcases for its new men, ships, and bands. Their primary purpose, however, remained the provision of facilities for building or refitting ships, and for routine maintenance. In the old navy, the yards frequently squandered funds rebuilding hulks at several times their replacement costs. They provided patronage jobs and slush funds—a trend only slowly and partially reversed in the new navy. Navy yards built during the nineteenth century are in figure 1.

Portsmouth at Kittery, Maine, 1800
Boston at Charleston, Mass., 1800
New London, Conn., 1868
New York at Brooklyn, N.Y., 1800
Philadelphia, Pa., 1800
Washington, D.C., became Gun Factory, 1800
Norfolk, Va., 1800
Port Royal, Charleston, S.C., 1861
Pensacola, Fla., 1825
Vallejo, Mare Island, Calif., 1853
Bremerton, Wash., 1891

Fig. 1: Navy Yards, Domestic

Philadelphia's League Island Navy Yard was among the first to be reformed in the revitalization of the 1880s. Throughout the late sixties and seventies, the old yard had provided a hospice for dying hulks of the Civil War. Antiquated ships were refitted at exorbitant labor costs, more to provide patronage jobs for political favors than to build effective fighting ships. Change came slowly to such a corrupt institution. A dozen years later, the department started to clean up League Island's administration. Still, in 1891 Secretary Tracy could call it "one of the most undesirable duties to which an officer could be ordered."[12] League Island waited for the new century to join the ranks of progressive and efficient naval institutions.

Most of the other yards were charged with corruption into the 1880s, but they underwent serious changes in the early years of the new navy. This occurred when Secretary Chandler, who had previously served as the navy's first solicitor and judge advocate general, took office. Having served as the congressman of the district that included Portsmouth, New Hampshire, Chandler had an idea of what went on in yard cities. His report of 1883 called for no more than 30 percent of a vessel's replacement value to be spent on repairs. The next year, with the approval of Congress, the cutoff was reduced to 20 percent.[13] This gave the secretaries the power to limit work being done on the ships, a power that they exercised to rid the navy of its most decrepit ships. As early as 1886, Congressman John G. Ballentine, Democrat from Tennessee, noted with approbation: "Uncle Sam's 'naval repairs' teat having run dry, and the voracious cormorants tugging at it for twenty years having let loose their hold, it may be assumed that we are now in the condition to enter upon a new era for the restoration of the Navy." As a result of this movement, in each year following, the annual report of the secretary of the navy could list the several ante-bellum and Civil War sloops struck from the lists.[14]

One example of the corruption that the 20 percent rule was meant to battle can be found at Mare Island, the department's major repair station near San Francisco Bay. The first post–Civil War Democratic secretary, William Whitney, earnestly endeavored to clean up the Republican trough at Mare Island. In the spring of 1885, he investigated the work in progress since 1872 on the *Mohican*. The restoration had already cost $900,000, or three times the replacement value of the ship, two-thirds of the "work" (i.e., two-thirds of the expenditures) having been done since 1882. Whitney wrote Comdr. John Russell, commandant of the yard, that this "certainly does indicate the most extraordinary mismanagement and wastefulness," and thereupon formed a board of investigation and summarily dismissed "certain foremen of the yard." Soon after, continuing his sweep, Whitney appointed another board to investigate business between the bureaus.[15]

Whitney's reform zeal led to even more effective administrative decisions; acknowledging the impossibility of closing bases in certain politically powerful districts, Whitney took to reassigning them. For example, in 1887 the Boston Navy Yard, one of the nation's oldest, was transferred to the Bureau of Equipment and Recruiting, and was no longer to make major repairs. Closing yards would have caused the department to lose political support and was, consequently, economically unsound policy.[16] There were too many corrupt yards in the East, while the burgeoning West lacked sufficient repair facilities. Four years later, a new yard was opened at Bremerton, Washington, following the recommendations of a board chaired by Captain Mahan.

As well as reforming the yards, the department encouraged efficiency and cooperation on the other land berths, including those devoted to the scientific fields related to sailing and the engineering fields involved in ship or gun construction. The navy had a longstanding tradition of supporting good scientific research—extending back to the hydrographer Matthew Fontaine Maury and the explorer Charles Wilkes—for which it received ample recognition. The centers of navy research were at the observatory in Washington, D.C., and the Nautical Almanac Office in Cambridge, Massachusetts. Command of the observatory was a plum usually reserved for the vice admiral or senior rear admiral of the navy, providing easy living in a pleasant situation.[17] This flag officer, as a rule, would not interfere much with the scientific research under his command.

The navy's researchers, at the Almanac and elsewhere, included the astronomers Simon Newcomb, G. W. Hill, David Peck Todd, and E. S. Holden. Albert Michelson was at the academy when he started his career's work of measuring the speed of light for which he eventually earned America's first Nobel Prize in Physics (1907). To encourage research, the department granted its researchers considerable autonomy, perhaps, in part, to thwart the National Academy of Sciences' efforts to detach the observatory from the navy. In 1889, the observatory did get increased autonomy within the department and by 1893 had a new location and new buildings in northwest Washington, D.C. It "had achieved a permanent place in the government scientific establishment."[18]

Ships

While scientists were observing and recording, naval engineers and constructors were building the ships of the new navy. The ships of the 1880s and 1890s were cleaner in design and intended to be more beautiful and respectable than their predecessors. These ships were popular; civilians loved to visit their uncluttered decks and spacious cabins, and to view their great rifled cannons. For most observers, the new navy's modern steam-driven, steel cruisers compared nicely to the old navy's wooden sailing ships. The sinewy rigging gave way to great guns in hydraulically driven turrets. The immense double expansion steam engines, electric lights, and shipboard telephones represented the awe-inspiring technical advances of the late nineteenth century making the officers and crew, as well as the taxpayers, proud.

Steel had advantages over wood and even iron: it was more durable, repelled shot more effectively, was more easily cleaned, required less upkeep, fostered an industry increasingly important to the nation, and received strong support from the Pennsylvania congressional delegations that represented steel-making districts. To some, however, steel ships lacked the romance of their wooden predecessors. One officer later noted nostalgically the sensual beauty of the older ships:

> Like a beautiful woman, a handsome ship attracts all eyes and has the great initial advantage of eliciting pleased attention; and that simple attention held us until displaced by pride in her great qualities of seaworthiness, stiffness, handiness, and speed. The two smoke pipes could be lowered in sections, telescope fashion, or reefed, as we called it, until entirely concealed within the hull.[19]

Yet sea- and battleworthiness were enhanced in the new cruisers, leaving the old ships only greater cruising ranges and a romantic advantage—the latter was soon remedied by the propagandists of the new navy.

The superstructures of the new ships presented a much less cluttered perspective. The nation itself was experiencing a change in its dominant residential architecture, turning from stick- to shingle-style. The mid-Victorian stick style resembled the bric-a-brac appearance of a warship of the 1860s or 1870s; vertical masts or columns were laced with lines or lattice. As the trends in architecture gave way to the horizontal lines and planar spaces of the shingle style, so too the ship designs emphasized unbroken horizontal sweeps and turrets in echelon reminiscent of walls and windows by architects McKim, Mead, and White. The uncluttered look was especially appealing to naval philosophers who wanted clean slates upon which to write America's destiny. The new ships also featured guns in turrets projecting more boldly from the ships' decks than had the cannons that had previously been set into the sides, below decks. In fact, the images of projected rifles and ships so impressed the editors of *Scientific American* that they included them on seventeen of their fifty-two cover engravings in 1887. The appeal of the guns and "gee-whiz" technology, which in other ages might be termed "battleship envy," cannot be overstated.

Another aesthetic advantage of the new navy lay in its choice of names. Adm. David Dixon Porter, and many politicians, had not liked giving ships native American names, a practice that he ended with the new navy. The *New York Times* agreed with him. When names were selected for the first four new ships in 1883—the *Atlanta, Boston, Chicago,* and *Dolphin*—the newspaper exalted the choices:

> These names are at once intelligible and decent. There is no more absurd delusion than that which leads to the infliction of wholly unfamiliar Indian names upon our men of war. Doubtless these names originally had a meaning, but that meaning has long since been forgotten. They are now mere aggregations of harsh consonants and sickening vowels. Our navy has borne on its lists such names as the Mosholu, the Naumkeao, the Shokokon, the Squando, the Umpqua, and the Waxsaw.

The editorial took the opportunity to denigrate Indians as well as the sailors who sailed their namesakes. It continued:

> These names hardly [any] of which could be pronounced by an intoxicated sailor or spelled by an accomplished naval officer, are as hideous to the ear as to the eye, and as meaningless as "abracadabra." Were a tribe of Indians to fit out a birch navy, there might be some excuse for them—being as ignorant as they are, ignorant and brutal savages—were they to name their canoes as we have named our men of war, but there is no possible reason why we should use such unintelligible and ugly Indian names.[20]

Moreover, the people of great cities were more likely to pay taxes and vote than were the native Americans.

The navy encouraged civic pride to support ships. A similar pride of place elicited national enthusiasm at the celebratory expositions of 1876 and 1893. The Philadelphia Centennial Exposition of 1876 and the Chicago Columbian Exposition of 1893 offered the navy opportunities to propagandize while in the process of revising its identity and goals. The following chapter examines ways the navy used the expositions to sell its vision of itself to the nation and shows how that act of presentation became a process of self-creation. It is worth noting that the navy hammered out this perspective while preparing for and experiencing these fairs. In 1876 the nation's progress was primarily attributed to efficiency and the great machines that helped to conquer the continent.[21] In 1893 the navy presented its greatest machine—a battleship—as the tool for conquest beyond the continent.

Men

Manning the new cruiser and battleship navy required changes in recruiting. The navy attempted to obtain good men who wanted relatively little reward, and was always looking to increase its labor pool. In the early 1880s, the navy recruited mostly from seaports and from the international maritime arena. In 1882, the navy maintained permanent recruiting stations only at Portsmouth, Boston, New York, Philadelphia, Norfolk, Washington, and San Francisco. A few years later, the new navy sought to recruit men from all over America, especially from its interior.

The United States Navy, unlike navies of some other powers, depended completely upon voluntary enlistments, never resorting to a draft or impressment, for most of the nineteenth century, without offering decent pay or tolerable circumstances. Difficulties frequently resulted from the low priority placed on recruiting. Stephen Luce noted these problems as early as 1874 and was echoed as late as 1897, when the *Chicago Tribune* remarked, "Congress has authorized one big battleship after another, but has utterly failed to supply the men to man them." The indomitable Lt. William Sims echoed this thought to his superior in naval intelligence, "It is not logical or practical, and therefore not American, to spend millions on battleships, and thousands on the education of her officers, and nothing on the man behind the gun."[22]

While the emphasis truly was placed upon new construction, the department made some efforts to man the ships effectively. The Naval Militia of Massachusetts, the first of fifteen state militias founded before the Spanish war, offered the department a group of partially trained sailors and yachtsmen upon whom the professionals at first were hesitant to rely. By the time of the Harrison administration, however, any possibility of a federally supported merchant marine as a naval auxiliary had gone the way of rigged fighting ships and commerce raiders, leaving the naval militia as the only proposed naval auxiliary. After a slow start, in 1891 Congress appropriated $25,000 for it. By 1898, the combined strength of the various naval militias included numerous auxiliary ships and 4,125 men, many of whom served in coastal defense and ran dispatches during the Spanish war.[23] Manning the regular navy required more drastic changes.

Everyone agreed that the navy needed higher quality personnel, and the 1880s and 1890s brought concerted efforts to improve its men. In addition to new strategy, equipment, and navigation, the navy recruited and trained superior men; at each level the new men of the navy were the culmination of decades of efforts to form a professional corps of dependable and skilled boys, men, and officers.

In terms of personnel, cleaning up the act started at the bottom. The new navy can be dated from the initial implementation of the apprentice system, which recruited good "American" boys to build an efficient, trustworthy, and polite service of men. The innovative Commodore Luce had participated in inauguration of the Naval Institute in 1873. In the first issue of the *Proceedings,* he called for the reorganization of an apprentice system to provide boys trained and educated explicitly for service in an American navy.[24]

Although potentially useful, the apprentice system never paid off. In 1875, the navy initiated the program, taking fifteen- and then fourteen-year-old boys into the service and detailing four antiquated ships for their training. By the early 1880s, the navy was training 750 of these boys at a time. The numbers and conditions fluctuated through the years, while the navy attempted with little success to retain as well as to educate its own sailors. Retention increased slowly, but as late as 1893, only 10 percent of apprentices remained in service after their formal tutelage.[25]

Sailors also changed in the late nineteenth century, as the nation's feelings of nativism, a form of isolationism, encouraged development of a workforce that was more American—harvested in the heartland, a single race, literate, and athletic. To fit the new navy to contemporary professional standards, the quality of sailors had to be improved. To this end, the department made naval careers for the lower ranks more enticing. By 1898, the navy promised a professional career to its sailors, with education, promotion, reasonable care, benefits, the possibility of a pension, and finally a decent burial. Fifteen years earlier, the service had been ashamed of its men.

The nation had been shocked in 1883 to hear of the sinking of the *Ashulot* in the Pacific and then relieved to read that only 19 of the 111 lost crew members were native-born Americans. The percentage on the other stations balanced out the numbers a bit, as "approximately one-half of the enlisted force was foreign-born" with the trend shifting more toward the American-born by the late 1890s.[26] By 1897, 74 percent were United States citizens and 12 percent more intended to become such. The Americanization of the crews was succeeding.

As the navy increasingly enlisted American citizens, it also brought in fewer African Americans. According to historian Frederick Harrod, in 1880, 14 percent of the enlistees were black, but in 1890 there were only 9.5 blacks in every hundred men. Increasingly, those blacks who served did so as servants in the mess: cooks and stewards. As victims of a segregationist vision of race relations, blacks endured deteriorating work conditions, while the work conditions for whites were generally improving.[27]

Cdr. F. J. Higginson described the ideal sailors of the new navy:

> What we want must come from the country, from the other side of the Alleghanies and south of the Ohio. We want boys who have never seen, and do not know, any other flag than the American, who have good American backgrounds, and who have no old world allegiance or affiliations. We want the brawn of Montana, the fire of the South and the daring of the Pacific slope.

Articles in magazines, especially boys' literature, focused on the Montana brawn with some success.[28]

To maintain the brawn in the age of steamships posed a challenge. Physical punishments were de-emphasized and the labor of running ships no longer provided as much regular exercise in hoisting and scrubbing. Organized sports were arranged to compensate for the alleged loss of vigor. For a while, boat racing (crew) stood alone as the sailors' only organized sport. Robley D. Evans was among the first commanders in the new navy to make serious efforts to institute other games, perhaps because of his longstanding concern that "steamer men look pale; they have no physique comparatively; they cannot stand work so well" as sailing men.[29] Evans emphasized baseball, although the fleet-tactics game of football won out for popularity.

With hygienic quarters and aerobic exercise, the last remediable complaint of the "Jack Tar" while in the service remained the food. In 1896, the *Iowa* became the first ship to experiment with centralized messes and enlisted men specializing as cooks. The new battleships could on occasion even cool enough water with their great compressors to make ice for ice cream.[30]

As the sailors were better cared for and more likely to serve longer stints, they increasingly specialized. In the effort to increase efficiency, the navy adopted modern management techniques that encouraged specialization; the number of sailor ratings grew accordingly. In 1885, the service adopted a six-step grade (or rank) line, which divided the men into three branches based on specialization: seaman, artificer, and special branch. By 1897, there were seventy-one such ratings.[31]

Despite all these changes, annual desertions between 1880 and 1890 increased from 8 to a remarkable 12 percent as labor resisted rationalization. To encourage retention, Congress passed measures to make postservice life more appealing. In 1894, Congress enacted legislation offering foreign-born sailors with five years service and honorable discharges the privilege of U.S. citizenship. And while there was no formal retirement plan, sailors contributed to a pension fund, which, although far from regularized, did provide some relief for the ill, feeble, or old.[32] Additionally, sailors invalided from service could live in the Philadelphia Naval Home. While some improvements were given to the sailors, changes at all levels affected officers more directly.

The officers' circumstances underwent significant changes in the late nineteenth century, despite or within the continuity described by historian Peter Karsten. Although they would not admit it, the officers ceased to be the adventurous heroes of the premodern era, becoming instead steam and gunnery engineers, personnel managers, and bureaucrats. The *New York Times* encouraged this change and others, letting the navy know of one area it had still to reform in the early eighties. Following a collision involving the *Ashulot* due to drunkenness of the commander, a stinging editorial called on the department to shape up and to punish those who "have brought discredit upon the service." To encourage a more trustworthy breed of man, the navy offered to its line officers careers full of many of the rewards and expectations of corporate life. It was considered a response to professionalization of the service.[33] The offer started with junior officers and reached up to the flag rank.

The status and expectations of junior officers in the navy improved drastically through the late nineteenth century. The reasons for this included better training, more room for advancement, higher pay and retirement benefits, and better jobs. For some time after 1882, only the top 25 percent of the Naval Academy class were commissioned in order to thin out the ranks and speed promotion; the remainder was given the free education and released. In 1884, the Board of Visitors of the academy noted that political patronage appointees were not always people of the finest character or academic ability, and that some were even boys who had previously been rejected by the academy. The board further recommended that the entrance exam be given across the nation instead of just at Annapolis, to allow the poor also to take the exam.[34] As well as widening the selection pool, the academy continued to increase its emphasis on science and engineering.

Naval education produced some exciting thinkers. While Albert Michelson (USNA 1873) was the new navy's only great scientist, the academy did produce several engineers of merit. Bradley A. Fiske (1874) designed and patented numerous useful machines including his range finder. His comrade William S. Sims would probably be called a systems engineer today, one of the first rank.[35]

The new navy saw to it that education did not end upon graduation from the academy, improving upon a conspicuous shortcoming of the old navy. The Naval Torpedo School in Newport had been the navy's first postgraduate school, founded in 1869 to test various underwater machines and tactics for destroying ships. The commanders of the school narrowly focused their efforts and did little to change the shape of the navy as it was downscaling in the 1870s. In this time of decreased expenditures, the school missed the opportunity to design an inexpensive defense, which its machines might have provided. These "infernal devices," however, had to wait until Arthur Whitehead perfected the automatic torpedo in the eighties. The old navy's effort at postgraduate education had failed, but the new navy would soon succeed.

The United States Naval Institute, a semiprivate, member-funded organization established in Annapolis in 1873, offered officers and other navalists a forum not only to speak but also to publish their ideas. Although Adm. David Dixon Porter was the first president, the organization owed its vigor to Stephen B. Luce, Foxhall Parker, and William T. Sampson.[36] Within a few years, the institute's *Proceedings* had started to spread the navalist gospel, and soon there were a dozen chapters nationwide. Some of the same navy thinkers who had founded the institute decided in the early 1880s that the navy itself needed to support concerted naval studies. These men, with Luce's leadership, urged the secretary to establish another postgraduate school.

Secretary Chandler established the Naval War College at Newport in 1884 to provide officers with a forum for postgraduate study of tactics and strategy. Its first president, the ubiquitous Stephen Luce, inaugurating the college that year, also opened the most voluble debate to date concerning the direction the service should take in terms of construction and strategy. Luce wrote, "No less a task is proposed than to apply modern scientific methods to the study [*sic*] and raise naval warfare from the empirical stage to the dignity of a science."[37] Luce found a most convincing spokesman for the college's new forward maritime strategy in Captain Mahan. In the several years that followed, Mahan, first as lecturer and then president, focused the college on creating an offensive-defense-oriented navy. In this, the college was frequently assisted by ONI and other offices of Walker's Bureau of Navigation.

Soon after the Naval War College opened, the *New York Times* editors advocated a goal that it should design a program to instruct in modern shipbuilding. This particular goal was not quickly achieved, as the engineers and design specialists continued to study at the Royal Naval College in Britain, as well as at Paris and Edinburgh.[38] In 1897, Assistant Naval Constructor Richmond P. Hobson was able to find American alternatives to Europe at Massachusetts Institute of Technology and then at the Naval Academy. Still, the new war college did produce innovative studies of war, most famous of which were Captain Mahan's sea power books. The war college, therefore, did advance the study of war and define the intellectual discourse of the profession.

As naval officers professionalized themselves, they had to eliminate certain options and distractions. Many supported the move to phase out the Marine Corps to create more berths for naval officers.[39] Some officers lobbied to close the torpedo school in the effort to create a battleship navy. Some obstacles were overcome slowly. It was not until 1899 that the navy instituted a system for weeding out bad officers. Before then, anyone who enlisted early enough and lasted long enough was virtually assured flag rank before retirement.

For those who survived to receive their pennant, roles changed—with the advent of the new navy, they lost some control of their commands on distant stations. Commodores and rear admirals assumed many new roles in managing, philosophizing, and planning, thus becoming the corporate elite of a vast and far-flung system instead of independent rulers of distant fiefdoms.

To some extent, they lost local authority due to the expanding worldwide communication network. Rear Adm. Casper Goodrich explained: "The cable spoiled the Old Asiatic Station. Before it was laid, one really was somebody out there, but afterwards one simply became a damned errand boy at the end of a telegraph wire."[40] Goodrich was correct in that a flag officer could no longer attack or invade nations on his own initiative as John Sloat had in Mexican California in 1846, or as John Rodgers had in Korea in 1871. Moreover, between 1865 and 1898, the nation was nominally at peace, so even the skirmishes and Central American invasions would have offered few of the opportunities of which naval heroes are made.

Officers were encouraged to leave the top-heavy service before retirement, causing the corps to shrink from 1,866 officers in 1881 to 1,399 in 1897.[41] Retirement itself improved the service, giving the bad officers a graceful exit, and allowing those more capable to stay and serve until the end of their careers, secure that they need not leave early to obtain a pension. Congress enacted mandatory retirement at age sixty-four for all but the most senior officers. All these measures encouraged officers of the old navy to retire, leaving the service to those educated in the new navy.

From the foundations laid by the navalist historians, through the training naval personnel received at all levels, the new navy emphasized the consciousness of a professional and competent modern force. This new American navy had children reading boys' magazines; boy apprentices and sailors learning trades; midshipmen joining the guild; and officers writing journals or studying tactics. Education went beyond the schools as the modern service emphasized ethics, sobriety, and efficiency. At each level, the navy reorganized, modernized, and professionalized to earn the support of the nation. At the same time, its proponents attempted to educate civilians as to the merits of this modern, efficient force.

CHAPTER THREE

Selling
—*the*—
Navy

Popularization of the Service

Between 1882 and 1893, the United States Navy emerged once again as a cherished institution in American society. As part of its efforts to professionalize and modernize, it struggled to counter a longstanding identification with the corrupt, the decrepit, and the functionless. Navalists—officers and civilians— saw the need to reestablish the service as a symbol of the big and heroic in American society. The agents of these changes were numerous and not coordinated by any self-identified group. Early popularization efforts began with the first reform bills and authorizations of 1882 and culminated with 1893's Columbian Exposition in Chicago. These efforts came from inside and outside the ranks of the navy. In addition to a revised historiography of the War of 1812, this new image was promulgated in such diverse media as literature, journalism, statuary, expositions, expeditions, and military societies.

Famous navalists such as Theodore Roosevelt and Alfred Thayer Mahan have generally been accorded the greatest responsibility for the creation of the new navy.[1] A good case can be made for Roosevelt as a popularizer, for he had done much by the 1890s; Mahan, on the other hand, had limited influence in the United States until the end of the century. The challenge for Roosevelt and the other navalists of the 1880s and early 1890s was, then, to sell the navy to the nation at large. That America's democratic process necessitated popularizing the service explains many of the differences between it and others that emerged in the late nineteenth century. While the navalists paved the road with new historical justifications and generally improved the service, the greatest obstacle to building a great navy remained the nation's traditional distrust of a standing military. These two themes contended with one another for primacy: on one hand, the democratic tradition of antimilitarism, and on the other, an enthusiasm for bigness and heroism.

Although the blue-water navy was not an expression of popular origin, a complex cultural negotiation between elite and nonelite forces determined the shape of the emerging force. As the elites attempted to sell the ideas of navalism, the rest of the populace showed a selectivity in what they were willing to accept. The result was a navy without balance. It emphasized the popular elements of bigness and heroism as embodied in the battleship and consequently slighted the navy's traditional but less salable duties: coastal defense and protection of shipping.

To Be Read

America in the last decades of the nineteenth century was a nation of extraordinary literacy. Taking advantage of this fact, the navy increasingly appealed to the nation's fondness for the large and heroic through widely circulated magazines and newspapers. *Youth's Companion*, a boy's monthly, ranked consistently among the most widely circulated magazines. It succeeded because the editors changed formulas and substance to suit the readership.[2] Into the early 1880s, the content generally encouraged the boys to behave, stay at home, and be good to their mothers. The *Youth's Companion* mentioned the navy only once in this era, briefly alluding to what a good boy David Farragut had been, and how he and other good little boys grew up to be successful men. The stories generally showed boys as rewarded for remaining within the women's domestic sphere, coddled in a mid-Victorian respectability.

Starting in the late 1880s, however, the content of *Youth's Companion* changed, increasingly showing boys who abandoned their mothers' apron strings for adventure and heroics in the man's sphere. *Youth's Companion*'s stories encouraged boys to enter the world unabashedly in search of adventure and success, often using the navy as a backdrop for the new ethos. In the mid-1880s and early 1890s, technology and war, the staples of the modern boy's literary diet, took command. For example, in 1889 Stephen Luce contributed his first piece, "Just the Boy That's Worked for the Navy," an engaging article on the sense of confidence and duty that apprentices received, and for which they were later greatly appreciated by employers.[3] Luce's contributions, and those that followed, increasingly encouraged this new attitude; *Youth's Companion* prospered and grew along with the new generation of American boys to which it catered.

An analysis of market reactions can help to gauge the response to this publicity. Advertising must find a certain resonance in order to sell, and through the 1890s, the advertisements increasingly turned to the naval motif that the new editorial style had embraced so firmly. Illustrations of boys in sailors' outfits advertised everything from oatmeal and soap to the patterns for clothes in *Youth's Companion,* as well as other magazines, such as the circulation leader, *Ladies' Home Journal.* As further evidence of the success of the new *Youth's Companion,* circulation increased to an impressive 500,000 copies a month.[4]

Adult magazines were also increasing their navy-related content. Between 1889 and 1897, the percentage of navy-related articles in *Harper's New Monthly* increased from zero to 3.3 percent. In the same time period *Century's* numbers went from 4.8 percent to 5.8 percent, and those of *North American Review* went from 4.8 percent to a remarkable 8 percent.[5] These articles covered a broad range of ideas, but each contributed to the navy's sense of security as a standing force within the republic.

Comparable to the shift within *Youth's Companion,* the tone of the adult magazine articles changed as well. The prestigious *North American Review* underwent a dramatic change in the late 1880s and early 1890s.[6] In the 1880s, the *Review* had rarely discussed the navy, and when it did, the theme usually involved corrupt business deals. The majority of the navy-related articles in the early 1880s mentioned John Roach, the reputedly fraudulent shipbuilder. By the early 1890s, navy officers and administrators were writing, and the articles specifically discussed the U.S. Navy. Their focus was the virtues of rebuilding and modernization of ships and yards. The *Review's* editors chose to allow the proponents of the new navy to present their case unopposed. The articles reflected editorial policies that were increasingly positive toward the navy—a trend paralleled by an increase in empire-oriented, non-navy articles appearing at the same time.[7]

Mostly the *Review* helped to popularize the navy by allowing its leaders to extol the military buildup's progress, essentially providing free advertisement space. In July 1889, Admiral Luce published one of the first public arguments for a battlefleet, taking his lessons on sea power in part from Captain Mahan's Naval War College lectures. In 1891, Secretary Tracy argued for the battleship navy and in 1893 Secretary Herbert described the splendid turnout of the American fleet at the International Review in New York. While these activist secretaries reported to the readers how well the navy spent appropriations, the naval propagandists also discussed what was being done to improve the caliber of the personnel.

Early in 1890, for instance, Adm. David Dixon Porter wrote on the increased discipline among sailors. The next year, he contributed a piece on officers' heroics, while his colleague Stephen Luce discussed how the contemporary navy would wage war.[8] In each case, the officers extolled the ability of a large navy to save the nation.

Luce also was among the first to recognize the mushrooming market for books on navy topics. He wrote many articles on his own and he encouraged Mahan to publish his lectures on sea power. Book publishing in the 1870s and into the early 1880s had largely ignored the navy, but by the 1890s almost every publisher offered naval selections.[9] Book publishers discovered that the navy sold extremely well, and the two expanding enterprises matured together. By the 1890s, readership had skyrocketed, with publishers releasing their own version of heroic epics, in the form of historical or technical celebrations. This was demonstrated most enduringly by Mahan's first sea power volume but also by the generally increasing interest in naval affairs.

Newspapers, especially the "Yellow Press," also found that the navy commanded a huge audience, especially if discussed in sensationalist language. The late nineteenth century was a time of extremely fierce competition, and editors' standards frequently wavered in the effort to bolster sales. Although playing consistently with the successful themes of vastness and derring-do, they often turned also to racism or gore to sell papers. The quintessence of yellow journalism can be found most clearly in the almanacs it produced. These almanacs allowed the editors to express their views of the world unimpeded by the uncertainties of daily news.

Joseph Pulitzer's *New York World Almanac* of 1891 sold 605,980 copies, swiftly becoming one of the nation's most popular reference works. The 1892 edition included several relevant entries. "American Naval Progress in 1891" noted with great pride, "the success of our guns must be very flattering to Americans." This account followed directly after a lengthy description of the "armed strength of Europe" including charts of "rifles used by European and

Asiatic powers" and their "modern heavy guns," which were demonstrably larger than those of the Americans. The relative size of the potential enemies' guns was apparently intended to arouse envy.[10]

At least as menacing was the alleged deterioration of the American fleet. While building new ships, the navy department was decommissioning or losing several of its Civil War-era sloops. Pulitzer depicted these efficiency measures in a frightening manner. A list of the ten craft struck from the navy's rolls further illustrates the alleged dangers of a feeble navy, as the frigate "Galena— went ashore off Gay Head [Martha's Vineyard]" and nine of the remaining ships wrecked or were scrapped. If this was insufficient to convince the reader of the precarious position of the United States regarding its naval power, the next entry closed the case as the almanac encouraged the reader to ponder the range of naval guns: "Whether a foreign warship could lie in the outer Harbor and bombard New-York is an interesting question to most New-Yorkers. The following is a list of foreign warships with guns which have a range of ten miles or more." The names of twenty-seven ships of five European powers followed.[11]

Nor were these idly threatening guns, as the next chart indicated. In "The Partition of Africa by the Nations of Europe Among Themselves" was displayed the rapid and systematic advance of Europe. France and Britain each had recently expropriated two and a half million square miles of territory, with a total subject population of sixty-one million—approximately the same size and population of the United States in the early 1890s.[12] Furthermore, few people needed to be reminded that British bombardment had destroyed Alexandria, Egypt, in 1882—effectively sounding the starting gun in the scramble for Africa.

These threats encouraged the nation to reconsider the usefulness of a strong navy for expressing state power. After the horrors of the Civil War, the nation had generally turned its back on the navy; for over a dozen years, the nation erected very few monuments to its dead. But the late 1870s and 1880s brought an increased sentimentality, as the recollection of the cruelties of the blockade and naval warfare gave way to somewhat imaginary memories of epic naval battles suitable to the great American tragedy.

To Be Seen

The new lessons were written not merely on paper, but upon stone. In Washington, D.C., for example, the first memorial constructed was the Navy Monument, placed directly in front of the United States Capitol in 1877. This impressive memorial was cut from marble to create an imposing forty-four-foot-high figure of America weeping on the shoulder of History, mourning the loss of her brave sons.[13] Accompanying characters include Mars and Neptune, the classical gods of war and the sea. Memories of the dirty tedious blockade gave way to visions of a classical epic. The next major naval statue erected in Washington, D.C., honored the Union's greatest naval hero, the officer who had ordered "damn the torpedoes, full speed ahead." Dedicated in the spring of 1881, the ten-foot-high cast of the fearless commodore David G. Farragut was set upon granite and struck from metal that had previously protected his flagship, the *Hartford*, from the mines of Mobile Bay.[14] The elegant bowsprit of the *Hartford*, meanwhile, was sent to Connecticut where it still dominates the main hall of the capitol.

By the mid-1880s, such statements were being reiterated locally across the nation, at times on an even larger scale. The emphasis of New Haven, Connecticut, on naval heroism and greatness typifies these efforts to affect political culture. Secretary William C. Whitney ordered the entire North Atlantic Squadron to New Haven Harbor to participate in the unveiling of that city's Soldiers and Sailors Monument, in June 1887. The dedication ceremony included cannon salutes from the *Richmond*, *Galena*, and *Yantic*. Seventy-five thousand visitors watched, including dignitaries who overlooked the spectacle from the monument's site at East Rock Park, high above the city.[15] Similar monuments decorated cities across the nation.

Moreover, people admired and respected these monuments rather than relegating them to the neglect they later suffered. On Memorial Day in 1887, for instance, New York honored the dead with speeches and decorations, as well as a parade. In the city of New York, "the Governor of the State, the Lieutenant General of the Army and the Mayor received salutes of the National Guard and the Grand Army of the Republic. . . . Statues of Washington, of Lafayette, and Farragut were garlanded with unusual taste and profusion, especially that of the old admiral." The last was a genuinely popular piece, having been designed by French sculptor Augustus Saint-Gaudens for Madison Square Park in 1881.[16]

Even when the navy was not explicitly the object of commemoration, it found a way to take part. Admiral Luce brought the North Atlantic Squadron to New York to inaugurate the Statue of Liberty.[17] To celebrate the sea power that had liberated America, Luce gave the city and its guests a grand show similar to recent decades' display of tall ships, leading a flotilla up the Hudson River.

Naval music contributed to the festive atmosphere of the memorial events. Between 1880 and 1891, John Philip Sousa and his Marine Corps Band became the navy's most singular attraction. Sousa presented the excitement of navalism to the nation, and was the most popular American composer of the late nineteenth century. For a dozen years, he directed the USMC Band, performing for millions of cheering people in hundreds of concerts, parades, reviews, and pageants each year.

Sousa's music was more than just entertainment. One of his best-loved pieces, "Semper Fidelis," set the first words of the marine corps motto to music in 1888. Playing up the broadly agreeable theme, "always faithful," Sousa's piece contributed to the new image of the navy/marine corps as a force always on guard and protecting the nation. This idea was ingeniously packaged for a nation that had traditionally distrusted standing armies.[18] Another inspired dedication, his march "The Washington Post," did nothing to slow the selling of the marine corps and the navy.

The USMC Band was not the only group heralding the department's new image. The navy yards and larger ships also had bands to play for civil and naval parades or reviews.[19] Sousa's work also inspired countless city and high school bands that soon became a mainstay of civil celebrations. They performed for the holidays and the regular reviews that provided summertime entertainment on town commons across America. The navy bands also played at parades launching exploration and rescue expeditions mounted in the 1880s and 1890s.

The expeditions initiated in the navalist spirit of high adventure were public relations events as well. They gave the navy some of its most dramatic opportunities to impress the nation with its worth, as well as with the importance of having well-funded fleets. Previous successful excursions had been small; one, for instance, brought astronomers to West Africa to photograph a solar eclipse. Others were dedicated to exploring and charting the seas. Renewal of Arctic exploration made the greatest splash. The subject of controversy, it had been abandoned after the disastrous *Jeannette* expedition.[20]

The *Jeannette* was a navy ship that was lost in 1881 while exploring the northern Pacific. The navy subsequently turned over responsibility for Arctic exploration to the army.[21] In 1884, however, it reentered the picture to save the army's Greely Arctic expedition.

Lt. Adolphus W. Greely, United States Army, Signal Corps, led an exploration force of twenty-seven into Lady Franklin Bay, between Baffin Bay and the Arctic Ocean, in early spring 1881. Cdr. Winfield Scott Schley, noting the poor planning, said, "this means that some Navy officer will have to go up there and bring them back."

When two years of successive army relief expeditions failed to reach Greely on Ellesmere Island, President Chester Arthur assigned the task to the navy.[22] Navy secretary William E. Chandler recognized an opportunity for publicity and played it for all it was worth. Having secured support from Congress, Chandler had ONI buy two whalers, the *Bear* and the *Thetis;* the Royal Navy donated the *Alert.* He then chose the dashing if pessimistic Schley to command the Greely Relief Expedition.

On 23 April 1884, Schley's fleet sailed from the Brooklyn Navy Yard amid great enthusiasm. It was seen off by hundreds of visitors who had covered the foredecks with floral displays. Sailing under the new Brooklyn Bridge, the fleet encountered thousands of well-wishers waving and cheering from the bridge and thousands more on the Battery and the shores of Brooklyn. Small boats dotted the East River and ships festively blew their whistles. Even the generally dour Lt. John Lowe of the *Bear* noted in his diary, "New York gave us a send off as good as only New York can."[23] The navy had mounted a big expedition, and the nation's greatest city responded in kind.

Despite the ice that cluttered the North Atlantic, the relief expedition arrived at Ellesmere Island on 22 June. Of the original twenty-seven explorers, only six, including Greely, survived.[24] All were weak and near death, for they had spent the previous year nearly without food. Several of the party had evidently cannibalized deceased comrades. The grim stories had not yet dampened public enthusiasm, however, when Schley brought the survivors home to Portsmouth, New Hampshire. A crowd of fifteen thousand cheered and welcomed them, providing just the occasion Secretary Chandler had wanted. In the face of human tragedy Chandler, ever the politician, arranged for the relief expedition to land first in his hometown, perhaps so that his speech would be delivered before a particularly friendly audience.[25]

Chandler's show, carried off with verve and shrewdness, served the modern navy well. Chandler described Schley as "energetic" and his lieutenants "efficient" and replete with "fidelity and skill." He turned his attention to Greely and his deceased and cannibalized lieutenants with "tenderness." Chandler successfully set the tone.[26] His remarks were duly transcribed and published by Rev. William McGinley in a government-sponsored document.

The next published account of the Greely Relief Expedition, that by Schley in 1887, proved even more successful. The initial reception of Schley's volume in *Public Service Review* typified the mixture of horror and delight with which the public viewed the affair: "[The] publication of Commodore Schley's work will revive a melancholy interest in the miserable affair in which the lives of fourteen [*sic*] brave and hardy Americans were wantonly sacrificed to the red-tape, tom-foolery and incompetence of [War Department] martinets."[27]

Schley's report did express a dramatic mixture of heroism and tenderness, leaving the reader with the impression that only the navy could have done the job correctly. His reports were printed along with the engravings of the handsome naval officers and the great frozen frontier that they had conquered. His words were starkly descriptive:

> Poor Sergeant Elison was found in his sleeping bag, in which he had lain for months, with his hands and feet frozen and sloughing away. His comrades had secured a spoon to the stump of his right hand that he might feed himself. . . . He suffered less waste than the others, and if the rescue had been delayed another forty hours he would in all likelihood have been the only one left to tell the tale.

Schley's longest single description paints Elison as completely passive and yet the strongest of the lot.[28] As in the navalist reinterpretation of the War of 1812, the army's reputation was tarnished, leaving the navy as the sole untainted claimant to the military-heroic tradition.

To Be Done

While expeditions greatly contributed to the glory of the navy, expositions brought to the public a participatory immediacy. They provided the navy with a dramatic and tangible forum for popularization, as they provided the nation with grandly appealing visions of empire.[29] The differences between the expositions of 1876 and 1893 clearly demonstrate the advances made in public relations and successes on the part of the new navy.

The last major exposition before the creation of the new navy celebrated the centennial of America's independence. The navy's exhibit at Philadelphia in 1876 typified the service's feeble and scattered political agenda of the day. It centered on machines, uniforms, and scaled-down ship models. The department sent several of its most recent uniforms, archaically bedecked with inlays, braids, and epaulets. It also provided a display of arms, including shot, projectiles, firearms, edge weapons, and Civil War cannons.[30] The most expensive exhibit the Department of the Navy provided was the set of ship models of historic but antiquated ships. All in all, the navy in 1876 showed poorly—with none of the interactive displays that might have excited crowds.

By 1893, however, the navy had transformed its representative apparatus. The Chicago exposition that marked the four hundredth anniversary of Columbus's first voyage proved to be a great public relations extravaganza. In 1876 the exhibits had been of antiquated paraphernalia; in 1893, the department used fifty thousand dollars and a great deal of ingenuity to provide the real thing—or the next best thing.

In Chicago's Lake Michigan, the navy constructed the USS *Illinois*, a 348-foot-long full-scale model of a battleship on stilts. The *New York World* claimed "few people who see the formidable guns and turret over the Fair grounds [that] protect them from invasion by water, will realize until they come very close to her that she is not a floating ship of war." One workman installing galley equipment allegedly expressed his concern to a naval architect that, "if she gets outside in a blow, I'm afraid that those stoves may cut adrift."

It was, said the *World*, "as fine a battleship to the eye as there is in the Navy." A model of awe-inspiring fighting power, the *Illinois* sported modern rifled cannons in place of Civil War smoothbores. Real officers and men fired guns and performed mock rescue missions. The *Illinois* was not only fine but also stunningly popular.

At that moment, the navy had no first-rate battleships in commission. But the *Illinois* did not remain the navy's finest for long. In one way, this ship *became* the new navy, not merely the model for it; indeed, the six-inch guns went to the *Oregon* as a secondary battery. Less tangibly, however, the *Illinois* and its hale crew personified the navy for the twenty million exposition visitors and countless readers of such papers as Pulitzer's *World*.[31]

In addition to the Columbian exposition, the navy found fora to celebrate its new image. In 1892, the service had hosted its own spectacle, the International Naval Rendez-Vous and Review, in celebration of Columbus's voyage to the West. The most modern fleets from each of the naval powers attended the show, first at Hampton Roads and then in New York Harbor. Thousands of curious spectators lined the banks of the James River and the piers and streets of New York, while international crews paraded through the city led by navy bands and local fire and police units. The event converted the greatest city of the new empire to big-ship navalism.[32] The ships metaphorically provided the technological answers to Americans' fears of vulnerability.

In the quest for absolute invulnerability, however, Americans overlooked something. That was the undramatic but potentially more useful small craft toward which much of the world was turning at that time. What most viewers did not see at this review was the alternative and auxiliary to the battleship—the torpedo boat.

The European powers were building scores of torpedo boats at this point. At the urging of its torpedo boat clique, the *jeune école*, France had already deployed 215 such vessels, leading the pack. The British navy had 199, the kaiser's *Kriegsmarine* [navy], 180, Italy and Russia, 165 and 152, respectively. Even the minor powers had torpedo fleets.[33] The United States had but one prototype, the *Cushing*, which impressed few except Lt. Cdr. J. D. J. Kelley, who observed unheeded: "In the naval Parade [in New York Harbor] of the Columbian Celebration in October of 1892, the Torpedo-Boat Cushing elicited the greatest wonder from those who, for the first time, realized what this country is capable of doing and has not done for the development of this type of auxiliary war vessels."

These vessels offered a potentially Davidian solution to the Goliathan problem of battleships. This strategy was most easily applied to nontraditional powers and especially to those with many dispersed harbors to defend. But torpedo boats failed to catch the popular attention with their diminutive size and lack of impressive guns. Instead, what was successful at the 1892 review was big—the bigness of the guns, of the ships, and of the fleets.[34]

The publicity worked. Twenty million people attended the Columbian exposition at which the navy portrayed itself as one of the nation's great symbols for the modern era—big and heroic. Tens of thousands more had watched the preceding naval reviews and celebrated the great battle fleets. Responding increasingly to navalist publicity, private citizens demonstrated their enthusiasm, vastly increasing the recruiting pool. Tens of thousands more joined fraternal or patriotic orders, which required firm commitments to building up the navy. Into the 1880s, these organizations drew phenomenal numbers once they learned how to take advantage of the genuine and widespread popularity of the reborn navy.

As was the case with the expositions, this took more than one effort. Such groups as the United States Naval Veterans Association were founded to "promote the growth and prosperity of the United States Navy."[35] When these organizations opened ranks to the multitude of supporters, they were successful. Among the largest were Sons of Veterans, USA, with a hundred thousand members in 1892, and the Patriotic Order of the Sons of America, also with a hundred thousand joiners. The United Confederate Veterans and the Regular Army and Navy Union were each founded in the 1880s with overtly political agendas, often including support for the first peacetime military buildup.[36] The Grand

Army of the Republic led all organizations in sheer numbers; but the Naval Militia had more influence, considering the active role its fleet of private craft played in the Spanish war.

Even among less-military societies, the navy's influence can be found. Since 1863, the country's greatest scientists have comprised the National Academy of Sciences. In 1892, navy scientists were playing a disproportionate role in its activity. In the early 1890s, for instance, the home secretary was Asaph Hall, of the navy. The eleven-man governing council included three navy scientists: Hall, Simon Newcomb, one of the world's premier astronomers, and Samuel P. Langley, who pioneered heavier than air aviation. Each of these men presented the navy's case eloquently, writing for major journals, giving popular speeches, and explaining the importance of well-funded navy science.

In sum, navalism spread across America between 1882 and 1893, not merely as the cause of a few scheming imperialists, but as a national movement growing up with the burgeoning nation, sounding two of the most important cultural chords of the day—great size and heroism. Yet, the cost of emphasizing the big may have been an inflexibility of construction that led to five decades of over-reliance upon battleships. Certainly, an unbalanced fleet lacking torpedo boats or submarines must be included among the costs. But without the appeal to the popular diad—gigantism and heroism—the public doubtless would not have responded to the idea of the new navy. As it was, support came from across the land and was genuinely enthusiastic. By 1893, America was dressing, humming, and voting to the tune of the navy.

CHAPTER FOUR

The Old Navy's Pacific

Throughout the 1880s, leading naval officers generally accepted an ethos that viewed the Pacific basin as a place for commercial and heroic enterprise. While a shift should not be viewed as either sudden or complete, the new navy generally adopted a different set of views—more imperialistic and militant— although the change came slowly. The perspective of the old navy was most cogently expressed by Robert W. Shufeldt and was typified in the writings of other senior officers, such as Daniel Ammen, Thomas O. Selfridge, Samuel Franklin, and Albert Barker. The department's official Pacific policies, which lasted well into the eighties, reflected the philosophy of the old navy.

Pacific and Asiatic

In the late nineteenth century, the Pacific region was becoming more closely merged as the great distances appeared to diminish. Exploration, hydrography, faster ships (first sailing, then steam), telegraphy, and free-trade economics enhanced communications and expanded commerce—shrinking the ocean. Regularized trade, for instance, increasingly brought Japanese silk, Hawaiian sugar, and Indonesian spices to the United States in ever less-expensive quantities. By 1880, American imports from China and Japan alone totaled $36,280,432, up from only $5.5 million at the close of the Civil War. From then until the depression of 1893, trade increased inexorably, and the development of commercial, power, and knowledge infrastructures continued. The nations of the Pacific, including the United States and imperial Britain, were growing together, prodded by flourishing international commerce. Some historians have called this integration "informal empire," but theories that suggest an integrated and maturing world economic order better explain the circumstances.[1]

Although growing structural interdependence suggested that the Pacific was increasingly becoming one community, the Navy Department continued to treat it as two regions, organizing its efforts into two squadrons. The Asiatic Squadron was based in Hong Kong and cruised the waters from approximately Midway Island through the Indian Ocean, generally staying in the western Pacific. In time of peace, the navy's ships could resupply at almost any port in this region, taking on stores, new sailors, and mail, doing so most often in China and Japan. Although the United States had annexed Midway in 1867, it established no permanent base there until 1903. Nagasaki and Yokohama had served as the Asiatic Squadron's major coaling stations, the latter also housing a storeship and hospital beginning in 1871.[2]

The remainder of the ocean was patrolled by the Pacific Squadron, then based in San Francisco Bay and nearby Mare Island/Vallejo shipyard. The ships of the Pacific Squadron cruised the waters east of Midway from Tierra Del Fuego to the Bering Sea. By the end of the century, the squadron had stations at Bremerton in Puget Sound, at Pichilingue in lower California, at Tutuila in Samoa, and at Pearl Harbor, Oahu. Generally ships could also resupply at Valparaiso, Callao, and other ports along South America's western coast.[3]

Thus, through the 1870s, the navy was relatively comfortable on the Pacific Ocean, with numerous ports of call and generally peaceful relations with the fleets of the other powers on station. Officers bonded chiefly with the British, who apparently never tired of toasting Josiah Tattnall's claim that "blood is thicker than water."[4] In doing so, they recalled that in 1859 American commodore Tattnall had interposed his troops at Tientsin (Tianjin) to save British invaders from a Chinese counterattack. His justification of consanguinity proved for decades to be the leitmotif not only of Anglo-American naval relations on the Pacific, but also of a myth rationalizing America's benign neglect of European aggression in that region. In reality, throughout this era, the fleets of the European powers and the United States cooperated more than they competed, particularly in the ways in which they experienced the twin hardships of distance from home and proximity to alien cultures. While the navy split the ocean organizationally, officers retained a notional consistency in their camaraderie with the other white men who served on it. They shared nostalgia for a common vision of home and a common vision of Anglo-Saxon heritage.

Into the 1880s, the United States remained essentially an Atlantic-oriented nation, and men on the Pacific were far from home; the mail took weeks or months to deliver, and even telegrams to connected stations were far from instantaneous. Telegrams to nonwired stations frequently took months to complete.[5] The hardship of distance meant that an officer's assignment on one Pacific station would rarely be followed by assignment to the other. The opposite was true for the polyglot and peripatetic crews. The cooks and attendants were usually Chinese (or Filipino) instead of the African Americans who served on the larger Atlantic stations. The men, sometimes known on the Asiatic Squadron as "China sailors," frequently made their homes permanently on station, marrying local women when their enlistments ended. For the naval officers, the Pacific remained a distinctly backwater region.

For the officers, Pacific service was distinctive in these and many other ways. Most important for identifying the Pacific as one coherent region were the writings of these officers. Whether on the Pacific or Asiatic Stations, their written discourse treated as one unit the ocean and frequently its littoral lands, except those close to the United States. This treatment changed dramatically with the creation of the new navy, but it still remained a cohesive discourse—one notion of an ocean.

Shufeldt's Pacific

The old navy's Robert Wilson Shufeldt (1822–95) generally viewed the Pacific Ocean as a place of challenge and excitement, the people as active and having their own initiative, and the markets as well suited for exporting to the United States. Shufeldt has sometimes been called an imperialist or a proto-Mahanian, but his views on the Pacific clearly put him in a completely different camp, that of the old navy. When disappointed, enthusiasm waned and his views approached those of European imperialists whose "orientalist" worldview derided the Asian character; but Shufeldt always rebounded, regaining his enthusiasm and genuine respect for the region and its inhabitants.[6] This type of respect died with the old navy.

Shufeldt, probably the most complex and far-sighted American naval officer in the Civil War and postwar era, represented these attitudes well. His navy protected America's interests abroad, specifically tending to the commerce outside Europe. In these regions (especially those taken over in the post-1884 "new imperialism"), Shufeldt saw the opportunity for America to play a greater part in a worldwide marketplace—to participate in the free-trade, Cobdenite world at just the time when it was on the verge of collapsing into the closed competition described more successfully by Hobson.[7]

Shufeldt's world, constructed along the lines of Richard Cobden's philosophy of free trade, had found stability in British worldwide economic hegemony and a political concert of European powers. He understood this system and wished to take advantage of the stability and prosperity for his own nation, while demonstrating little interest in taking part in the European type of political domination. Toward the end of Shufeldt's naval career, changes in the economic and political situation in Europe, combined with a disintegration of the power of local collaborator-rulers, triggered the new imperialism, which overran the Pacific in the last two decades of the nineteenth century.[8]

Embarking in 1878, Commodore Shufeldt took the antiquated frigate *Ticonderoga* on a three-year world tour, to encourage American trade and show the flag where it was rarely seen. Shufeldt had conceived of this commerce-aiding tour and had easily convinced leading congressmen and Secretary of the Navy Thompson of its potential importance. His three-year mission was sponsored by both the Departments of State and Navy and was intended to expand trade and regularize relations, not to establish or take colonies. He emphasized free trade and opposed increasing America's formal rule in the Pacific, with the notable exception of the Panama-Nicaragua isthmus.[9]

Shufeldt's post–Civil War writings reveal an officer concerned with the broad economic, political, and military needs of his nation. Indeed, his writings comprised a grand strategy.[10] He painted a realistic picture of a nation essentially self-sufficient but prospering from certain types of commerce, especially from an enlarged import trade that increased the standard of living. He hoped to balance trade with exports of American surplus, the primary goal not being to extend rule but to obtain those select items that America could use to improve the lives of its citizens. Shufeldt never considered foreign resources worth a war.

Shufeldt did not complain about the type of navy existing in the so-called dark ages, for all he needed could be provided by any ship with cannons large enough to enforce good manners between local traders and Americans. Significantly, he did call for the navy to have ships in better condition but not of a different type. His ships did not control the seas, but rather policed them in time of peace. "Low down as the American navy is to-day, I think I could select a fleet which would make a respectable demonstration in these Eastern seas," he wrote for a San Francisco newspaper in 1887.[11] He may have developed some of these ideas during his tedious service in the Mexican and Civil Wars. He certainly practiced them on his voyage around the world on the *Ticonderoga*.

Shufeldt's views of the Pacific typify the old navy at its finest. For his successes and despite his notable setbacks, he was consistently rewarded with praise, fame, and promotions. Shufeldt's advancement was due, to some extent, to his having been appointed an officer decades before the Civil War appointment hump, although he attained rear-admiralty at approximately the same age as those of the later generation.[12] His career nevertheless was also advanced by the fact that he was a natural leader and philosopher of the old navy.

Shufeldt briefly attended Middlebury College before his appointment as a midshipman in 1839, six years before the founding of the Naval Academy at Annapolis. After a brief training period, he embarked for the Brazil Station where he helped protect Americans from riots in Rio de Janeiro. After a respite for more training, he left for Africa's gold coast in the squadron that shared arduous duty with the British navy in suppressing slave trade.[13] By 1853, however, it became apparent to the adventurous, ambitious, and still young officer that the navy was facing extremely slow times and was failing to provide excitement as well as the financial rewards needed by the father of a growing family.

Shufeldt left the service and spent the years before the outbreak of the Civil War in command of commercial ships between New York, New Orleans, Mobile, and Havana, all the while cultivating connections in business and government circles and making money. He used political and commercial connections freely—a trait that attained for him these positions and the ability to use them effectively.[14] When Fort Sumter fell, he was United States consul general in Havana, a post from which he was able to assist the Union cause by arranging for his friend Capt. Charles Wilkes to pull John Slidell and James Mason off the British packet *Trent* on their way to serve as the Confederacy's representatives in Britain and France.[15]

This controversial action and the concomitant diplomatic uproar only whetted Shufeldt's thirst for adventure. In 1863, he rejoined the navy, commanding a monitor on the blockade—only to find this too tedious. He groaned to his admiral: "I am unsuited for service on an ironclad—being too large & too full blooded for such a confined space." Shufeldt received a steam schooner instead and set out to chase blockade runners.

Soon after Grant and Lee met at Appomattox, Shufeldt set off for the Pacific, for the first time seeing the lands and waters of East Asia where he eventually earned his greatest fame. Shufeldt found the Asiatic Squadron exhilarating and enjoyed being there and seeing the sights. He took great pleasure in sailing the sea and writing poetry. He noted, "I believe that God made Heaven and Earth—but I am sure that He made *the sea*."[16] The space, the freedom, the relative power of his ships' old cannons, even his purchasing power thrilled Shufeldt.

He expected amity, trade, and general cooperation between the United States and the nations of the Pacific: "China & Japan—are both looking towards America—with most friendly gaze—not only for trade & intercourse which they expected from the Pacific but with an element antagonistic to that European power [Britain] whose encroachments they dread."[17] Thus he identified the East Asians and the North Americans as Pacific peoples, both fearing the advance of the new European imperialism. Shufeldt felt sympathy for the people and for their rights, and he came to feel at home among them. Shufeldt saw a harmony of interests among all the distinct nations bordering the great Pacific common. He wrote, "The Pacific Ocean, with its long swell & gentle breezes is waiting for the American flag. Alaska and the Aleutians form the arm which America is stretching out to embrace the nations & the commerce of the East."[18]

Shufeldt steamed home from his first Asian tour in the *Wachusett,* intending to promote America's cooperation and interaction in the Pacific. He started several years of lobbying to obtain an Isthmian canal to encourage the commerce that would sustain his vision of the Pacific as a sector of free trade. In 1870, Captain Shufeldt attempted to recruit young Lt. Cdr. Alfred T. Mahan to help him survey a Nicaraguan site for such a canal, but Mahan had other plans that kept him in New York.[19] Here, perhaps, Shufeldt lost a great opportunity to convert the still impressionable Mahan to his own vision of sea power and its relation to commercial empire.

Several years later, Commodore Shufeldt expounded his own theories on the influence of sea power upon America in his modestly titled *Relation of the Navy to the Commerce of the United States*. This pamphlet more accurately depicted his grand strategy than any of the pieces he published in newspapers. First, he advocated a naval service that would foster commerce in peace, while halting enemy shipping in war. For Shufeldt, sea power meant the power to cultivate trade along the great ocean waterways; he thought that trade made a nation great, drawing lessons from the historical success of the British Empire and the failures of the Chinese.[20] The United States needed adequate sea power to police trade with the peoples of the Pacific but did not need the power to fight the great battlefleets of the European powers.[21] This policy certainly called for renewing the navy. As Shufeldt noted in a letter to the politically powerful former congressman John Sargent, "The United States, strange as it may appear, is pursuing a policy which, at no distant day, will make her in like manner as formidable beyond her limits as China or as a turtle in a shell."

Conduct of national policy abroad required the United States to build some fast cruisers, but not the battlefleets that the European great powers maintained.[22] Shufeldt favored the traditional American balanced defense strategy—strong coastal defense combined with the deterrent of commerce-destroying cruisers. The cruisers had to be strong enough to destroy commerce and swift enough to avoid battleships. Coastal defense, for Shufeldt, relied mostly upon monitors and coastal fortress guns large enough to repel invasion. He never engaged in the quest for the ultimate machine of national defense such as battleships or armored cruisers designed to outrace and outgun any opponent. Rather, Shufeldt's strategy relied upon a system of interlocking defenses including the monitor, fortress, and cruiser combination.[23] Such a scheme, after all, had adequately defended America for three generations.

Within this framework, Shufeldt also advocated subsidizing a steamship line that would trade between Asia and America in peace, and would fight a *guerre de course* (attack shipping) in war. These same steamers might also serve as troop and supply transports.[24] The transport idea shows Shufeldt's flexible thinking. He clearly placed importance on plans to seize and hold land during war.

Shufeldt's ideas regarding sea power embodied the best strategy of the old navy, as did his geopolitical views of the Pacific. His pamphlet *Relation* (1878) contained his views on China, although he had aired some preliminary fulminations in semipublic addresses over the previous few years. In 1878, he regarded China's primary problem to be its failure to adapt to the changing world. China was "an aggregation of people without external force" who suffered from "the absence of interchange of ideas through the absence of interchange of commodities." Typical of the nations of the Pacific, China was a closed society and would not learn modern ways without commerce being brought to it, according to Shufeldt. His specific warning was not for China, however, but for the United States: it should not remain static or it would become more like China, merely another Pacific nation without external force, "cultivating the contempt of nations and cultivating our own insignificance."[25] Shufeldt sought to shape American grand strategy using observations from the historical and contemporary worlds.

Also typical in Shufeldt's perspective was his opinion of the Chinese as potentially dangerous because of their backwardness. They were not first-rate soldiers or sailors, but they posed a possible threat to Americans nonetheless. As he noted a few years later, "China has a Navy of about 60 vessels of the modern type" in addition to "a partially trained force of about 35,000 men, armed with breach-loaders & a complement of field pieces. [The viceroy] has also in store 200,000 or 300,000 stand of arms & several hundred pieces of artillery."[26] Shufeldt, who was generally optimistic, viewed the Chinese soldiers as a potential force for good.

He hoped that they would not be turned against America and comprised rather a force that might be used for Shufeldt's own good. Shufeldt himself hoped to take an important leadership position in the Chinese defense organization upon his retirement from the United States Navy. Apparently, the viceroy, Li Hung-Chang [Li Hongzhang], deceptively encouraged Shufeldt in this fantasy. To Shufeldt, then, the menace of Asians was very real, but it could be contained if properly channeled by white intelligence. Soon after, in 1883, the U.S. Navy once again acknowledged the reality of China's military capacity; during the Canton riots of that year, its navy protected European residents and property from real threats. This illustrates the old navy's graduated response doctrine, which enabled the department to act with sufficient but not catastrophic force to a particular threat. With the riots and with the promise of his Chinese appointment having fallen through, Shufeldt temporarily soured on the Chinese even as he was engaged in a diplomatic mission in China and Korea attempting to open Korea to American commerce. At this point, he wrote the undiplomatic Sargent letter decrying the "inscrutable" Chinese.[27]

In this letter, Shufeldt retreated to a more imperialist rhetoric. He "orientalized" the Chinese by detailing the inscrutable nature of their diplomatic discourse, the rhetoric of which he had taken many years to learn. The Chinese were "down-trodden people of the earth." Shufeldt commented with fear upon their potential power:

the 400,000,000 of people, [who] if turned in any intelligent direction— unrestrained by any moral obligation—unhindered by any physical obstacle— over-running Countries—exterminating races—I am forced to agree with the experienced diplomats, that Chinese progress in the art of war, is a thing to be checked rather than accelerated by the European powers.

Shufeldt here did not fear their arms or capacity for modern-style war as much as their sheer numbers and senseless force. With his personal hopes dashed, he temporarily fell into the orientalist dialogue of defining and limiting in order to control.[28]

Shufeldt, in his disappointment, fits the description of an "Orientalist" for reasons given by Edward Said. Despite his limited efforts, wrote Said,

> the Orientalist remained outside the Orient, which however much it was made to appear intelligible, remained beyond the Occident. This cultural, temporal, and geographical distance was expressed in metaphors of depth, secrecy, and sexual promise; phrases like "the veils of an Eastern bride" or "the inscrutable Orient" passed into the common language.

During the bitter period of his rejection, Shufeldt did not limit his version of orientalism to military affairs. An embittered view of the Chinese civil leaders also came out in the bitter Sargent letter. He viewed Li as an "absolute and despotic leader . . . who lives on the mere breath of the Empress, an ignorant, capricious and immoral woman." Much like the nineteenth-century British historians of India, Shufeldt wrote of Li, "he is a thorough Oriental and an intense Chinaman. This implies contempt for Western nations and hatred for all foreigners. . . . He keeps together an incongruous Empire and an effete dynasty."[29]

The letter caused a huge stir among the fledgling China hands in the United States who were fearful of insulting the Chinese. Commodore Shufeldt was recalled by the State Department, but the press supported him. The *New York Times,* for instance, stated that the letter "revealed the hollowness and unsavoriness of oriental diplomacy . . . and gave a graphic picture of the espionage, theft, and promiscuous blackmailing that prevail in the Chinese government from the bottom to the top." Nonetheless a buoyant character, Shufeldt returned to East Asia and opened Korea the very next year with the invaluable assistance of the "inscrutable" Chinese and the "despotic" Li.[30] He had recovered enough faith, at least, to accept their help.

Despite his diplomatic blunder, Shufeldt succeeded. Actually, the Chinese leaders were not seriously perturbed except that Shufeldt had insulted a woman, the dowager empress. Even so, the court reaction was mild. Shufeldt still managed to open Korea on terms satisfactory to all involved.[31] Promoted to rear admiral soon after, Shufeldt retired to Kumamoto, Japan, after a long pleasant visit with his new friend, the king of Korea. Eventually even Shufeldt tired of living away from the States, and rejected an offer to be minister to China.[32] After a few years in East Asia, Shufeldt returned to a different America, which viewed the Pacific in a different light. He died several years later, having already outlived his importance as a spokesman for the Pacific policy of the service and of the nation. The new navy's policy was based on principles completely opposed to his—on a battlefleet and an imperialist agenda.

Even when he despised them, Shufeldt had always taken Asians seriously: they were to be feared or loved. They were to be helped or hurt, but always they were real, interactive people with an agenda of their own and equal to Americans in many ways. Even the orientalism to which he once turned was personal, and he never viewed the orientals as anything less than representing a real power with which Americans had to reckon. While his view of Asians even included a stereotypical female despot, Shufeldt never disenfranchised them. That blow was to be struck by a later naval philosopher who never really was able to know his competition.

Pacific Policies of the Old Navy

Several episodes typify navy Pacific policy debates and demonstrate the ways in which Shufeldt's perspective was paradigmatic for the old navy. The views of particular officers will demonstrate the pervasiveness of these attitudes. The disastrous *Jeannette* expedition, mentioned in chapter 3, set out for the Arctic via the Pacific at approximately the same time that Shufeldt's world cruise began on the *Ticonderoga*. In many ways, the *Jeannette* tragedy mirrors the experiences on the *Ticonderoga,* as the officers of each ship came to acknowledge the overwhelming physical realities of the Pacific—its deadly threats as well as its lustrous promise of adventure and wealth. Reports of the experiences of the officers on the lost *Jeannette* as they vainly wandered the northern Pacific contributed to a general respect for the unforgiving physical character of the ocean and for the lives of its people, while reinforcing the view that the Pacific markets were valuable mostly for their exports.

Lengthy reports and hearings following the disaster noted the overwhelming physical perils of the ocean. With the ship trapped in the ice for two winters, and during escape efforts across ice-laden waters, the officers consistently displayed a respect for the power of the Pacific. They clearly recognized its power over their lives. This humility diminished during the decades following when the officers had less to fear, and their strategies were less respectful of the vicissitudes of the great ocean.

The navy's reaction to the calamitous *Jeannette* expedition of 1879 set the tone for a decade's perception of the northern Pacific. In many ways, it reflects Shufeldt's attitudes on the proper role of the navy in the northern Pacific, Bering, and Arctic regions. Shufeldt valued geographic places for their inherent qualities. For example, he did not favor a continued U.S. naval presence in the northern Pacific because of its apparently marginal economic value. He did not favor holding the region for some vague idea of a potential strategic value, and the navy followed this evaluation for the time being. Almost alone in his position that the navy should continue to explore the far-northern Pacific, Chief Engineer George Melville posited for it a Turnerian significance; the last frontier motivated progress and kept the nation vigorous and growing. Gleefully noting the danger of Arctic exploration, Melville cited the heightened spirit that adventure gave to a society.[33]

Lieutenant Jonathan Danenhower, in the *Proceedings* of the United States Naval Institute, debated Melville on the wisdom of continued Arctic exploration after the loss of the *Jeannette*. Danenhower wrote:

> After having served with one Arctic expedition and having devoted seven years to the study of the subject, as well as the watchful observation of the numerous efforts and the comparatively insignificant results attending sacrifice of human life and treasure, I unhesitatingly record myself as opposed to further exploration of the central polar basin.

Danenhower's argument fell within the sphere of Shufeldt's notions of the Pacific, emphasizing the practical uses for the time. In contrast to Melville, Danenhower wanted tangible results. Danenhower's argument carried the day. Throughout the eighties, however, the navy avoided the northern Pacific.[34]

In the western Pacific, the navy adopted an equally reasonable policy of minimal interference, as demonstrated during the little-known Ponape (Pohnpei) crisis.[35] This island in the East Carolines had considerable strategic and economic potential, yet its imperial crisis has received far less attention than others, because it was settled with surprising harmony. Ponape provides some interesting insights into the changing attitudes within the navy regarding the relation between the Pacific islands and the defense of the United States.

American Protestant missionaries were among the first whites to settle there, in 1852, and they soon won the hearts of much of the population for their inoculations against smallpox, which had periodically ravaged the island. Many of the survivors of the 1853 smallpox visit converted to Protestant

Christianity in the following years, and the mission grew, founding a school for girls in 1882.

Three years later, Germany started to form a Pacific empire of its own, hoisting the kaiser's flag over all the Carolines. But Germany's position in Ponape quickly proved untenable, and the flag was soon lowered. The Spanish took possession four months later in 1886. The United States Navy, meanwhile, remained oblivious to any problems. The commander of the Asiatic Squadron reported, "affairs in the East are quiet." The Spanish, however, proved even more problematic than the Germans. Rebellion started almost immediately, with Protestant proselyte-natives firmly opposed to Catholic Spanish rule. American Protestant missionaries may have instigated this insurgency, as the Spanish claimed. Logical as the argument seems, the Protestant minister, Mr. Doane, was cleared of just these charges after being hauled off to Manila for trial.[36] While Doane was in Manila, the natives killed the Spanish governor and his troops, on the fourth of July 1887.

The United States consul general in Manila characterized the massacre as a logical response to the excesses of the late Spanish governor. "The natives, probably driven to fury by a crazy Spaniard of a Governor, have risen in fearful rebellion and driven the Spanish, after killing almost all their land forces—49 being dead—out of island."[37] Fearing that reprisals against the rebels would also harm American missionaries, the consul called for navy protection.

A new Spanish governor, Don Luis Cadares, took charge of Ponape in November, followed shortly by a visit of the USS *Essex* to oversee American interests. The commander of the Asiatic Squadron had sent the *Essex* and its skipper, Charles Jewell, because of his "good judgement and tact" as well as the proximity of his ship.[38] Although chosen for diplomatic skills, Commander Jewell was instructed to arrive with Cadares's expeditionary forces, which he did, assuring the secretary of navy that the Americans on the island would "receive full protection" from the Spanish forces and from the natives. This act showed a willingness to extend diplomat-like protection to the missionaries—a policy that the United States applied only in nonwhite lands.[39]

The *Essex* was one of the newest and finest ships in the U.S. fleet, but as a wooden screwsloop with one eight-inch gun, it would not have inspired much fear among the European powers. Jewell was armed, however, with "a synopsis of the rights and privileges of Germans in the Carolines and [knowledge from] subsequent correspondence between [U.S.] Department of State and that of Spain" that Americans' rights would be equal to those of Germans in the region. The *Essex* protected the Americans and watched as peace was temporarily restored; she left a few days later.[40]

The truce continued only three years, as the Protestant natives continued to chafe under their Catholic rulers. In June of 1890, the Spanish began a small buildup of forces, and soon after the Ponapeans again massacred the soldiers. The governor surrendered that summer, but 1 September brought ships from Manila with a thousand troops. Fearing for their safety, many of the missionaries fled the island two days later. On 13 September, the Spanish shelled the island, without discrimination. A week later, three hundred troops landed and burned "all property including that of the American Mission."[41] When the missionaries returned in late September, they were greeted with new restrictions, including one against holding meetings.

Commander Henry Clay Taylor brought the *Alliance* to Ponape in late October and immediately reported on the situation to the commander of the Asiatic Squadron, George E. Belknap. "I found the situation here unsatisfactory. The rebellion still continued." Hoping to end the bloodshed without any extra change in the status quo, Taylor noted the opinions of both sides. "The feeling among the Spanish here has been and continues to be very bitter against the American missionaries, who are accused of inciting the natives to rebellion." As for the missionaries, Taylor "made a thorough investigation and [found] them innocent." While taking the side of the missionaries and islanders in the debate, Taylor assented to the Spanish-proposed solution—the removal of the missionaries.[42] In return, the governor promised reparations for the Americans' losses. Three years later, the United States government sent Taylor to London and Madrid to conclude the settlement discussions.

Throughout the entire process, the United States Navy had attempted to protect the rights of the civilians on Ponape. The two rebellions expressed the genuine interests of the natives, which the navy attempted to protect. No official mentioned the possibility of the United States taking over the island, despite the fact that Americans were far more popular than, and had priority over, the Spanish or the Germans. The State Department had dispatched Herbert Rand from Carthage, Illinois, to Ponape in October 1890. Rand, the brother of a missionary couple on the island, naturally expressed considerable interest and concern for the well-being of the Americans in Ponape. However, he arrived at Ponape on 11 November 1891, after the troubles had passed. Ten days later, the State Department recalled him.[43] This left negotiations in the hands of the navy, and, in particular, Taylor.

For the old navy's officers, Ponape posed no outrageous soul-searching. Following the Shufeldt view of the world, the officers involved saw no reason to extend U.S. control over the island. The new navy might have insisted that the missionaries stay, in hopes of grasping this strategically important region, while also advancing the interests of the American missionaries and manufacturers. By 1890, the old navy, the islanders, and Spain had essentially resolved the issue, leaving the new navy a settled situation.

Henry Clay Taylor served faithfully by these old navy principles until he attended the Naval War College in the 1890s, at which point he converted to the new navy or Mahanian perspective on the Pacific. As late as 1893, however, Taylor was still laboring to resolve the situation without conflict. But when posted to Newport, he became one of the strongest supporters of the new precepts upon which the new navy was being built.

—————— Officers of the Old Navy ——————

Taylor was young enough to learn the ways of the new navy, but the generation that had entered the service before the Civil War reflected a common set of values, as delineated in their various memoirs. Most would retire by the late 1880s, allowing Taylor and his cohorts to take command. Among those who published memoirs, a few old navalists stand out: Daniel Ammen, Thomas O. Selfridge, Jr., Albert Barker, and Samuel R. Franklin. Ammen's memoirs, *The Old Navy and the New,* present a likely voice for the old navy.[44]

Ammen's first cruise had been with Lt. Charles Wilkes on his famous exploring expedition around the world between 1838 and 1841. Striking the tone typical for nineteenth-century adventurers, Ammen recounted a Pacific full of peril from the geography and the people. Ammen attributed to the Fijians, for example, more active evil intent than he could have known them to have. His mate, a Mr. Underwood, was killed "at the feejee islands by the savages, who endeavored to carry his body into the interior to roast, but were driven off, and his remains were taken on board ship." For this old salt, the interior represented death and cannibalism and American sailors were safe only at sea. So nefarious were the Fijians' presumed intentions that "Wilkes soon after attacked the natives living on the small island where the outrage was perpetrated; he burned their villages and butchered so many of the inhabitants that not a single visitor has since been killed for the purpose of feasting upon him."[45]

Although Ammen's understanding of commensurate response and even causation lacks enlightenment, his writing clearly reflects the gravity with which the old navy treated the people of the Pacific. His words also underline the respect for the geography of the Pacific region. In the quotations cited above and many others, the interior represents a place of violent and even unjust death, in the first case for the sailor and the second for the villagers. For Ammen, the interior was the scene of a sailor's worst nightmares.

Local enemies, on land and sea, continued to present a threat throughout Ammen's cruise in the Pacific. In China, he encountered imperial forces that appeared to him eager for a fight. "The [coastal defense] boats, it was said, were principally employed against opium-smugglers, but going by in review they did not fail to beat their gongs to inform us that they were ready to fight."

Again Ammen assumed that the Pacific people were threatening. Reflecting on the navy's propensity for firing cannons in respectful salutes, gongs might not appear so ominous. Also it must be noted that United States Navy vessels had been known to escort opium into China, furthering the trade that embarrassed and weakened the Celestial Empire, and that Britain engaged in its first "Opium War" only a few years later to ensure this immoral trade.[46] The Chinese forces, therefore, had good reason to resent American naval ships that cruised their waters apparently immune to a ban on drug trading. They might well have threatened the American ships.

Even when the land was not physically threatening, Ammen found it physically remarkable and used the language of explorers to describe it. He went on to Japan, which he liked, and to Guam: "Nowhere in the wide world has Nature been more lavish than on the island of Guam, or more earnest in sparing [man] pain and injury." Ammen concentrates on Guam's physical aspects, much as he did for the threatening places; the description is of a reality, not merely a potentiality. His successors in the new navy discussed it for its conceivable value as a market or strategic base. Ammen even took an interest in the welfare of the Pacific islanders including the peaceful Hawaiians, who "would soon be extinct, as they would have no chance in the struggle for the 'survival of the fittest.'"[47] Ammen did not predict that the Hawaiians might flourish as valuable members of the worldwide economy, because life was so precarious in their ocean.

Ammen took the Pacific extremely seriously. It was a place of excitement, challenge, and pleasure. His colleague, Thomas Oliver Selfridge, Jr., shared these views. Born in 1836, several years after Shufeldt and Ammen, Selfridge still shared and propagated many of the attitudes of his officer-father's generation. The son of an admiral, Selfridge acted as one of the bridges between the original navy and the more modern but still traditional navy.[48]

Given his upbringing, the nonchalance with which Selfridge remarked on his first tour of the western Pacific seems natural. "In due course we reached the Orient, where the remainder of the time was spent in the usual visits to Chinese and Japanese ports." Familiar and comfortable, if not at home on the Asiatic, Selfridge did not express any of the alienation from the geography that later officers did. Those who felt alienated, he suggested, did not survive. "We [had] cruised on the West Coast of South America for about a year" when one Lieutenant Mooney while "under surveillance for insanity" jumped overboard and perished.[49] The Pacific was a tough place.

Selfridge also discussed the people of the region as real entities with their own distinct characters and initiative. He included in his autobiography a segment of his orders from Secretary George Robeson, presumably to emphasize the importance he and the department assigned to human relations on the Pacific. He noted of the natives of Darien, "It will be necessary to take every precaution to propitiate the Indians on the isthmus, who may be of great service." But these careful relations did not necessarily signal friendship. The orders continued, "a proper display of force . . . may prevent hostilities which would otherwise occur."[50] The secretary and the officers of the old navy took seriously the people of the region. Several other officers important in the creation of a perspective of the Pacific and the United States Navy's strategy there also grappled with the Pacific at personal and policy levels.

Samuel R. Franklin, a contemporary of Selfridge, received his appointment in 1842 and sailed almost immediately for the Pacific. Valparaiso, the port city of Santiago de Chile, greatly impressed Franklin as "the largest and most important seaport on the Pacific Coast." His first cruise lasted an unusual five years, during which Franklin learned a healthy respect for the sea and a fearful respect for its littoral peoples. Near Tahiti he noted, "we had now been cruising amongst the islands of the Pacific for some months, and we were not sorry when the time came to get under way for the coast. Savage and half-civilized life become irksome when the novelty is worn off."[51] Franklin's admiration for Pacific people was limited, but he did interact with them and learn something of their customs.

Franklin, like his contemporaries, spent years on station actually dealing with the problems of people. Interestingly, when he wrote of pleasant experiences, he did so in present tenses (am, are), and for disagreeable incidents, he used the past tenses (was, were). Franklin retired in 1889, and wrote his memoirs in 1897–98 for the audiences of the new navy era. Yet his work revealed the old navy evaluations of the Pacific Ocean as a dangerous home, on the shores of which dwelt real people with their own, often oppositional, agendas.

Albert Barker joined the navy during the Civil War buildup; his views of the ocean, its people, and even the development of markets place him distinctly in the realm of the traditional navy.[52] Still, he represents something of a transitional figure, for while he frequently came to the new navy solutions to problems, his reasoning remained that of the old navy. For example, Barker took singular interest in the people of the Pacific, and based his opinions on what he saw there. Often these ideas mirrored those made by men who based their considerations upon geostrategic, not local, criteria.

Barker's first command, the *Palos,* brought him to China in 1876. He took every opportunity to see and understand the land and its people. Optimistically, he noted that the Chinese "seemed good-natured and perhaps are as happy living this way as though they lived in palaces." While in Canton, he "visited nearly all the different places of interest, including temples, pagodas, markets, the temple of horrors, the execution grounds, and the water-clock." Twice Barker broad-mindedly explained Shanghai's reputation as a "gay, immoral place" as due to foreign influence, not the nature of the people. Continuing his tour of East Asia and his sympathy for its inhabitants, he noted, "Europeans even in Korea were apt to treat Koreans with little respect and [that] this was repugnant to" him.[53]

The individuals of Asia invoked more than passive images for Barker. Some gleaned an officer's highest compliments. In 1884, he saw France fight China, noting, "so far as personal bravery is concerned, the Chinese equal any Europeans." These vigorous people played roles in deciding their own destinies. For those who did not, Barker agreed with Ammen, they would be eaten by the more fit. He remarked that the Australian aborigines were "becoming scarce." Not content with the euphemism, he clarified: "rapidly dying off."[54]

By the 1890s, Barker was coming about to a new navy perspective, although in so doing, he retained his old navy rationale. In command of the new cruiser *Philadelphia,* Barker landed in Honolulu soon after 1893's Hawaiian revolution in which his very recently deceased colleague, Capt. Gilbert Wiltse, had played so pivotal a role. Fearing another renegade action like those of the *Boston,* the department kept its local commanders under close scrutiny. Capt. Barker operated the entire time under directions from the rear admirals in command. Still, he attempted to justify Wiltse's moves, and the refusal to restore the monarchy with his fear of Queen Liliʻuokulani's anger. She was "bloodthirsty" and not to be trusted with sovereignty. His having taken the queen seriously shows that Barker retained his old navy vision of the Pacific up into his service in the new navy. He continued to respect the initiative and power of local actors at a time when American naval officers and vessels could easily have overpowered them.

Perhaps appreciative of Barker's understanding of the Pacific, President William McKinley called on Barker to brief his cabinet on the Pacific strategy soon after the *Maine* sank. McKinley trusted Barker to make the briefing. Barker noted on 24 March 1898, "I again saw the President on official matters and pointed out to him at his request on the globe in his room, the position of Guam and some of the islands of the Philippines."[55] The president soon called in new navalists to comprise his war board, but as the crisis shaped up, he continued to rely on the less politically engaged Barker for his great personal familiarity with the ocean.

Barker, like Franklin, Selfridge, Ammen, and Shufeldt, treated the Pacific with the respect of intimacy. None expressed much interest in changing it, not because it was immutable, but because they respected the integrity of the indigenous cultures and economies. None of these officers called on the navy or the nation to alter the region significantly, although each certainly called for some American participation in what they found there. The officers of the old navy chose to serve and protect. The navy of conquest replaced these attitudes in the years closing the century.

CHAPTER FIVE

The
New Navy's Pacific

To create the new navy, reformers cut across intellectual, cultural, technological, and even economic seams. By the 1890s aggressive new notions dominated the naval officers' perspectives of the Pacific: the ocean became important for its offensive strategic value, and the people and lands became passive
players on the stage of international relations. In some ways, Alfred Thayer
Mahan, the author, was responsible for the new set of views, and in many ways,
he, the officer, typified it. In his perceptions and those of his fellow officers in
the new navy, there developed an alienation from the Pacific—a distance that
allowed them to look at the region for its strategic potential, instead of for its
cultural or personal value.

The writings, diaries, and recollections of several other officers indicate
how representative Mahan's views of the ocean were. These views were shared
by many officers who set the new tone—George Dewey, Robley D. Evans,
Winfield S. Schley, Charles E. Clark, and Seaton Schroeder—as well as by two
young men who went on to lead the service in the twentieth century, Harris
Laning and William Leahy.[1]

The new perspectives stemmed from numerous changes in the United States
and world culture including the rise of Social Darwinism, nationalism, and jingoism, as well as changes in technology and world markets. Most important,

however, were the changes within the navy itself: the new ships, the increased professionalization, and the new aggressiveness. These cultural and techno-logical changes eroded the cultural relativity that had characterized the old navy, promoting instead the rigidly hierarchical worldview of the new navy.

The officers of the new navy had greater familiarity with the ideas of the Social Darwinists than had their predecessors. Karsten notes their use of the phrases introduced by philosopher Herbert Spencer and sociologist William Graham Sumner, such as "struggle is a law of nature" and "righteousness is evolution." Yet, for the most part, their willingness to adopt these notions was predicated upon the earlier experiences that would have supported the Darwinian conclusions.[2] The backgrounds of individual officers help explain the origins of this new imperialist discourse.

Mahan's Pacific

Alfred Thayer Mahan shaped the navy and the nation only after he started to teach at the Naval War College in 1886, and especially after the publication of *The Influence of Sea Power upon History 1660–1783* in 1890.[3] But Mahan's career prior to these events is perhaps more revealing of the reasons behind the recreation of the Pacific in the minds of late nineteenth-century officers. His alienating personal experiences, as well as the larger cultural, political, and economic situations of the day, shaped his perspective.

Mahan's notions of sea power were, prima facie, efforts to satisfy the re-quests of Stephen Luce to examine historical conflicts in order to derive some timeless theories of sea power and its influence upon the rise and fall of great powers, so as to instruct his officer-students at the war college. Through his-torical studies, mostly of Great Britain's imperial wars between 1660 and 1815, Mahan did eventually derive what were deemed "timeless principles"— a science of power.

Mahan identified three critical elements of sea power: (1) weapons of war, primarily first-class fighting ships and their supply bases; (2) a near-monopoly of seaborne commerce from which to draw wealth, manpower, and supplies; and (3) a string of colonies to support all of the above. His theories, however, rested upon two serious fallacies. First, his over-reliance upon the notion of concentrating forces falsely denied the importance of coastal defense, and un-dervalued commerce raiding. These assumptions forced planners to search for a decisive, war-winning battle, often in vain. In short, he rejected any value for what in the late twentieth century would be called low-intensity conflict.

Second, Mahan grossly overstated the strategic benefits of controlling seaborne commerce and colonies. While in peacetime these components of empire frequently did contribute to wealth and consequently to long-term strength, in war they often proved to be liabilities. Mahan's timeless principles, as enacted along the lines of late nineteenth-century navalism, had the effect of turning America's strategic vision of itself on its side; instead of remaining an unassailable continental power with maritime reach, it became an over-stretched island power with global weaknesses.[4]

The origins of the sea power science are not derived from some essential truth, rather they reflect many of Mahan's own intellectual, political, cultural, and personal experiences. His biographers tend to emphasize the intellectual history of Mahan's works: the works of Henri Antoine Jomini as interpreted by Dennis Hart Mahan, *The History of Rome* by Theodor Mommsen, a summary of naval wars by naval ensign William G. David, or the directions of Stephen Luce. Historians naturally emphasize the impact of the era: the cult of technology, Social Darwinism, and progressivism.[5] And each of these works has great explanatory value. To these should be added the personal experiences of Alfred Thayer Mahan, and especially those on the Pacific.

No one would claim that Mahan's prickly personality was typical, but his experiences give perspective and instruction. He was born in 1840 at West Point, the first son of the military academy's famous professor of civil engineering and tactics, Dennis Hart Mahan. Young Mahan went to Columbia College, before transferring to the Naval Academy. Rarely challenged by the academic work, Mahan graduated second in his class in 1861. As a midshipman, Mahan was distinctly unpopular with most of his messmates and often out of step with their ways. Soon after graduation, he served with little distinction on the West Gulf Blockading Squadron and the South Atlantic Squadron. After the war, Lieutenant Commander Mahan found himself in a diminished postwar service, frustrated by slow, antiquated ships and even slower promotions.

Mahan served in the Asiatic Squadron in the late sixties and on the Pacific Squadron fifteen years later.[6] He rarely enjoyed his Pacific tours, and his dairies, letters, and dispatches record his acute alienation and frustration on that ocean. Directly after the second tour, Mahan wrote his lectures on sea power, intent on educating Naval War College officer-students on the historic and geostrategic factors that established the framework for America's international relations. These addresses frequently expressed Mahan's perspective of the nation's relation to the Pacific—an understanding that had been shaped to a great extent by his own experiences on that ocean. His views were characterized by a finite-sum world, one in which nations won or lost based on their vigor and resourcefulness.

Mahan's most apparent personal reactions to the Pacific were boredom and alienation. He never found constructive amusement while at sea and in port was inflexibly tied to American ways. Boredom pervades much of Mahan's extant writing from this era. Seeing noncolonial China for the first time in 1867, he described it merely as "rather a slow drag." The boredom continued through Japan and 1868. In a letter to his father, Mahan noted, "Our Hakodate trip is happily drawing toward its close. . . . This town is uninteresting to the last degree."[7] He wrote this after riding ponies in the countryside, camping in the mountains, and finding a ship that had been pillaged by pirates.

The next year the boredom had grown to despondency as he noted in his diary, "More tendency toward drinking. . . . Have displayed temper. . . . also somewhat morbidly depressed at times." More than ennui gnawed at Mahan. He felt painfully rejected by Theron Woolverton, passed assistant surgeon in the *Monocacy*. Mahan had spent months on the effort to convert Woolverton to his own more fervid Christianity, writing him instructional letters, badgering him to attend church services, and sermonizing him at every chance. Beyond the Christian love, Mahan had expressed in his diaries an almost pathological attraction to Woolverton. If not romantic, this love was romanticized. They rode horses in the country, attended cultural exhibits, and enjoyed long, bacchanalian dinners together. Except for the drinking, none of this resembled the normally taciturn Mahan. He moaned:

> The human regard and affection I have [for] Woolverton, more than any I have felt for anyone in a long, long time, my regrets at our separations, & my anxiety to see him hold fast to the profession [of faith and Christian behavior] he made before many witnesses and to which by his own confession he has not adhered; all this mixture of human &, I trust, also Christian affection makes me anxious & depressed & morose.

Dejected and disoriented, Mahan abused alcohol through much of his tour of the Pacific Station, often noting, in literary self-flagellation, how much he drank. For a New Year's resolution in 1869, he went so far as to limit himself to "a glass of sherry before and a pint bottle at dinner," a vow that he violated on nearly half of the recorded days of the first month.[8]

Mahan's ailments were not limited to those induced by excess. Debilitating bouts of an undiagnosed illness punctuated his Asiatic tour. He wrote his mother:

> I was feeling a little sick with a cold in my stomach, for which I took some castor oil, but without remedying the evil. . . . As night came on, the weather grew worse . . . the doctor was giving me morphine, and so although I was aware that we were in some danger, I was perfectly quiescent & indifferent.[9]

Aside from a possible organic illness, Mahan's diary notes greater trepidation than one might generally expect from a naval officer.

In addition to alcohol and morphine, Mahan turned increasingly to God, saying prayers several times daily.[10] A high Episcopalian, he loved to attend the Church of England services whenever possible. Mahan's proselytizing Christianity and moralizing tone were similar in spirit to that of the American missionaries then serving in the Far East and Pacific islands. Only his profession set him aside from this increasingly important class of American imperialists.

Although supportive of missionary work and tithing to his church, Mahan's Christianity sparked little personal compassion. He scorned the non-Christians, not just the "barbarian" heathen but all those disciples less fervent than himself. He sulked and was rude to the officers and men of the *Iroquois*. He noted, "I lost my temper very wickedly and burst out at Dixey for what was not his fault."[11] Despite his humbling reflection, Mahan comported himself among his messmates and men with airs of superiority, a position boosted by his faith. Indeed, often he derived only the sanctimoniousness from his religion. Other times, it was the pomp.

Mahan's admiral, a flag-lieutenant, and six sailors drowned at Hiogo in January 1868, but Mahan was not "distraught" for he had not lost any intimate friends, as he wrote his family. The drowned sailors and officers afforded Mahan a spectacle of high-church pageantry combined with a display of naval ceremoniousness—a flawless combination of the religious and secular: "We had a beautiful funeral over the remains of our dead officers and seamen. The day was fair and cloudless, and the bay perfectly smooth—neither rain nor wave to mar as they very frequently do, the naval display."[12]

Mahan was always impressed with "smooth" water; his later strategic writings routinely relied on the water to be smooth and unobstructed—a blank sheet upon which he could plot his own will.[13] On this page he would plot complicated evolutions of many ships. His letter continued:

Thirty two boats [of] English and Americans took part in the procession many of them very large. When they took up their march the Admiral's flag ship began firing minute guns—and was followed by the *Shenandoah, Oneida* & *Iroquois* each one giving him thirteen guns, the number to which he was entitled as a salute when alive.[14]

Mahan's later strategic writings promoted an ordered battle, in which the guns fired perfectly while the men comported themselves in as orderly a fashion as had their ships. For the funeral, the guns were grand, the men "beautifully" arrayed: "On shore the English seamen in the left column, in blue shirts, and the Americans on the right in white, looked beautifully from the ship. . . . But it was a very sad and solemn sight to see that long line of coffins borne as they were on men's shoulders in the ancient fashion."

Mahan concluded, "I have never seen anything more impressive," nor was he ever happier than at this funereal display of naval power. In the next paragraph, he continued along an apparently different vein. "I am enjoying glorious health just now, I do not remember any time in years that life has been so pleasant as it is now."[15] The juncture between the funeral and the paragraph following suggests that Mahan never felt so happy as when the entire fleet was sad, solemn, and on display.

Apart from the funeral, Mahan's first cruise in the Pacific had proven miserable. Despite being given his first command and having had the opportunity to meet a variety of people and being introduced to several of the world's oldest and most varied cultures, Mahan isolated himself from most influences, dejected and alienated. He was distinctly not an orientalist, exhibiting almost no inclination to try to understand the Asians or islanders. Immediately following this tour, Mahan spurned Shufeldt's offer of more Pacific duty in order to find a wife and start a family—which he quickly did.

Mahan found his second tour of the Pacific no more engaging. Between 1883 and 1885 he commanded the *Wachusett* on the Pacific Station, protecting United States interests along the western coast of South and Central America. The old *Wachusett* had seen proud service in the Civil War, even sinking a Confederate raider, the *Florida,* the sister ship of the notorious *Alabama.* The *Wachusett* had also been Shufeldt's ship while on the Asiatic Station. Yet by the 1880s, it was no longer considered an effective fighting ship —a point that Mahan naggingly reminded his superiors about. Still, the navy's policing role required Mahan to sail between ports troubled by the tumultuous politics of the 1880s, especially by the War of the Pacific then concluding to the advantage of Chile.

Mahan rued every minute in the *Wachusett*. Again the Pacific meant painful separation from the primary object of his love, this time his wife from whom he had not been separated in over a dozen years. He missed Ellen and fretted that his children would forget him. Unimpressed by local problems and remarking that the United States had no real interest in the eastern shore of the Pacific, Mahan complained about his exile. His correspondence with the department detailed each of the ship's numerous problems, including personnel, stores, and equipment. The dispatches comprised a checklist of what could go wrong with a ship. He lobbied the department in vain for early relief.[16]

Another commander might have found some pleasure in the tour, either from meeting local people or from sailing the ship. But Mahan was not another commander. He ran the ship aground and soon after came close to wrecking it in a collision. Mahan was not even the "indifferent" sailor he has been called. As for the natives of the region, apparently they were not even people but "aliens" and nonentities. Writing soon after about American progress, "now, arrested on the south by a race wholly alien to us, and on the north by a body of states of like traditions to our own . . . we have come upon the sea. . . . in our natural, necessary, irrepressible expansion, we come into contact [at Hawaii] with the progress of another great people," the British.[17] The Polynesians did not inhabit the Hawaiian Islands; in Mahan's view, the British did.

Missing his family, on a third-rate ship, and ignored by the department, Commander Mahan found the eastern Pacific as alienating and frustrating as he had found the western waters. Four years later, in 1889, Comdr. J. A. Greer, commander of the Pacific Station, recommended to the secretary of the navy that the station be given enough modern ships to make possible tactical fleet maneuvers.[18] Mahan seized upon this idea to alleviate his old frustration—the American feebleness on that station.[19] He and his planners at the Naval War College, as well as those at the Office of Naval Intelligence, immediately started to develop fleet operation plans. The ship requirements were not even partially fulfilled until the *Baltimore* affair of 1891, but Mahan, Greer, and ONI had the blueprints for a Pacific fleet.

Mahan's alienation from the Pacific was expressed in many ways. His writings about the potential uses of the Pacific often reflected his personal experiences. His discussion of America's growth and destiny in the Pacific sounds strikingly autobiographical. His attempts to intellectualize the Pacific as a clean slate upon which the navy would write its own history sounds almost like an attempt to efface his collisions and dismal experience on the Pacific Station, replacing them with the heroic victory he had never achieved.

According to Peter Karsten, Mahan was among those officers who "both accepted and vigorously and frequently employed much of the philosophy of social Darwinism." On the other hand, historian Cynthia Russett suggests, "Mahan wrote his enormously influential *The Influence of Sea Power upon History* without benefit of Darwin. Mahan's arguments . . . rested [instead] on a close study of contemporary international relations and intimate familiarity with the great European military and naval theorists." Russett shows that Mahan was at sea for most of the early 1880s, the time when social Darwinism was really first making its popular debut into the American intellectual forum.[20] Mahan's experiences in the years leading up to the formulation of his strategy, including his apprehensions and misadventures on the Pacific in the several years preceding his posting to the war college, indicates a predisposition to the position he finally developed.

Mahan's 1890 article "United States Looking Outward" in the popular journal *Atlantic* clearly laid out his contemporary political agenda—his overt reasons for taking up writing. Mahan followed this successful article with a prolific career writing on American foreign policy. Most notable among his essays in the pre-1898 years are: "Hawaii and our Future Sea Power," "The Isthmus and Sea Power," "Possibilities of an Anglo-American Reunion," "The Future in Relation to American Naval Power," "Preparedness for Naval War," "A Twentieth-Century Outlook," and "Strategic Features of the Caribbean Sea and the Gulf of Mexico." In late 1897, Mahan published these works under the title *The Interest of America in Sea Power, Present and Future*.[21] Although several of these articles appeared after the depression had started in 1893, Mahan formulated his basic understanding and agenda in the years of boom that preceded it. While his other books claimed some objectivity and impartiality, this volume explicitly presented Mahan's political agenda.

In "United States Looking Outward," Mahan displayed an agenda for the United States that at first glance might not differ significantly from that of Shufeldt, published a dozen years earlier. Mahan echoed Shufeldt, complaining "the home market is secured; but outside, beyond the broad seas, there are markets of the world, that can be entered and controlled only by a vigorous contest."[22] The similarities end there, and the differences are more important than the similarities.

Picking up on the Samoa and Ponape crises, Mahan called for increased American assertiveness in response to European and especially German aggression. "All over the world German commercial and colonial push is coming into collision with other nations: witness the affair of the Caroline Islands with Spain . . . ; the Samoa affair; the conflict between German control and American interests in the islands of the western Pacific." Furthermore, Mahan found Germany's long-term agenda expressed in these isolated acts of aggression.

> It is noteworthy that, while these various contentions are sustained with the aggressive military spirit characteristic of the German Empire, they are credibly said to arise from the national temper more than from the deliberate policy of the government, which in this matter does not lead, but follows, the feeling of the people,—a condition much more formidable.

Perhaps this demonstrates where Mahan learned the grammar of his strategy. American naval officers' perspectives on the ocean itself changed by the 1890s into viewing it as a region of interest for its military-strategic value—in which the great power war games would be played.[23] Changes in technology, strategy, and European power politics were the overt causes of this new situation. Yet personal reasons must not be ignored.

Despite, or perhaps because of, the desperate alienation he felt on the Pacific, Mahan wanted to redraw the ocean. His own personal maturation required that he master the Pacific on paper, while his actual command of the *Wachusett* had proven so ineffective. To command the Pacific properly, he needed the great new tools of American destiny, as well as a blank slate upon which to write his own destiny. For Mahan, battleships were the tools, and the Pacific, the "ideal of a vast plain unbroken by obstacles," was his blackboard.[24]

Officers of the New Navy

George Dewey, a near-contemporary of Mahan, shared many crucial perspectives about the Pacific.[25] Dewey was truly the "Admiral of the New Empire," as his biographer claims. Although old enough to be an officer in the old navy, his attitudes and actions also place him in the vanguard of the new navy. His notions of the Pacific illustrate this statement. From his earliest exposure, Dewey viewed the Pacific as a place of boredom relieved only by its potential for American conquest.

In 1873, during the *Virginius* crisis, Dewey was cruising on the Asiatic Squadron, aboard the *Narragansett*.[26] According to his autobiography, the members of his wardroom expressed concern that they would miss the action should war break out with Spain. "On the contrary, we shall be very much in it," he said. "If war with Spain is declared, the *Narragansett* will take Manila." Like Mahan, Dewey viewed the Pacific as an arena for American conquest and victory over the other powers. For all his time there, Dewey devoted little of his memoirs to commentary on the people he met in the Pacific. Initially thwarted in war and finding the people unnoteworthy, Dewey expressed little interest in the region until he could change it. Like Mahan, he viewed daily work on the Pacific as basically dreary. Instead of assigning him to Manila in 1873, the department assigned him to "two years in the Gulf of California [which] means practical isolation."[27] Yet not all officers of the new navy found Pacific service so isolating.

Winfield Scott Schley served extensively on the Pacific, and his autobiography reflects his more optimistic, enthusiastic outlook. Schley, born in 1839, had graduated at the bottom of the academy's 1860 class. He was an extremely popular officer, at least until the divisive Sampson-Schley controversy over credit for the battle of Santiago Bay (1898). Although Schley found some Pacific islands to be "ideal" and "happy, friendly," he always regarded American or European interventions as just and salutary, subscribing as he did to a teleological Darwinian conception of progress. In 1865 he took a Gatling gun ashore in San Salvador, El Salvador, to "guard American property in the custom house" during a civil war. In fact, he ended up taking sides, offering protection to the losers, whom he called "political refugees."

Despite some appreciation for indigenous cultures, Schley generally believed it important to sustain the imperial powers. After safeguarding American property and friends in El Salvador, he sailed for Peru where his troops "put down a coolie riot." Consistent, he soon thereafter fought against "advances upon the foreign settlements" in Tientsin (Tianjin). This indicates complete adherence to the idea that the North China territory belonged to the whites who controlled it. His ship, the *Benicia*, went then to Shanghai, "to protect the common interests of her own and foreign citizens [to] repress all possibility of an up-rising, thought to be probable, in view of the unreasoning excitement among the Chinese."

The idea that the Chinese people would have an "up-rising" in their own city and that they were "unreasoning" to do so, promotes the justice of denying the Chinese sovereignty in their own land. The next year, Schley had to go a step farther, when his squadron bombarded the premier Korean port at Chemulpo (Inchon). This brutality was made necessary because "the right to humane treatment had to be insisted upon." Schley concluded of the Korean affair, "the punishment inflicted was great and the lesson it impressed upon that hermit kingdom ultimately brought it into fellowship with our Western civilization and made for friendship."[28] Compare this justification with that of Daniel Ammen (discussed in chapter 4), who considered the shelling of Fiji justified because of the murder of an American. In the case of Korea, Schley's ship fired because the Koreans did not want to trade with Americans or promise the return of shipwrecked smugglers.

Winfield Scott Schley—named for the general who had conquered Mexico and secured U.S. acquisitions in the Southwest—shared with his colleagues of the new navy assumptions about the role of the United States on the Pacific frontier. According to Schley's reasoning, native peoples had no idea as to what their best interests were. The ocean was merely an arena for American and European commercial interests. Consistent with this view, the actions described above took place in cities at the interface between growing American commercial needs and markets of the basin: Batavia, Valparaiso, San Salvador, Tientsin, and Shanghai.

Another near contemporary who led the navy into the twentieth century, Charles E. Clark, also found the people of the Pacific at best worthy of contempt and at worst of genocide. Soon after William Seward negotiated the Alaskan purchase in 1867, Clark's ship was wrecked at Hope Island, off British Columbia. The Royal Navy was able to rescue all but thirty of the Americans who remained on the island confronted with natives who failed to understand American superiority. Fortunately for the natives, they did understand Clark's howitzer, for he had a jar of smallpox virus in reserve with which he was prepared to infect the entire group.[29] Clark's disregard for the peoples of the Pacific, however, was relative and not absolute.

In China, Clark found the exception who proved the rule that other peoples were inherently inferior to whites.

> There is a general impression that the China-man is a soul-less machine in his relations with other races . . . with no sentiment toward his employer, however well he may be treated. And yet you will come across an exception occasionally, as in the case of the comprador Ah Tee.

This comprador, or middleman, proved loyal to his white patrons. Apparently, the only good "China-man" was he who arranged for trade between his people and the Americans.[30]

The new mood among naval officers also colored the worldview of Seaton Schroeder. After graduating in 1868, his first cruise brought him to newly purchased Alaska, evidently to master America's newest frontier. He observed, "It was important to let the inhabitants of the few scattered villages see the American flag and learn what it meant. . . . and several times our little guns had to do more than send a warning that white traders must not be molested."

Evidently, Alaskan territory and people were to be bought and conquered, more like American Indians than foreigners. Schroeder continued, describing the villages his ship shelled and burned, in "prompt retribution" for allegedly killing two traders. The brutality of these experiences allowed Schroeder and his colleagues to rewrite the American notions of the Pacific, treating it much like the frontier of the American plains where the nation's wealth and character were forged.[31]

Harris Laning's experiences (1873–1941) and those of William Leahy (1875–1959) demonstrate how the opinions of Mahan and the new navy extended well into the twentieth century. Laning, who entered Annapolis in 1891, eventually ascended to the presidency of the Naval War College (1930–33) and then to the command of the United States Battle Fleet. An athletic Episcopalian born to a leading rural Illinois family, Laning typified the young candidate whom the new navy hoped to recruit. In addition, his specialization in ordnance complemented the battleship-heavy service.[32] A battleship man of the right age, Laning represents the most successful of the young navalists of the late nineteenth century; he was a member of the "Gun Club," the conservative flag officers of the 1930s navy who insisted upon a near-complete reliance upon dreadnoughts at a time when submarines and aircraft were changing the face of naval warfare.

Laning's classmates called him "Ching," a nickname that stuck throughout his career. Ching Laning's first Pacific experience came after graduation. At his request, the department assigned him to the *Philadelphia,* flagship of the Pacific Station. Laning, in his description of this assignment, discussed America's role in the Pacific in Mahanian terms: "In 1895, the United States was attempting to become a great Naval power. The population of our country had so increased that it was rapidly changing from being a mere producer of food products and raw materials for the rest of the world, to being an industrialized one." He continued, showing the inexorable rise of American sea power in the Pacific: "as we changed from being primarily agricultural to industrial, our people had to compete with other nations and a larger Navy was necessary to ensure us free use of the trade routes across the sea."[33] That it seemed natural for the nation to build a large navy because of increased industrialization implies that industrialization would lead inexorably to exports to the Pacific. These views typified the new navy.

Laning also shared many cultural assumptions with his peers on duty in the Pacific. He, like his messmates, tended to reduce the Pacific islanders to mere shadows of the whites who ruled them. Of the Hawaiians, he noted, "The Islands were, even then, strongly for annexation." Maybe the "Islands" favored it, but the nonwhite majority did not, or there would not have been such a strong monarchist following. The nonwhites whom Laning encountered during his long stay seem sometimes to have existed merely for his entertainment. First, he encountered the "boat boys" who ferried the officers from their ships at Pearl Harbor. Laning gave a quarter to a special "boy," a certain Sam, with the condition "when I return ashore in about an hour you had better be good and drunk." This "tip" implied the power and willingness to serve retribution if he were not sufficiently intoxicated within the hour. "Sure enough there Sam lay as thoroughly drunk as could be,"[34] thus reinforcing Laning's perspective that he was free to write the destiny of the islanders.

Laning's second experience with Hawaiians indicates no more respect for them or their culture. "One night we were asked to an old time Hawaiian hula dance which in those days decidedly lacked any refinement whatsoever." He picked his entertainment based on one set of criteria and judged it by another. Leaving early, Laning did not make any friends. "Just what the final outcome of an ancient hula was, I can only guess, but it evidently was to offer the dancers to the guests."[35]

The saga continued: "A week or two went by before Dan and I were invited to another party, this one was to be a luau, or native feast, attended by the leading Hawaiians of Honolulu, a very fine affair of its kind and Dan and I were the only white people invited." In this case, "leading citizens" meant those who had most adequately adapted to American ways: "all speaking English perfectly and dressed in the height of American fashion." Laning, having lost his appetite tasting a snail, did not enjoy the luau, despite the fact that "after two or three hours [the guests] moved to a large lanai where native musicians had assembled and [they] danced in the usual formal European way." Unfortunately for Laning's evening, "that form of dancing did not continue long as the musicians, having imbibed freely of swipes [a beer], ceased playing waltzes and two steps and from then on there were only native airs gradually becoming more and more temperamental and seductive."[36] Again he and Dan left early. Again, Laning had visited a native gathering where drinking and sex might logically have been found, and he left indignant when it was.

Soon after, Laning served in the war to free Cuba. Laning's sympathy for freedom, predictably, did not extend to the people of the Philippines, against whom he fought during the insurrection. Laning's Pacific, like that of his contemporaries and of Mahan, featured weak, lascivious, or even nonexistent people, useful only as entertainment.

Like many of his contemporaries and Mahan, William D. Leahy viewed the Pacific as a region devoid of virtue, save for its strategic potential. Typical of his day, Leahy's views of its people erased motivation and reduced them to shadows. On board the battleship *Iowa* steaming from Seattle to Cuba in 1898, Lieutenant Leahy condescendingly noted in his journal, the "land on the south side of the straits is named Tierra del Fuego, and is inhabited by a stunted race of Indians; who until recently, are said to have been cannibals."[37] Where they could once have been identified by their diet (albeit the importance of cannibalism was greatly distorted), these people no longer had even that identifying feature, leaving them unremarkable among other "Indians." These Indians were reduced to passive instruments in Leahy's construction. They merely scratched at the earth without any lasting presence or significance.

Having acknowledged that these people had ceased their cannibalism (and consequently lost their only active role in international relations), Leahy went on in the present tense to describe how they would formerly have attempted to capture wrecked seamen.

> These natives are not often seen except when a ship is wrecked in the treacherous channel when they are said to collect by hundreds in answer to signal fires. Not having yet learned the use of fire arms, they are not very dangerous in battle, and wrecked sailors have little difficulty in driving them away.[38]

This description of the Indians as almost jackal-like comes, as noted, in the present tense, despite the changes with which Leahy opened his discussion. In so doing, he fits these people into another colonialist paradigm in which the natives are timeless. Their past is their present and the two are not worth differentiating, for the people are not sophisticated enough to experience change, shifting positions only in response to temporary phenomena.

Leahy was a keen and frequently sympathetic, if biased, observer; he put these people into the context of his navy's view, a perspective that was conquering the Pacific. If even a sensitive and apparently well-adjusted officer like Leahy could feel this callously toward the Pacific, then the navy had caught up to Mahan, or at least to his attitudes regarding the Pacific and its peoples.

---------------- Policy for a New Ocean ----------------

The changes in personal attitudes paralleled those in the policy of the new navy; the navy's relations with Chile, for instance, reflect the same predispositions as the memoirs of various officers. Through the early 1880s, the navy continued to respect the sovereignty of the nation and people of Chile, but by the late 1880s, callous intimidation had replaced consideration.[39] In 1882 a minor crisis had erupted in the United States when a vague threat from Chile appeared. Rumors flew that Chile's warships might even have embarked for San Francisco, to bombard that allegedly defenseless city. These claims fueled the intense naval policy debate then raging in Washington, D.C.

In any case, the scare passed and relations normalized. While America's relations with Chile remained far from friendly, they were not in conflict. Accordingly, during the scare, the department told the commander of the Pacific Station, "It is the desire of the Department to continue to maintain a reasonable Naval force upon the west coast of South America for the present."[40] But shortly thereafter, Rear Adm. George Balch was ordered to disperse the ships in the waters of the eastern Pacific, not to concentrate them near any particular nation, even those of a potential enemy.

With the new navy, however, the American military in Chile took on a more ominous presence. Throughout February of 1887, without a crisis, for instance, almost the entire squadron either anchored in or cruised the waters of Chile. And by 1891 as Chile underwent a revolution, the United States played an even more aggressive role to undermine the popular movement.[41] First, the United States Navy seized the *Itata*, a ship loaded with supplies for the revolutionary government. Soon after, the navy provided asylum and free passage for deposed president Balmaceda. Schley, in command of the *Baltimore*, refused to bow to Chilean sovereignty—in Santiago's port. While anchored in Valparaiso, Schley allowed his men shore leave despite the obviously hostile environment. When two were killed by mobs, Schley, and eventually the State Department, held the Chilean government responsible. Finally, President Benjamin Harrison, generally a taciturn man tempered by Civil War experiences, pressed claims against Chile, threatening war.

Taking a position hitherto used only to justify navy interference in Chinese or Central American riots, Harrison conflated the mob action of Chileans with the perceived policy of the Chilean government.

> I am clearly of the opinion that where such sailors or officers are assaulted by a resident populace, animated by hostility to the Government whose uniform these officers and sailors wear, and in resentment of acts done by their Government, not by them, their nation must take notice of the event as one involving an infraction of its rights and dignity—not in a secondary way, as where a citizen is injured and presents his claim through his own Government, but in a primary way, precisely as if its minister or consul or the flag itself had been the object of the same character of the assault.[42]

In one long sentence, Harrison assumed and thereby acknowledged that the attacks had been provoked by American official actions. Harrison decided that the unofficial mob reactions had been official, as well as immoral, responses; he brought the nation to the brink of war in support of Schley's infelicitous effort to redress them. Yet the war would have resulted from the unfortunate decisions of the United States while attempting to advance American power in Chile.

George F. Hoar, the "mugwump" Republican senator from Massachusetts, saw the mob actions in Valparaiso as efforts to resist American imperial power. But at this point, Hoar still approved of the salutary effects of the power that the United States was asserting. Hoar claimed to view the murder of U.S. sailors on Chilean soil as tantamount to an attack on American territory. "Some citizens of the United States have been wantonly murdered and [illegible] outraged," he wrote his friend Charles F. Adams. Responding to President Harrison's ultimatum, he noted, "It was not a common or ordinary brawl, but an outbreak of passionate hatred toward the American people which moved the mobs in Valparaiso." Hoar went on to note, "Great Britain, under such circumstances, would have been likely to threaten bombardment."[43] Even mugwumps were waxing belligerent.

The negotiations followed in this extremely heated environment, during which time the navy sent Robley D. "Fighting Bob" Evans and his modern cruiser, the *Yorktown,* to relieve Schley and the *Baltimore.* Evans wrote in his diary, at one point in the tense standoff, "I wish I could have a scrap with the [Chilean cruiser] *Errazuriz* for I feel confident we could have taken her." Evans demonstrated attitudes typical of the new American navy. His diaries scarcely mask his contemptuous disregard for Chilean authority. Offended by the behavior of dockside crowds, which had harassed his gig, Evans addressed the

> senior officer in command of the city . . . then read him the riot act . . . and served notice on him, then and there, that a repetition of the offence would be sufficient evidence that they could not control their people, and that I should arm my boats and shoot any and every man who insulted me or my men or my flag in any way.[44]

This attitude reflects aptly the new navy; Evans assumed an insult to be just cause for military intervention in the major port city of a sovereign state. Evans's "riot act," whatever it was, had no relevance to the Chilean legal code. The *Yorktown's* boats had no inalienable rights to access Valparaiso. No American officers had the authority to open fire on a crowd because of an insult.

With typical contempt for their level of sophistication, Evans justified his position, claiming "the Chileans understand nothing but force." Actually, the Chileans had understood national sovereignty, and Evans needed the threat of force to undermine it. Yet in the end, Evans and his navy bullied their way to a success he could only attribute to the observation that "the American flag is a wonderful thing when all is said and done."[45] Chile acceded to U.S. demands and agreed to pay an indemnity. That matter settled, "Fighting Bob" Evans sailed for the northern Pacific's Bering Sea, where he was to lead the efforts to combat what was viewed in the United States as excessive pelagic sealing.

Evans was given a newly created Bering Sea Squadron, comparable in size to any of the American standing stations, and set out to capture millions of dollars worth of Canadian ships and seal pelts, while in international waters.[46] As noted in chapter 3, the navy had decided to leave alone the far northern Pacific in the years following the *Jeannette* expedition. Having found the region relatively unpromising in terms of their ability to import America's excess produce, the navy had virtually forgotten about it for a decade, until 1889.

In that year, Charles Stockton, one of Mahan's first students at the Naval War College, took the *Thetis* on an expedition to the Alaskan waters. He cruised the coastal waters, blazing trails for the new American navy. In his journal, he detailed the way in which he typically carried out his mission.

> At Cape Prince of Wales: During the morning I had a conference with some [of] the leading natives. . . . Told them what I wanted to communicate . . . that

they had a bad reputation, and that if they maltreated white men they would be punished, but if they treated white people who were ship-wrecked properly they would be rewarded.

Stockton wrote in the language of the new navy. The local people no longer had convictions or cultures of their own, at least not that he respected. "What a pity that nothing is done for the elevation of these people."[47] The journey of the *Thetis* marked the resurgence of American interest in the far northern waters.

Even the memory of the *Jeannette* tragedy was resuscitated for the sake of supporting the new navy. In late 1890, it finally erected a memorial to the disaster. Assistant Secretary of the Navy J. R. Soley dedicated the monument at the Naval Academy. By 1889–91, the new navy, in conjunction with the State Department under some pressure from California and Washington sealers, was ready to reconsider its role in the northern Pacific.[48]

Evans's mission in this region continued in the aggressive manner with which he had treated the Chileans. He seized enough "prizes," as he called them, to underwrite the entire fleet's summer cruise.[49] The Canadian sealers were acting in international waters off Alaska, yet the United States claimed the right to police regions beyond national boundaries. Evans's use of the term "prizes" implies a legally declared war or blockade, which was far from the actual situation. This debate between Washington and London (acting for Canada) lasted into the twentieth century, with numerous rounds of arbitration —each acknowledging the increasing power of the United States.

The *Baltimore* crisis was not resolved until the Chilean government agreed to pay indemnities to the families of the dead sailors. By 1891, therefore, the navy had initiated a new aggressive style of diplomacy along the extremes of the eastern Pacific. The year after these two "crises" began, 1892, the department created a "Special Service Squadron," which consisted of the best new ships of the Pacific fleet under Rear Adm. Bancroft Gherardi. This squadron cruised the Pacific, and then moved to the Atlantic, the envy of every flag officer. When John Grimes Walker was given Gherardi's squadron, political string pulling was blamed, setting off a bitter controversy. These two powerful admirals wanted to be at the forefront of America's new policies.

The Pacific was the embryo of the nation's imperialist expansion. From it flowed her imperial attitudes as well as the theoretical justifications for her battle-oriented fleet. Each of these officers, from Mahan to Leahy, shared the new navy's perceptions of the ocean—that the Pacific was a blank slate upon which the United States should write its imperial destiny. They had learned contempt for the Pacific people in the late nineteenth century, and when they found themselves empowered to act upon it, they did so. Mahan merely provided the intellectual abstractions that justified these activities. The attitudes themselves had been forming for decades.

Photographs

The New State, War, and Navy Building in Washington, D.C., from which the three departments controlled U.S. foreign relations for decades. Today it is called the Old Executive Office Building. (Beverley R. Robinson collection, U.S. Naval Academy)

Rear Adm. Robert W. Shufeldt had probably the most complex and far-sighted view of American greatness among naval officers in the Civil War and postwar eras. However, his vision lost out to a simplified, aggressive, and imperial model.

Theodore Roosevelt led the navalists as historian, strategic analyst, assistant secretary of the navy, and president of the United States. Here he poses with the faculty and staff of the Naval War College, home of the new navy.

James Russell Soley, a figure now almost lost to history, was a leading intellectual of the new navy. Like Roosevelt, Soley was a Harvard graduate and an assistant secretary of the navy. But he was a professor, not a politician.

Alfred Thayer Mahan is still one of the most influential military strategists ever. Here, Captain Mahan lectures at his beloved Naval War College—presumably on the influence of sea power upon history.

The ill-fated *Jeannette* left San Francisco in the summer of 1879 to explore the Bering Sea. Soon it became stuck in the ice floe that crushed it over the course of a year and a half. The survivors abandoned ship in three small boats and sailed for the nearest land, Siberia. One of the three was lost with all hands. Only twelve crew members ever returned, and the navy temporarily abandoned its proud tradition of exploration. The *Harper's* reproduction is from May 13, 1882. (Beverley R. Robinson collection, U.S. Naval Academy)

The Portsmouth Navy Yard in New Hampshire, as it appeared in 1883. Many of the practices and materials depicted here had remained virtually unchanged since the *Constitution* was launched in nearby Boston in 1797.

The Mare Island Yard, in San Francisco Bay, reflects the new navy's urban roots and its focus on the Pacific Ocean.

Antebellum steam frigates like the *Powhatan* remained in service until the 1880s, patrolling remote waters and protecting American interests. The sails gave them the mobility needed for commerce raiding and peacetime patrol duties.

Cdr. Gilbert Wiltse had command of the old navy's *Swatara* in 1884–85. In 1893 Captain Wiltse would order men from his new steel cruiser, the *Boston,* to intervene in the Hawaiian revolution. Note the cluttered rigging; by the early 1880s, that was being phased out.

An inventive weapon system, the *Vesuvius* fired dynamite out of three huge pneumatic tubes. Her guns could move only up and down. To aim, the ship had to be maneuvered into place. The guns' high-tech air chambers are shown here.

The first major ship of the new navy, the hybrid cruiser *Atlanta*, was far better suited for steaming than for sailing.

The USS *Maine* was designed to chase commerce, to fight cruisers, and to flee battleships. She served as a symbol of the new navy and of the United States. An explosion in her coal bunkers brought the nation into war with Spain in 1898.

Although the *Olympia* was only a protected cruiser, Comdr. George Dewey felt confident about leading her into battle against the Spanish fleet at anchor in Manila Bay on 1 May 1898. Here, she fires a birthday salute for George Washington earlier that year.

Illustrators Currier and Ives joined the navalists' campaign to popularize the notion of American sea power with this drawing of the cruiser *Philadelphia*.

With four 12-inch guns, the USS *Iowa* was probably the most powerful fighting ship in the world when it was launched in 1896. Authorization, but no appropriations, for the $4 million ship was slipped into a bill after it had left the naval affairs committees. Seen here in dry dock, it is clear what a feat of engineering her construction represented.

A first-term congressman from Iowa, Daniel Kerr, insisted that he would not support appropriations for the 10,000-ton battleship *Indiana* unless it was built in his home state. But Kerr was no match for Henry Cabot Lodge.

The Best Defense *Is a* Defense

Origins of the New Navy

In the early 1880s, the debate surrounding the construction policy and strategy of the navy determined the course the nation would follow in reshaping its international role as a great power. Many options were available to the United States at this crucial juncture, as the courses of other nations indicated. Facing shifting global geopolitics, declining imperial ambitions, and near-farcical military capacities, Spain retrenched in the effort to retain some fragments of its empire. Two emerging great powers, Germany and Japan, each concentrated on building an efficient domestic infrastructure to set the stage for seizing places in the sun. Britain and France, through renewed naval building programs, generally sought to retain the status quo. And Russia was unable to change, despite the agonizing circumstances of its restless people. As in Japan and Germany, certain American elites rebelled against the U.S. traditional commercial and inward-looking ethic and against a world ordered by British and French interests. Several of these elite groups, and in particular the navalists, hoped to redirect the United States along more timocratic and imperial lines. Their greatest success was in the creation of a new aggressive navy between 1882 and 1893.

Many domestic and transnational factors contributed to a dramatic shift in America's world position: changing technology and shifting international markets, the "closing" of the western frontier, the long recession that began in 1873, the massive influx of eastern and southern European immigrants, the emergence of Japan and Germany as hungry new powers, and the international land scramble known now as "new imperialism." Furthermore, the immense distance from European and Asian markets, the state of technology, and the historical tradition as well as a favorable political culture fostered by some ambitious men, ensured that the navy would lead the United States into its new position. Yet the shape of this new navy was formally prescribed by Congress, not by naval professionals. Between 1882 and 1885, the United States abandoned its traditional strategy that had balanced offensive and defensive measures in favor of a near complete reliance upon the offensive-defense formula of the *guerre d'escadre*. This shift was dictated, to a great extent, by the ships that Congress provided, and this chapter concentrates on the public debate over these authorizations.

The navy, one of the largest and most courageous in the world at the close of the Civil War, by the early 1880s had decayed due to a sordid combination of corruption, neglect, inactivity, and lack of a clear mission for its vast fleet of ships initially designed for inland and coastal blockade duty. Within a few years, its ability to provide an effective defense against even third-rate powers had come into question. In 1880, the journal *Nation* condemned the service as a "satirical semblance of a navy." *Frank Leslie's Illustrated Newspaper* ran a cartoon in which Uncle Sam reviewed his decrepit fleet moaning, "Good gracious! Is that the navy on which I have spent so many millions of good money?" Reflecting this decline, the standing naval war plans called for coastal defense with the possibility of commerce raiding.[1]

By 1882, mounting criticism led the way toward the building of a new American navy. This would be a navy initially funded on the cheap, one lacking a strategy while the nation defined its military needs for the late nineteenth century. The first new navy would reflect this lack of consensus. Some writers or politicians protested against wasting money on a "sham" fleet that could neither fight nor run, but their voices were drowned out in the call for ships that would have something for everyone: some speed, some cruising distance, some armor, some guns, and some economy.[2] Because popular, or at least congressional, support was needed to create the new navy, the lines along which it developed reflect the tailoring of the strategic philosophy to the most fashionable hardware. The ships authorized in the early eighties were designed to do everything—yet they could do nothing well. The strategy developed for this fleet proved equally defective as its function followed its misbegotten form.

A descendant of ships of the line, the battleship is heavily armed and armored and designed primarily to fight other ships of war in fleet operations known to the French as *guerre d'escadre*. Cruisers, fast ships with light armor and smaller guns, traditionally cruise seas to sink enemy commerce, engaging in *guerre de course*. Battleships and cruisers each had roles in some offensive-defense strategies, as they were supposed to take the war to the enemy—forward maritime strategies. On the other hand, a defensive-defense traditionally included coastal guns, harbor mines, harbor-based boats, and a militia designed primarily to repulse enemy attack.[3] The debate had raged in defense circles from the first days of the Revolution through the early national period, at which point it fell into abeyance as the nation settled for a standing defense of fortresses and cruisers augmented as immediate circumstances required. This timeless debate reopened in Annapolis soon after the end of Reconstruction.

Young John C. Soley, an avid big-gun navalist, told the Naval Institute in 1878 that "our harbors are easily protected from an enemy; [thus defended] hostile squadrons will not be able to cruise on our coasts."[4] Assuming that the fortresses would protect the harbors and cities, Soley wanted a navy that would be capable of asserting American power beyond the coastal borders. He called for a larger "cruiser" that would be capable of destroying not only the enemy's commerce, but also its cruisers. The defense establishment generally ignored this call for a ship for battles. The nation would not construct such vessels for another fifteen years, although the idea of such a strategy was resuscitated from its half-century hibernation.

By 1880 the debate had spread from its origins in Annapolis to Washington, D.C. Congress noted the navy's state of disrepair, and the Naval Affairs Committee recommended rebuilding along the lines of a compromise between a defensive-defense and an offensive-defense: "We cannot expect at once to build up a Navy powerful enough to meet in mid-ocean and successfully contend with the monster iron-clads of England, France, and Italy, nor do we desire that the attempt should be made." Relying upon the ocean to continue to be America's best defense against foreign entanglements, the committee went on to reaffirm a Jeffersonian anticolonialist position, one that the nation's Hamiltonian republicanism had constantly challenged. The report opposed a forward maritime strategy as being precipitously close to imperialism. It observed, "We have no colonial dependencies to hold in unwilling subjection, nor jealous rival nations upon our border to overawe by an exhibition of power. We have no temptation to make aggressive war for conquest upon any trans-oceanic nation."

Rather than an extraterritorial empire, the committee continued, Americans ought to concentrate on building a stronger democracy at home: "We have an empire equal to our ambition, not too large, let us hope, to be successfully governed as one nation upon republican principles." In its conclusion, the committee offered to augment the defensive forces with monitors and torpedo boats, also calling for (offensive) cruisers to

> extort from an enemy terms of honorable peace, by aggressive war upon the high seas. . . . [with cruisers of] speed sufficient to enable them to chose time and occasion and fight or flee at will, and administer just retribution upon an enemy by the destruction or capture of his commerce.[5]

At this point, the Naval Affairs Committee reflected a more aggressive agenda than the voters and Congress at large were willing to accept. For although cruisers were officially on the lists and designated for commerce raiding in war, their antebellum works made this offensive doctrine theoretical at best until modern steam-driven ships could be constructed. That time was a few years away. Sowing the seeds of a naval revival in 1880, the naval enthusiasts had to wait several seasons for their first harvest. The Naval Affairs Committee persisted in this philosophy of a balanced strategy, though the congressional resistance temporarily halted its implementation.

A proposal that mixed the two defense strategies failed in 1880, due to lack of widespread support. To upgrade the navy, navalists worked on two fronts: first, the broader political culture had to be nudged into navalism, as was illustrated in chapters 1 and 3; and second, the navy itself had to be changed, as noted primarily in chapter 2. Failure to gain support, however, was probably due to the dual nature of the strategy: to attack abroad and to repel at home. Only with a simplified formula were the naval enthusiasts able to win wider support. In the meantime, they would have to clear the fields of torpedo boats, monitors, and coastal defense guns, to prepare for the forward maritime defense. To rid the defense debate of its confusing second factor, navalists attacked the institution of research and development, which supported a technologically driven but politically naive navy.

Defense on the Defensive

The battle between the Torpedo School at Newport and the Naval War College has traditionally been viewed as the reactionary forces of slow-thinking conservatives versus the vigorously patriotic Mahan and the "Young Turks," his progress-minded successors. The winners write the history and the Mahanites won the day, as indeed they dominated the decades following: battleships constituted the bulk of the nation's defense until December of 1941. Still, the Torpedo Station, the navy's first postgraduate school, had been established at Goat Island near Newport, Rhode Island, in 1869, to "facilitate a full examination of the purposes, functions, and limitations of naval power and allow officers to formulate effective strategy, tactics, and logistics."[6]

The school was designed to investigate and develop noncapital ship strategy. Following these directions, the commanders of the Torpedo School were just a few of the victims of the destructive power of the battleship. Others deprived of history's laurels include high-ranking officers of the old navy, such as Daniel Ammen and David Dixon Porter, as well as the journalists, pacifists, and anti-navalists who stood in the way of America's expansive urge.[7] To some extent, the partisan historiographical battle has even gone so far as to separate the ideas and beliefs of the Torpedo School from its politics, depicting it merely as a counterprogressive institution—the enemy of the enterprising War College. The once powerful presidents of the Torpedo School, especially Frank M. Ramsay, have been viewed as fanatical leaders of an atavistic movement. They were vilified both in their time and subsequently, just as were later proponents of a defense that did not rely solely upon the battleship, Billy Mitchell being the most infamous example.[8]

From the beginning, the difference in opinions involved personalities. Alfred Thayer Mahan had never enjoyed doing what naval officers did: cruising, maintaining, and practicing. As related in chapter 5, he had served for two bitter decades marking time until Stephen Luce offered him the post at the Naval War College. Ramsay, on the other hand, was an officer's officer who believed in the navy in which he served. As superintendent of the Naval Academy, as chief of the Bureau of Navigation, and as commandant of the Torpedo Station, Ramsay played the nemesis to Mahan. The clash of personal styles could not have helped the situation. Mahan's biographers never tire of repeating Ramsay's alleged sniping at Mahan, "It is not the business of naval officers to write books."[9] Even if Ramsay did say it, War College proponents treated him no more charitably or open-mindedly.

In reality, Ramsay and his colleagues were forced to wage a decade-long defensive action, against an array of enemies, to maintain the type of strategically balanced, technologically feasible, and economically viable navy that had adequately served the nation in the years following the Civil War. Although Ramsay himself had some sympathy with new navalism, he did not want it at the expense of maintaining national security.[10] By 1890, however, after only six years of struggle against the War College, technologists (like Ramsay) favoring investment in torpedoes lost the struggle for a place in the new American navy. Ironically, some torpedo boats were actually built in the 1890s—not for coastal defense but for the offensive-defense of battleships, a dramatic sign of the extent to which their strategic function was subsumed to a tactical role in the battleship navy.

Navalists had bitterly criticized the defensive weapons for impeding the construction of the modern aggressive American navy that would have made the United States a great power. Initially they based their attacks on the grounds of the alleged dysfunction of these defensive weapons. Soon after, they based their more deadly attacks on strategic assumptions taken enthusiastically from Mahan's moot historical proofs. The reasons for their success, however, are quite different. The offensive-defense won out because the politico-cultural climate favored the big and heroic symbols provided by the largest ships for the day's political iconography. Through the 1880s, however, the debate within navy circles still contended seriously with the question of providing security for the harbors and cities.

At that juncture, torpedo boats played a vital role in American defense strategy, if not in the practical defense of the nation. They played a role in the strategy, because the navy proposed construction of these inexpensive craft. They could not play a vital role in the nation's defense, however, until some were actually built and deployed. Before they could be built on any scale, they needed to be tested in field conditions.

Ironically, Spain provided the first such opportunity in the post–Civil War era during the *Virginius* crisis, which prompted the navy to collect its fleet off Key West in 1873. Admiral Porter commanded the fleet with the navy's chief signal officer, Comdr. Foxhall A. Parker, assisting. Porter and Parker were dispatched to maneuver the fleet, at a cost of five million dollars, to demonstrate America's commitment to gaining satisfaction from Spain. While failing to impress the great naval powers, the fleet proved sufficient to convince Spain of

America's commitment.[11] Strategically, therefore, the exercise succeeded completely.

In 1874, Parker gave a speech at the Naval Institute entitled "Our Fleet Manoeuvre in the Bay of Florida, and the Navy of the Future." The maneuvers tested, among other things, the efficacy of torpedoes. He noted, "for our long line of sea-board the torpedo is invaluable." Parker insightfully if incorrectly declared that "the fleet of tomorrow must consist of rams, torpedo boats, and artillery vessels" as well as commerce-destroying cruisers.[12] Yet the technology of torpedoes (in both propulsion and guidance) was not advanced enough, and U.S. naval strategy had not, and would not soon, cultivate torpedo warfare.

Parker had assisted in the command of a fleet of ships left over from the Civil War, which were outdated but not yet completely obsolete. In addition to the defense craft, Parker included cruisers in the balanced philosophy that he retained from his successful Civil War experience. Furthermore, he also proposed fleet evolutions. He believed that with new first-rate ships, the navy should practice more fleet tactics, for *"a unit of force acting under one head"* is worth maintaining. He thereby anticipated Mahan's dictum by fifteen years. Parker's tactical goal for these ships focused on "the art of concentrating a greater force than the enemy upon a given position." Further foreshadowing Mahan's adoption of Jomini, tactics were "simply an adaptation of military to naval."[13] Yet he also recognized the necessity for nonbattleships within his fleet—a concession to the fog of war that Mahan would not make.

The next year, in 1875, Lt. F. M. Barber presented a series of lectures on below-surface weapons, including his *Lecture on Submarine Boats and Their Application to Torpedo Operations,* which opened up the field for advanced strategic thought.[14] Previously, strategists and the public had viewed the submarine as a suicide boat, because of the notoriously unsuccessful experience of the Confederate submersible CSS *H. L. Hunley,* which sank six times in Charleston Harbor. Barber's lectures were published and widely circulated. They recalled in considerable and rosy detail a revised history of America's submarine warfare efforts, from David Bushnell's trials during the Revolution to John Holland's more recent and praiseworthy efforts. He demonstrated how the submarine boat and the torpedoes were traditionally American inventions and uniquely suited the American timeless geostrategic defense principles.[15] In other lectures, he recounted the accuracy of the Whitehead torpedo and called on the nation to adopt it and submarine boats for coastal defense. Consistently and with considerable prescience, Barber still believed in 1886 in the defensive-defense. He said, "Since the United States is eminently a nation of peace, its defenses should be made invulnerable, for its power of offense will never be great, except possibly towards the end of a long war."

In the 1870s, Barber's practical and theoretical work, done at Newport's Torpedo Station, pointed to a strategic vision that the navy would most likely have implemented if there had been any funds for development.[16] The meager funds required, however, failed to appear, in part because the department did not follow up aggressively and in part because torpedoes were not generally popular enough to receive wide support.

Several years later, the *Proceedings* of the United States Naval Institute translated and published a major piece, "The Employment of Torpedoes in Steam Launches Against Men of War," by French naval lieutenant Charles Chabaud-Arnault. The lieutenant listed the various efforts to use torpedoes against warships, and despite evidence of some considerable failures, he came out in favor of their application.[17] The *Proceedings* gave Chabaud-Arnault a larger platform from which his work could reach all those concerned with what form the new navy would take. In 1880, the editors of the *Proceedings*, leading naval officers, were still earnestly attempting to add torpedo boats to America's defense. Within six years, the editors' efforts had failed completely, and they had to abandon their flexible strategy for the more rigid strategy of massive ships.

Through the 1880s, as the institute expanded to twelve chapters nationwide, the defense debate opened up to an even wider body of participants. With increased attention paid to foreign affairs, and to the navy in particular, the debate reached into the popular press, a medium from which it had been informally banned for over a decade. The press significantly assisted in the simplification of the defense strategy proposals.

───────────────── The First New Navy ─────────────────

Widely popular President James Garfield was assassinated in 1881, but his navy secretary William H. Hunt had already been able to set in motion the reforms that built the first new navy. Most important was Hunt's constitution of the first Naval Advisory Board, known generally by the name of its president, Rear Adm. John Rodgers. Composed of nine line and six staff officers and convening on 29 June 1881, the Rodgers Board set immediately and aggressively to the work of deciding the construction plan the navy should follow. Reflecting the strategic balance if not the small size of the day's navy, the board proposed a buildup, which promised more of the same but better. The board's report on 7 November called for the construction shown in figure 2, with a total cost of $29,607,000. Significantly, Chief Engineer Benjamin Franklin Isherwood and the three naval constructors dissented, issuing a minority report, which called for ocean-going, heavily armed ironclads instead of the smaller cruisers.[18]

8	first-rate cruisers
10	second-rate cruisers
24	wooden cruisers
5	steel rams
5	torpedo boats
10	cruising torpedo boats
10	harbor torpedo boats

Fig. 2: Rodgers Board Proposals, 1881

The more conservative line officers responsible for the majority report clearly called for a rebuilding, but not a reformulation, of the navy, which had served the nation so well for nearly a century. The heavy cruisers, in time of war, would range far and wide, the terror of any maritime nation. Meanwhile, the smaller boats would protect the shores from enemy attack. The "cruising torpedo boats" were fit to engage the enemies' cruisers or to serve as auxiliary to the cruisers on punishment excursions in less-developed lands. These had been the functions of the old navy. But for Congress, the Rodgers Board suggestions were still a hard sell. An expensive building program of "more of the same" lacked an ardent constituency. Only when separated from the small ships did the larger ships have a chance of receiving support.

Congressmen held their own various ideas about building programs. From late January through mid-February of 1882, the House Naval Affairs Committee held extensive hearings on the Rodgers Board recommendations. Capt. Montgomery Sicard, a line officer in charge of the Bureau of Ordnance, testified extensively in favor of the board's recommendations. He discussed torpedoes when the House committee's members seemed only to be interested in the big ships with the big guns. Although not enthusiastic about the use of torpedoes at sea, Sicard concluded that torpedoes would do very well "for such water as we have during nine-tenths of the year in any large estuary or bay."[19] Sicard was struggling, along with the board, to maintain a balanced fleet.

Commander Robley D. Evans, who later earned the sobriquet "Fighting Bob" during the *Baltimore* crisis, viewed torpedoes with considerably less enthusiasm. He preferred to emphasize great ships, which he would use as rams. "Two or three of these cruisers would have a great advantage over any ironclad afloat, either at sea or in smooth water." He "would fire the whole ship at her [opponent] instead of the projectile."[20] Congress also demurred at this potentially costly suggestion. It was, however, convinced to build steel rather than iron ships.

In March 1882, the House Naval Affairs Committee recommended that Congress authorize fifteen ships at a total of ten million dollars. The committee, like the navy witnesses, comprised men knowledgeable in the nation's traditionally successful defense strategy, had essentially accepted the Rodgers Board's recommendation. But the ensuing popular and congressional reaction to the report overturned the goals of the Rodgers Naval Advisory Board. The backlash proved devastating.[21]

Congress, as a whole, failed to support the measure because it did not want "more of the same." The majority of the floor debate during this time centered on the corruption and wastefulness of the navy. Most of the legislation that was passed addressed the efforts to end these problems, rather than to shape a new navy. In the end, the chairman of the committee was only able to force through authorization for two ships—and these went virtually unfunded by the Appropriations Committee.[22]

Joining the debate after the Rodgers Board reported, the *New York Times,* like many other journals and indeed the navy professionals, followed a contradictory policy regarding the proper balance of the fleet. Starting in approximately 1882, naval issues were becoming increasingly debated in the pages of the editorial and news columns of this moderate Republican newspaper.[23] The *Times* always maintained its growing enthusiasm for the navy, while never deciding on the most efficacious course for its development. The numerous construction debates demonstrate this lack of a coherent policy, as reported in the *Times*.

Through the seventies, the *Times* editorial policy had continued to support the traditional strategy, which combined *guerre de course* with coastal defense, but in the early 1880s a schism developed as the editorial policy tended to emphasize coastal defense, while the news and features articles frequently favored an emphasis on enhancing the commerce-destroying capabilities. Ten years later editors would switch support from the *guerre de course* to *guerre d'escadre*. The unifying passion of both positions was not actually the strategy of destroying commerce but the enthusiasm for bigger ships. In the early 1880s, this excitement took the form of emphasizing the commerce destroyers over the coastal defense units within the defensive-defense strategy. In the later era, when armor and larger guns became more available, the commerce destroyers joined Lincoln's monitors and Jefferson's gunboats in obsolescence. At the beginning of 1882, a letter to the editor stated: "the real point is that the United States Navy wants [i.e., lacks] first-class ships . . . with speed equal to the best merchant steamers."[24] The speed of great commerce destroyers, in the early 1880s, symbolized the excitement of the navy. The anonymous letter-writer presented the point, but the Committee on Naval Affairs declared it with considerably more bluntness.

Soon afterward a partial transcript of the report of the Naval Affairs Committee claimed that "to longer delay action looking to the building up of our Navy would, in the opinion of [the] committee not only be folly but even crime." Claiming that "there is an immense moral power in a fifteen knot ship," it concluded that the nation needed "at this time all the moral power which can be crowded into iron and steel."[25] Great speed marked the moral ship, both for the committee and for the *Times'* editors.

Other congressmen agreed, especially outside of the House and Senate Naval Affairs Committees where the support for the big ships would generally come at the expense of ships that would have balanced the fleet. Abram S. Hewitt, Democrat from New York and a leading businessman and later mayor of New York, opposed funds to the coastal defense monitors. He asked Congress, "Shall we have a Real Navy or a sham Navy?" Hewitt opposed completing the monitors as components of the "sham navy." They had already taken an undeserved three and a half million dollars, let alone the four and a half million dollars requested in the newest appropriation. Hewitt's movement only partially succeeded, as the 1882 appropriation for fiscal year 1883 failed to include money for the increase of the navy. Eventually, however, the department completed a handful of monitors in time for service in suppressing the Filipino insurrection; apparently by then even monitors required an offensive justification. In 1882, however, Hewitt asserted: "A navy we want, and a navy this country will always have. But, as I said the other day, it is a real navy and not a sham navy that the people of this country want."[26] He wanted to take the battles away from his coast through a more offensive defense.

Republican Congressman George Robeson disagreed with Hewitt, remarking:

> It is ridiculous to build an offensive navy to go out and strike at the commerce of foreign nations if you have nothing to defend your harbors and seaports; if you have the accumulated capital and property in the maritime cities at the mercy of any ironclad that may come in.[27]

Robeson, who had served as Grant's secretary of the navy, agreed with everyone that the navy needed reconstruction, but he did not want a "New Navy" with an aggressive strategy that would ignore defensive priorities.

The *New York Times* originally concurred with Robeson's strategic outlook: the United States Navy's offensive capacity should not go so far as to threaten battle with the great ships of other powers. The editors quoted with glee the review of an article by a naval officer in the *North American Review*. Not yet on the battlefleet wagon, they wrote:

> according to Commander Gorringe, we need no *fighting* cruisers . . . and he is undoubtedly right. It would be a folly for us to build a fighting fleet to match that of England, and it would be still greater folly for us to build a fighting fleet inferior to those of England, France or Italy.[28]

The *Times* editorial concurred with Gorringe that the nation needed primarily a defensive-defense with the potential for commerce raiding for an additional deterrent. It remarked on the pointlessness of showing the flag, commenting that if foreign nationals wanted to see the flag, then they could buy one. The *Times* wanted no battleships for the deterrent side of the defense equation, merely commerce-destroying cruisers like those that had long served as the nation's only forward deterrent.

For the *Times* of 1882, the best defense comprised a combination of the plodding monitors, the speedy torpedo boats, and an attractive

> fleet of fast ships armed with two or three long range guns each, with which the commerce of any nation with whom we may be at war can be destroyed. England will never be deterred from going to war with us through fear of our iron-clads, but if it were known that we had thirty *Alabamas* ready to be let loose on the British shipping, she would be very reluctant to bring such a scourge upon herself.[29]

On the other hand, in retrospect the British might also have noted that the *Alabama* had been sunk in 1864 by the Union screwsloop *Kearsarge,* and the North had won the war in part because its fighting ships enforced the blockade.

Perhaps because the lines of debate were not yet clearly drawn, the *Times* in 1882 also gave warm attention to one of the ascending stars in battlefleet navalism, Theodore Roosevelt. In a lengthy review of his *Naval War of 1812,* the writer agreed with the "rising young politician" on the importance of having a fleet-in-being. He approvingly surmised that Roosevelt had "been much guided and had his own conclusions strengthened by the statements of

Admiral Jurien de la Gravière in his admirable *Guerres Maritimes.*" By 1882, one *Times* reviewer, at least, appeared to favor the *guerre d'escadre* philosophy as propounded by the French admiral and Americanized by Roosevelt.[30]

The editorial writers, however, resisted the creation of a fighting fleet. In the spring of 1883, the editorials still favored a balanced defense, to the extent of remarking favorably on the monitors, which were then rapidly losing support in most other quarters.

> [These are] really formidable vessels. . . . [while] defending harbors the monitors will be fast enough to give good account of the enemy's vessels . . . and it will be unnecessary to find fault with them merely because they cannot play the part of swift cruisers intended to destroy the enemy's commerce. We might as well find fault with a submarine torpedo because it is not a floating iron-clad battery.

The editors were missing the point, however. The objections to the monitors lay not in a perceived uselessness for defense, but instead in the spirit that would stay at home to take the beating. This spirit was not in accord with the vocal elites. The strategic appeal of the cruisers had not been argued any more persuasively by the actual operations in or since the Civil War than had monitors. But the excitement of fast ships proved victorious over monitors, primarily in the historiography of the 1880s.[31]

Like the torpedo and the monitor, in the early 1880s, the ram had made a temporary resurgence as an idea for the defensive side of the defense formula, perhaps a result of the Austrians' successful use of them in the Battle of Lissa. Widely acknowledged as a good idea, the ram, especially that designed by Rear Adm. Daniel Ammen, received considerable attention. The *Proceedings* gave Ammen a soapbox in 1882. Robley Evans had propounded the idea before Congress in that same year. Ammen proposed spare, highly maneuverable, double-hulled rams, two of which were supposed to defend a major port city at relatively little expense. Publishing Ammen's proposal, the Naval Institute showed itself open to this or any construction, offensive or defensive, that could potentially gain support from citizens and Congress for a larger navy. In the following years of the early buildup, however, rams failed to gain popular support. In fact, the two experimental "torpedo rams" laid down in 1873—*Alarm* and *Intrepid*—were placed in ordinary at this time.[32]

Ammen's ideas for defensive craft dovetailed well with those of his superior, David Dixon Porter. In the early 1880s, Admiral Porter was calling on

Congress to appropriate money over the following two fiscal years for the construction of twenty torpedo boats to protect the coasts and harbors. Porter's torpedo boats would have played a significant role in the defensive strategy of the United States. Harkening back to Barber's lectures, Porter rued the fact that "comparatively little has been done in this country towards building torpedo-boats. We have only one, the Alarm, and she is uncompleted." However appealing an idea technologically, Porter's torpedo boats failed to receive political support. The *Times* had also seen some logic in having these little fast and inexpensive boats at home on the defense; the editors allowed Porter plenty of column space to speak his piece, in stark contrast to that allowed Congress's proposals.[33] They, along with the admirals of the old navy, hoped to modernize the navy with new defensive weapons. But in the end, Porter succumbed to Congress and the civilian secretary.

The 1883 appropriation responded not, however, to Porter or to Ammen but to the requests of Secretary William Chandler, who expressed in his *Annual Report* his concern for the two cruisers authorized but not funded. In correspondence with Congress on 2 January 1883, the cautious Chandler recommended that the first cruiser that Congress had authorized not be built just then, as "so large and expensive a vessel is not now required." Chandler explained that the first advisory group, the Rodgers Board, had called for building a ship that large only in conjunction with a balanced fleet at a total cost of nearly thirty million dollars.[34] Chandler recognized the importance of a balanced fleet and he told the House that he saw no reason to build two large, expensive ships if they were to be the only ships authorized. In the case of starting with only a few ships, he said, "Construction should begin neither with the largest nor smallest, but with the medium sized ships. This large vessel, when finished, would not be adapted to the present condition of our service."[35]

Noting that "undoubtedly the object of Congress in deciding to build so large a ship was to obtain room for engines and machinery which would give great speed," Chandler claimed that high speed could be had less expensively in a medium-sized ship. Chandler did not want to have an imbalanced portion of the Rodgers Board's proposed construction. Rather, he sought to preserve the strategically balanced combination of offense and defense. Here, he coincided with the Naval Affairs Committee, the Rodgers Board, and the admirals of the old navy.

While the Rodgers Board's massive proposals received support from within the House Naval Affairs Committee, they found considerable resistance from the Committee of the Whole, especially from the Democratic majority. Much of the reluctance came from fears that the new construction would be lost in the tide of rapidly changing technology. Typically, Representative Atkins said, "I do not believe that this government will lose anything by waiting another year. Let us see what the tests shall prove. Let us see whether inventions will be made. . . . there have been greater changes in the last five years" than could have been predicted, he concluded. This argument had postponed a large-scale naval buildup for several years and continued to be relevant if not successful into the 1890s. Some Democrats feared that the outgoing Republicans were trying to railroad them into swollen appropriations to cover the anticipated lean years ahead.[36] Chandler agreed that the new construction should not be hurried. He appointed the old navy's Comdr. Robert W. Shufeldt to chair the second Naval Advisory Board, which duly affirmed his devotion to maintaining the navy's traditional balance of offensive and defensive strategies.

The Shufeldt Board, sensitive to congressional restrictions and to Chandler's balanced vision, proposed the authorization of one armored cruiser, three protected cruisers, and a dispatch boat. Shufeldt and his board, however, emphasized the importance of the unarmored cruisers as part of his philosophy of free trade. Shufeldt envisioned these ships joining the old navy, as a commerce-destroying deterrent. As a champion and benefactor of the old navy, he distinctly opposed the construction of numerous armored "cruisers," which would more likely be engaged in actions against other fighting ships. Shufeldt opposed building ships to rival those of the European powers. He told Congress, "I do not propose such a ship as that for our Navy to-day."[37]

The appropriations debate following the Shufeldt report marks an important turning of the tide. Congressmen, especially ones outside of the Naval Affairs Committee, assailed Shufeldt's report as not new and progressive enough—for merely rebuilding and not recreating the navy. Congressman Thomas Whitthorne, Democrat from Tennessee, characterized the hyperbolic reaction on the floor.

> When the Secretary of the Navy selected this advisory board it was unfortunate for the country that he should have selected as president of that board the only living man, I believe, who, during the whole investigation of the Navy, was willing to be put on record as asserting that we have a navy, and that was Commodore Shufeldt.[38]

In the face of aggressive congressional assaults, Secretary Chandler attempted to hold fast to the strategic beliefs that he shared with many of the senior officers.

Chandler found Shufeldt's proposals strategically, if not politically, sound and based his requests upon them. He started with the expectation that Congress would fund the two steel cruisers, which it had authorized the previous year. Beyond that, he "deemed it [his] duty to recommend that Congress be requested also to authorize the construction of two of the second-rate, steel, single-decked, unarmored cruisers," one of the five steel rams, and one iron dispatch boat from the list that the Rodgers Board had recommended. These cruisers were to make thirteen knots, yet each cost less than a million dollars (completely fitted). The dispatch boat was to be armed with one six-inch breech-loading cannon and four Hotchkiss guns at a cost not exceeding $500,000. He also advocated authorizing funds to complete the four double-turreted monitors, which had been under construction since 1875. The House Naval Affairs Committee essentially adopted Chandler's plans, substituting a torpedo boat for the dispatch vessel.[39]

Although the big-navalists were willing to support Chandler's proposals as a starting place for naval rebirth, opposition in Congress, the Committee of the Whole, came from many directions. Members claimed that the navy was incompetent, that the United States could not produce the needed guns, or that the navy had no peacetime function and therefore ought not to be enlarged unless war were imminent. Finally, on 3 March 1883, pressured by the navalists to do something, Congress appropriated money to construct the ABCD ships, *Atlanta, Boston, Chicago,* and *Dolphin,* as well as to complete the monitors.[40] In so doing, Congress authorized the cruisers that Chandler had recommended, plus a larger cruiser and the dispatch boat. Lost from the program was the $60,000 torpedo boat, despite its strong support from the Naval Affairs Committee.

Congressional appropriations had little relevance to any pronounced strategy—the offensive-defense, the defensive-defense, or the traditional balance of the two. Yet the proponents of both, and even the antinavalists, agreed that the new ships should be built: the navalists because they were a start, the antinavalists because they were so weak, the defense strategy followers because they were partially rigged and consequently of limited offensive ability, and the offensive strategists because they were primarily steamers. Most saw the cup half full, few half empty.

Whether viewed as capable or crippled, the new ships certainly resembled the camel—proverbially a horse designed by a committee. Few ships have ever received as much adverse discussion as did the four authorized in 1883. The cruisers *Chicago, Atlanta,* and *Boston* and the dispatch boat *Dolphin* were each lightly armed, unarmored, and built upon completely original plans. They were so built because no existing plans would have satisfied the Congress, which was funding them. They had to be inexpensive as well as reasonably large and fast. The size and speed had therefore to come at the expense of durability, endurance, or power. They were even partially rigged, because of a mixture of technological timidity, nostalgia, parsimony, and the political compromises that made them more palatable to the antinavalist congressmen.[41]

The bidding by contractors took place soon after, and the new navy was launched, at least on paper. It would be approximately six years before the ABCDs actually formed the core of the famous "Squadron of Evolution." Once Congress had authorized them, the enthusiasm to build new ships temporarily abated, like steam loosed from a kettle. But the source of the heat remained constant, if redirected. After two years of intense lobbying to authorize four paltry ships, the new navalists tried a new tack; they founded the Naval War College in the continued effort to precipitate a great power navy.

While the new front was being opened, some sturdy souls carried on the battle of the budget. A staunch supporter of a big navy, Senator Eugene Hale, Republican from Maine, proposed constructing two cruisers, a dispatch boat, three gunboats, and a ram, as well as three torpedo boats. He also hoped to bring about further reforms to naval administration. President Chester Arthur strongly endorsed the bill, but it failed to pass the House, which had recently reverted to Democratic control.[42] Whether Democratic or Republican, the House would not support the smaller craft designed for the defensive-defense. A year passed while the defense establishment and the nation waited for results of their earlier efforts. Little attention was paid to the navy.

In the meantime, the little dispatch boat *Dolphin* underwent some trials in which it showed poorly. The sea trials quickly demonstrated the uselessness of the *Dolphin* as a ship of war, yet its proponents claimed that these reports were purely political efforts to discredit those behind the boat. Once in service, however, the *Dolphin* was widely recognized as a junket boat for VIPs, especially for members of government and the press who needed convincing of the merits of a new navy. Whatever its design, the *Dolphin* served with great distinction as a propaganda platform.

The *New York Times* generally supported the moves to create a new navy, going so far as to bury reports by virulent yet knowledgeable critics of the new ships. On 23 February 1884, the assaults on the ABCD ships were first reported by the *Times*—at the end of the news section. Although Engineer-in-

Chief Benjamin Franklin Isherwood disparagingly called the *Dolphin* "merely a steam yacht," the newspaper gave equal space to the Naval Advisory Board, which equated the dispatch ship with its six-inch gun to the Confederate raider *Alabama*.[43]

The editors of *Scientific American* concurred with Isherwood, opposing the *Times'* editorial stance. Of the designers of the ABCDs, an editorial commented, "it is hard to understand how [they] could have made so fatal an error. Here we have four slow and unarmored ships, or in other words, ships that can neither fight nor run away." The editorial concluded that trying to get both power and speed, "they have got neither."[44] Many people conceded the point that the navy had failed to get ships that would successfully serve as either commerce destroyers or coastal defenders. For the editors of *Scientific American,* the defensive side of this equation was less important, at this point, as they entitled their essay, "Our slow New Navy." Through 1886, the technical stories on the new navy received no editorial comment, leaving them alone with their specifications. The editors would only become more enthusiastic about the new navy in 1887 as their discourse became more political and more interested in the sexy technology of "big-ness."

The *North American Review,* on the other hand, encouraged support for Chandler's construction plans. Although only a handful of articles on the navy appeared in its pages in the period of 1881 and 1883, they each called for a buildup. John Roach, the private constructor who was awarded the contracts for the ABCDs, had in 1881 contributed two pieces on the necessity of building new ships. The journal also included the aforementioned piece by Lieutenant Commander Gorringe that reviled the condition of the navy's fleets as compared even to third-rate powers.[45]

While the new cruisers were battered in the high seas of politics and journalism, proponents of defensive-defense systems made their last concerted effort to retain a place for the cruisers in the navy's strategy. But increasingly Congress and popular opinion came to see coastal defense as best based only on land. A *Times* editorial in March, during the budget debates, claimed, "There will be no dissent from the thesis which [a Congressman had recently brought out] that we need a Navy [because] our whole coast, including Boston, New York, Philadelphia, Baltimore, Washington, New Orleans, and San Francisco is absolutely at the mercy of any naval power." A barometer of vacillating policy-elite opinion, the *Times* recommended remedying the shortcoming, according to an editorial two days later, with large coastal defense guns, proclaiming "if we cannot afford to supply ourselves with heavy guns, we might as well fall back upon pikes and bows and arrows as our weapons for defending ourselves." This Jeffersonian view did eventually result in the 1885 Endicott Board's support of reconstituting army fortresses along the coast, but very little popular enthusiasm built up for some form of coastal-based naval support for stationary guns. Unfortunately for the defensive equation, the press failed to support the navy's efforts to provide a coastal defense at just the time when torpedoes and rams, in conjunction with large guns, might have gained the upper hand in a contest with ships of the line. While the Royal Navy's 1882 bombardment of Alexandria scared many people, it came at a technological moment when modern coastal defense could have easily defeated Her Majesty's ships.[46]

Some in Congress agreed with the *Times* on the potential for coastal defense guns while also clamoring for a *guerre d'escadre* capacity. The new House Naval Affairs Committee chairman, Samuel S. Cox, spoke to Congress that spring "on the necessity for defenses on coast and at sea." Cox noted that "we have within our boundaries ample resources both of men and material to carry on a defensive warfare [*sic*] against any of the great powers of Europe or all combined." A blue-water or extreme navalist before his time, Cox would not build up a commerce-destroying navy. Already by 1884 the New Yorker wanted to take the "defensive warfare" away from his coast. "I am not inclined to favor the destruction of commerce. If we must have 'cruisers,' let them be of a class that can overhaul and destroy the cruisers of the enemy."[47] Cox did not demonstrate much tolerance for the navy's new commerce-destroying forward strategy. Already he was pushing for a more battle-oriented strategy in which armored battleships would be required. Although the Democrats are generally considered to have been less enthusiastic about building a big navy, Cox certainly typified some of the more zealous actors in the creation of a fleet-in-being. Cox's philosophy foreshadowed Mahan's condemnation for the *guerre de course*, which could not take "the possession of that overbearing power on the sea which drives the enemy's flag from it, or allows it to appear only as a fugitive; and which, by controlling the great common, closes the highways by which commerce moves to and from an enemy's shores."[48] Unfortunately for the Mahanites, Cox's party lost control of the House in the year the Naval War College opened; Cox and Mahan were never able to cooperate on their shared agenda.

Cox was a long-serving and particularly astute student of political culture. He had at one point served as a representative from Ohio before moving to New York. His strategic thought, however, presaged the sloppy, slippery slope of heavy cruiser construction. The nation was developing contempt for the navy's weak cruisers and for its allegedly ineffective coastal defenses, at just the same time at which it was increasing its general enthusiasm for the service as a cultural icon.

Both the old decrepit navy and the new "sham" navy were experiencing difficult times. While the *Dolphin* was being ridiculed, the old navy was literally bursting at its seams—each with a dogged press in attendance. The one-hundred-pound rifled Parrot gun aboard the *Standish* exploded in October 1884. The *Times* mercilessly (and sarcastically) pounded the navy on the question of its guns. "It may be all very well to provide ourselves with vessels and guns capable of doing injury to an enemy in case they are captured, but surely in time of peace it is little less than criminal to permit men to go to sea on our crazy hulks or to meddle with our murderous guns."[49] The *Times* advocated rebuilding the navy, at very least.

The *Times* further remarked on Admiral Porter's informal recommendations for authorizations of November 1884, that sixteen million dollars was too much for such a useless navy, despite the fact that most of the money would be going for almost exactly the same defense for which the *Times* itself had been calling. Furthermore, when the secretary's formal proposal came out the next month, the paper reported it without editorial comment.[50] This is surprising because the secretary's proposals coincided with the editorial agenda. When his proposals were hacked apart by Congress, leaving no new construction funds, the editors supinely approved. Perhaps by late 1884, the editors had changed their opinions about the best defense.

This notion was confirmed several months later when they came out in favor of the department's order to refit the *Intrepid* as a gunboat to patrol China's rivers. The *Times* appeared to be losing faith in the usefulness of the first new navy, at a time when the nation also seemed ready for a naval holiday after the early 1880s flurry. The *Times* editors clearly saw the buildup as increasingly problematic. Like many other papers and magazines, they carped viciously on the progress of John Roach's construction of the ABCD ships.[51] Mixed reception for the new ships imperiled continued support for the new cruiser navy. The buildup had already shown the lopsidedness of the new strategy, ignoring as it did the defensive side of the equation. This drew fire from many sides.

Not everyone in the navy had forgotten about torpedo boats. Despite their relative unpopularity among those who were funding the navy, certain officers recalled the defensive-defense roles of the service, at least until the early 1890s. Rear Adm. Edward Simpson, then president of the Naval Institute, reminded his audience on 4 December 1885 that "we are sadly deficient in vessels for coast or harbor defense." At just the time when the Torpedo Station seemed guaranteed some space in Newport, Simpson recalled its purpose. "Our instruction in [the stationary mine] is very thorough at the torpedo station at Newport, but the moveable torpedo is one that more especially demands study." He called for "supplementary squadrons of torpedo boats." Yet progress on torpedoes remained glacial. Noting this dearth of torpedo boats, the American builder Herreshoff laid down the *Stiletto* on speculation in 1885.[52]

Also noting the gap in the coastal defense system, the army stepped up its own research into the use of moveable torpedoes for coastal defense. The office of the chief of engineers asked for increased funding in 1885 as the army took up the navy's slack on torpedo defense. Maj. Gen. John Newton, chief of engineers, called for an appropriations increase of 50 percent, claiming, "I regard this particular item for experiments and instruction as one of the most important to be considered."[53] While the navy was moving into the glamorous world of fast cruisers, the army was increasingly tackling coastal defense encouraged by the Endicott Board's findings. The next serious major gap left by the navy that the army would attempt to fill was that of troop transports, but that was not until 1898.

Torpedoes had not been completely deleted from the nation's defense. The army took over the navy's interest in using them for coastal defense. After the turn of the century, the navy eventually got around to constructing some torpedo boats for battle groups. Torpedoes, however, had signified that last effort of the navy to maintain a modern coastal defense. The army took over the coastal defense, building up the large guns and fortresses first established on a large scale in the early nineteenth century. This left the navy with a minimal coastal defense role in war. It was freed, by 1885, to pursue a forward maritime strategy, contingent upon the continued construction of ships designed for such measures. Despite a few setbacks, these appropriations followed in comparatively fast succession: starting in 1886 with the second-rate battleships, the *Texas* and its near-sister, the ill-fated *Maine*, as well as cruisers discussed in chapter 7.

2 second-class battleships
4 heavy monitors
6 cruisers
1 dynamite cruiser
1 torpedo boat
3 gunboats

Fig. 3: Authorizations, 1883–86

The authorization of the *Maine*, for both those interested in symbols and those who believe in hardware, marks the tipping of the balance. By the end of the 1885 appropriations hearings, the navy seemed firmly committed to a new strategy—a strictly offensive-defense (see fig. 3). This new strategy had been devised within the department less on its own initiative and more in response to pressures from Congress and the press. Five years before Mahan published his Naval War College lectures, the stage was set for a Mahanian navy and America's imperialist course.

CHAPTER SEVEN

The Best Defense *Is an* Offense

Strategy and Construction

Between 1886 and 1893, the emphasis of naval construction shifted from protected cruisers to armored cruisers and then to battleships. Along with this change came a shift in strategy from one of *guerre de course* to *guerre d'escadre*. As other historians have noted, the shift reflected the paternal influence of Benjamin Franklin Tracy, the power politics of Henry Cabot Lodge and Theodore Roosevelt, relative stabilization of battleship technology, the sea power philosophy of Alfred Thayer Mahan, and the changing international geopolitical world that resulted from the emergence of Germany, Italy, and Japan as great powers.[1] Each of these explanations has been persuasively argued, and they certainly did shape the new American navy. But its form, initially and eventually, was decided by congressional politics and the popularity of big, steel ships. To understand the shift in this broader context, we must examine particular events, debates, and opinions of the late 1880s and early nineties.

As seen in previous chapters, the United States had already shifted naval strategies once since 1882.[2] In the crucial period of 1882–85, the navy had abandoned its traditional mixture of coastal defense and commerce-raiding

117

capacity, in favor of a near complete reliance upon the offensive-defense of a *guerre de course*. This enhanced commerce-raiding strategy, however, was limited in practice to the planning boards until the first cruisers were actually commissioned. The last of the ABCs did not join the fleet until 1888 (*Atlanta* 1886, *Boston* 1887, and *Chicago* 1888), by which time the construction plans, and the concomitant strategy, had already shifted to battlefleets. In 1889, Comdr. John G. Walker took command of the new Squadron of Evolution comprising those new cruisers recently designed for single-ship commerce raiding, using them as one might use ships of the line. To many observers in 1888–89 then, the enhanced *guerre de course* appeared as it actually was—a stratagem to lure the nation onto the slippery slope to battlefleet construction. At just the moment that cruiser strategy was becoming a potential rather than a dream, it was replaced by the even more aggressive battle-oriented philosophy.

Protected cruiser design had made some technological progress since the days of the early 1880s. The ships authorized in 1888 suffered slightly less from the awkward requirements and designs of the ABCs, although they were still called upon to act as cruisers as well as ships of the line. The new *Olympia*, for example, would make its fame in 1898 as Dewey's flagship at Manila Bay; fortuitously for mythmaking, the Spanish fleet was unable to return the fire from the *Olympia*, which itself could not boast any usable armor.[3] Designed as a cruiser, it was light and swift, capable of up to twenty-one knots. By 1898, however, the speed of the cruisers had become irrelevant because they acted as part of a fleet and were severely limited by the speed of the slowest ships—the notoriously sluggish colliers and supply ships. Using cruisers in the fleet, therefore, required the new strategy developed by navalists in the late eighties and nineties, a philosophy that reflected emerging political and imperial ambitions.

Strategy and Politics

A study of the political maneuvers in several key years is necessary to understand the shift from a cruiser to a battleship strategy. The year 1886 produced the first indication of change in the nation's strategy, almost imperceptible at first but then moving decidedly toward a more belligerent stance. These changes occurred at many levels including the subterranean tunnels of intra-party politics, at times leaving the historian to make informed guesses as to the events behind certain critical events.

Throughout the 1880s, the majority party Democrats had few major disagreements with the Republicans over naval issues.[4] The leading representatives of each party claimed to want to build up the navy so as to increase security. In reality, the actions of the representatives frequently reflected concerns originating in domestic politics rather than in concerted efforts to form a grand strategy based on geostrategic realities and international political threats. For the majority, the new naval strategy was an unforeseen outcome. The consensus had gone as far as building a navy for defense, but interparty rivalries, coupled with intraparty sectional and regional conflicts, cluttered the path for a new American navy—obstructing it so that only battleships could break through.

1886: The First Battleships

On 10 March 1886, the Naval Affairs Committee chairman, Hilary A. Herbert (a Democrat from Alabama), reported favorably to the House on H.R. 6664, entitled "Increase of the Naval Establishment." The Republican minority, under Charles Boutelle (Maine), had concurred heartily with this report. The report called for major increases in construction, while emphasizing the traditionally balanced defense. Herbert and his colleagues came out in favor of building ships of the line as well as cruisers and coastal defense boats. Their report marks a crucial phase in the transition of the type of offense the navy would provide; no longer content to build a cruiser offense, the House Naval Affairs Committee now called additionally for ships capable of fighting other warships.[5]

2 sea-going armored vessels at $2,500,000 ea.
3 protected cruisers at $1,500,000 ea.
4 first-class torpedo boats at $100,000 ea.
1 torpedo cruiser at $300,000

Fig. 4: Naval Affairs Committee Appropriations Request, March 1886

To start, the committee recommended the following: "two sea-going double-bottomed armored vessels" of six thousand tons and sixteen knots, costing two and a half million dollars apiece; three protected cruisers like the *Chicago;* four first-class torpedo boats; and one small torpedo cruiser of eighty tons (fig. 4).[6] In addition, the committee recommended completing the four double-turreted monitors, which were still cluttering the yards after a dozen years.

These proposals, although totaling a relatively ambitious $10.2 million in appropriations (plus those still needed to complete the monitors), would only slightly have altered the traditional balanced strategy. The torpedo cruiser could be used either at home for coastal defense or for actions on the rivers patrolled by the Asiatic Squadron. The monitors represented the strongest old coastal defense, while the torpedo boats would have marked the beginning of a new navy coastal defense. The light, protected cruisers were the trademark of the first new navy, while the six-thousand-ton armored vessels would serve as the beginnings of a "modern" battlefleet; interestingly, their plans called for torpedo outfits because the committee believed them to have "become a powerful engine of naval warfare." The torpedo cruiser was even more particularly an offensive weapon as it was intended to sail with the fleet in order to destroy enemy torpedo boats—presumably on the enemy's coast![7]

The committee's proposals would have shifted but not revolutionized the nation's strategy. Like its direct successors, the Democratic Naval Affairs Committee Report called on the navy to update its defensive capabilities and to augment its offensive-defense capabilities with the beginnings of a line of battle. These proposed additions promoted a strong offensive navy as a natural outcome of the nation's geographic situation.

> We have no rival on the western continent, and we justly feel secure against any attack an enemy might make upon us by land. But we are without adequate means of defending our foreign or our coastwise commerce, and the cities scattered along our long line of sea-coast are absolutely at the mercy of any second-rate power.

If the nation was worth protecting, naval historians and strategists had confirmed the crucial role of the navy in that defense. Like most contemporary educated discourse on the subject, the report cited the new historiographical trend that viewed the American naval tradition as dating from the Anglo-American War of 1812–15.

> Prior to the war of 1812 there were some serious differences of opinion among our statesmen as to whether the United States ought to attempt to become an important naval power, but from the moment when the news came of the brilliant victories of Hull and Lawrence at sea and Perry and MacDonough on the lakes, the question was decided.[8]

The lessons learned from that war, expressed by the report, were the futility of defending the nation on land and the importance of America's "capacity to become, *the equal, if not the superior of any naval power in the world*." While the nation had the capacity to build a navy second to none, the committee reminded the House that in 1885, it was second to most including Brazil, the guns of which "could easily throw shells into New York City from off Coney Island beach" as could those of Argentina, Chile, or any number of other powers.[9]

The committee urged the House to debate the bill, but the Democratic leaders of Congress would not allow the Committee of the Whole to discuss the bill until it had been reduced by two protected cruisers and three torpedo boats. When the long-postponed debate finally opened at the end of the session on 24 July, Herbert offered a different version of the bill; he called for only $3,500,000 to commence the building in 1887. Instead of the proposals detailed in figure 4, Herbert offered to build those ships listed in figure 5 and to provide the armament for those that had been authorized the year before (fig. 6) while paying for all of this over three years.[10] The first year provided no funds for the construction of the two battleships and funded only one of the original four protected cruisers.

2 sea-going armored vessels at $2,500,000 ea.
1 protected cruiser at $1,500,000
1 torpedo boat at $100,000
5 monitors (to be completed) at $3,178,046
1 dynamite cruiser at $350,000
PLUS: $3,649,300 for guns

Fig. 5: Herbert's Revised New Ships Request, 24 July 1886

Additionally, the bill offered the construction of a "dynamite cruiser," an experimental type of ship with three pneumatic tubes that erupted one-hundred-pound charges of dynamite. The new proposals also reduced the number of torpedo boats from four to one and struck out the torpedo cruiser altogether.[11]

These proposals drastically reduced the buildup, not merely in size but also in strategic composition. Instead of a strategically balanced authorization, Herbert's bill offered the promise of a battle-oriented fleet. Despite his attempts to mask the changes by dispersing them over three years, Herbert gave a dramatic plea for the construction of a new type of navy. He iterated pessimistic claims for the nation's feeble defense, and he cited President Cleveland's approval for the measures:

All must admit the importance of an effective navy to a nation like ours, having such an extended seacoast to protect. And yet we have not a single vessel of war that could keep the seas against a first-class vessel of any important power. Such a condition ought not longer to continue.

1 cruiser at $380,000
1 cruiser at $315,000
1 gunboat at $190,000
1 gunboat at $90,000

Fig. 6: Authorizations, 1886

Herbert picked up on the navy as a popular motif for the 1880s, reclaiming it from the predominantly Republican litany. After Cleveland, Herbert quoted at length from Andrew Jackson, who had told Congress to "cherish" the navy.[12]

Herbert could not afford to offend his voting constituents in Alabama who had only been "unburdened" of federal troops a decade before, so he interpreted the military history of his nation and his party to encourage unity: "It was the old Democratic idea that while a large standing army was dangerous to the liberties of the citizen, an efficient navy was the right arm of the nation." Herbert even managed to revise the history of the Civil War, only twenty years past. He incorporated the bravery of both navies, Confederate and Union, into one heroic heritage. Reuniting under one flag John Rodgers, Samuel DuPont, and David Farragut with Thomas ap Catesby Jones and Raphael Semmes, Herbert noted, "All these were officers trained in the American Navy."[13] Herbert's remarks represent an oratorical high-water mark in Reconstruction, which was reached by the majority of his constituents only in 1898 when the nation actually fought as one.

The members of the committee argued for the bill on the floor through July 1886. After Herbert's speech, Charles Boutelle took up the debate. Noting that he expected greater cooperation from the incoming Democrats on the issue of building a new navy, Boutelle carped loudly about Herbert's having forced a reduction in the recommendation. He accused three powerful congressmen of having eviscerated the bill so as to make it appear that the Democratic Congress was providing new ships while not actually having to spend the money on them.[14] He claimed that the House, marked with

all the beauties of Jeffersonian simplicity with Jacksonian energy combined, have dodged and evaded and hid away from their responsibility in this matter until at the close of the session they come creeping in with this substitute behind the coat-tails of three members of their party to whom they have delegated the power to say what kind of legislation the three hundred and twenty-five Representatives of the people ought to permit themselves to consider.

At the end of this speech, Herbert responded that, yes, the Democrats had changed their recommendations based on the acknowledgement of the

fact that the committee is simply a representative of the House; and when we found that there was an opinion in the House that we ought not to expend this year as much money as was carried in that bill and that we ought not to authorize the building of as many ships as were there authorized, we conformed to what we believed to be the sentiment of the House.

Despite the claim to be speaking for the House, Herbert then went on to try to limit debate and to force a quick vote.[15]

Congressman John G. Ballentine (Democrat from Tennessee), a member of the Naval Affairs Committee, took the offensive for his party's substitutions, claiming that armor would be of no use against the great guns of a cruiser, thus negating the worth of armor at all.[16] Most interesting, Ballentine's statement premises a cruiser in battle with the enemy warships. Yet, commerce-destroying cruisers were not theoretically intended to engage other warships. Ballentine thus tacitly acknowledged the offensive strategy that the nation was almost imperceptibly adopting, even without the ships designed to effect it.

After lengthy debate as to whether certain parts of the ships could be constructed outside the United States, the House passed Herbert's bill essentially as outlined in figures 5 and 6. From there, it proceeded to the Senate Committee on Naval Affairs, which voted favorably upon it with only slight amendments.[17] Although the House vote on the bill is not recorded, the vote on the last of Herbert's amendments clarifies several of the political tensions.

The voting on the last Democratic amendment to the appropriations bill broke down mostly by parties. Presumably because the Democratic leadership was attempting to reduce the authorization, the pro–big navy Republicans voted against it.[18] Here we have a case in which the Republicans voted against what was still a large increase in naval expenditures. The Republicans took a stand to demonstrate party loyalty as well as an alleged moral revulsion for the subversion of popular will, which Boutelle had mentioned. In the end, however, fear of losing all naval appropriations forced the Republicans to support the bill, even in its distorted final form.

Many Democrats failed to vote in favor of the amendment, whether by not voting or by voting against it. Among those fifteen Democrats who voted nay were ten representatives with districts or personal concerns that included naval or maritime interests.[19] Therefore, from both sides of the aisle, the bill was opposed by those who thought it too weak. The greatest part of the debate, furthermore, focused upon the conditions under which the secretary could purchase foreign-made materials for the ships. Remarkably little debate during the entire session went into a strategic discussion on the wisdom of building battleships. Those voices that had pleaded against their construction were drowned out in the scramble to ensure that the expenditures would be spent at home in the districts of particular powerful members. Here Congress abdicated its responsibility to establish national strategy rationally, allowing pork-barrel politics to determine the construction that consequently dictated strategy.

The House passed the amended bill only when assured that the money would be spent domestically, unless the steel manufacturers could absolutely not produce enough armor plate for completion. Congressmen, especially the Democrats, made their primary interests starkly clear in the course of this extended debate. The bill passed from the House to the Senate, which took up the issues with a slightly different agenda. Perceptibly less concerned with pork-barrel politics, the senators amended the bill so that the secretary could shop abroad if necessary. The Senate passed this amendment and presented the bill to the conference committee, which brought the changes to the House. After more acrimonious debate, mostly between Thomas Reed and Boutelle on one side and Herbert on the other, Congress passed the bill on to President Cleveland, who signed it on the fifth of August.[20]

The appropriations of 1886 (for 1887) included funds to construct the nation's first battleships, the *Texas* and *Maine*, as well the dynamite cruiser *Vesuvius*, the cruiser *Baltimore*, and the torpedo boat *Cushing*. Of these five ships, two eventually triggered international crises.[21] Thus the nation's construction philosophy started its second major revolution in four years. This revolution proved more enduring, as construction continued along 1886-defined parameters for over half a century.

────────────── 1887: Holding the Line ──────────────

The year 1887 brought little to alter the course of construction strategy. Congress authorized two more cruisers, as well as two patrol gunboats.[22] It also authorized the department to purchase the *Stiletto*, the new fast torpedo boat that Nathaniel Herreshoff had built on speculation two years before. The *Stiletto* was never given a chance to prove its merit; being virtually alone in the fleet, it had no opportunity to do so. Since torpedo boats would be most efficient in packs, patrolling the nation's seven thousand miles of coasts and numerous harbors, a sole torpedo boat could only have been disappointing. The purchase of the *Stiletto* shows more the feebleness of the efforts to support defensive tactics than it does any commitment to them.

More important to the composition of the fleet than the addition of one torpedo boat was the deletion of several old ships. Among the four ships (all Civil War-era screw frigates) dropped from the list in 1887 were the *Ticonderoga*, which had taken Shufeldt around the world, and the *Wachusett*, which had played formative roles in the notions of both Shufeldt and Mahan. The others were the *Shenandoah* and the *Lackawanna*. Striking the Civil War-era ships from the lists continued into the midnineties with 1891 as the peak year. The loss of these rigged warhorses curtailed the navy's ability to cruise distant waters for long periods without coaling stations.

The changes occurring in naval strategy met with little concerted opposition, although as late as 1887, there were still some informed observers favoring a balanced defense or even strictly defensive defense. As for the new ships, *Scientific American,* for one, expounded a "wait and see" philosophy until the summer of 1887: "The United States are yet more fortunate [than a geographically vulnerable Europe] . . . we do not believe that a feeling of insecurity should be created. War is not threatening us, and if it were, the danger would be provided for in some way." Expanding on the problems of preparedness, the editors noted, "The efficacy of heavily armored ships is still to some extent an unknown quantity." Neither were light cruisers to be trusted. Of the ABCDs the editors remarked, "Here we have four slow and unarmored ships, or in other words, ships that can neither fight or run away."[23]

Instead, as late as July 1887, *Scientific American* called for a more ad hoc approach to the nation's defense. "A fleet of small armored vessels of high speeds, and provided with rams, could be rapidly constructed and put afloat" in time of imminent peril. In the same issue, an article appeared that favored the construction of "Submarine Boats." Thus as late as early summer 1887, *Scientific American* trusted to Yankee ingenuity and flexibility for the defense of the nation.[24] Editorial policy changed only in summer of 1887 when the cruisers started their trials.

The ABCDs appear to have suddenly impressed the editors of *Scientific American* and caused them to abandon the defensive-defense in favor of whichever defense provided the most inspiring ships. Soon after the harsh editorial mentioned above, the editors executed an abrupt volte-face by embracing the new ships. In mid-July the magazine published a cover piece with the cruiser *Atlanta,* showing men dramatically posed for firing the small and great arms. The article that accompanied the picture adored the new ships for their modern, efficient appearance. "Everything here is hard, severe, straight."[25]

The author lavished Keatsian praise on the armaments. The adoration started with the gun-shields

> out from which extends the gun barrel, long, slender, tapering. The great perfection and finish to which these guns have been brought is better realized as soon as the breech is opened. The interior shines like burnished silver, and the grooves, threads, and rifling are as clean cut and perfect as the mechanics of a watch.[26]

Infatuated with the sexy new ships, the editors of *Scientific American* became their most devoted proponents. Later that month, they went so far as to attack Adm. Philip H. Colomb, RN, for suggesting that torpedo boats might negate some of the strategic advantages of a battleship. They published a quotation from a lecture at the Royal Service Institute at which Colomb spoke of the torpedo boat, which "for its cheapness, combined with its assumed destructive powers, makes it especially the weapon proposed for the driving off of" a blockade. The editors dismissed Colomb for his folly: "a well reasoned judgement cannot, however, accept this view."[27] By mid-1887, the editors of *Scientific American* had converted to the blue-water navalism.

———— 1888: The Rise and Fall of the Cruiser ————

Unlike the contemporary French Navy with its *jeune école* or the later German U-boat fleet, American *guerre de course* never achieved a moment of ascendance in American strategy in the age of steam. At the apex of cruiser enthusiasm, in 1888, the last of the ABCs (*Chicago*) was commissioned, three armored cruiser hulls were laid down (*Newark, Philadelphia,* and *San Francisco*), and six light, protected cruisers were authorized (*Olympia, Cincinnati, Montgomery, Raleigh, Detroit,* and *Marblehead*). Yet 1888 also marked the demise of America's commerce-destroying strategy, with the laying down of the battleships *Texas* and *Maine* and the authorization of their half sister, the armored cruiser *New York*.[28] With these additions, the navy marked its new commitment to a policy of engaging the enemy's own warships.

The armored cruiser *New York*, like the ABCs, exemplifies a misbegotten ship of war designed by a committee carried to new extremes by the confused strategy of the mideighties. The very term "armored cruiser" posed an oxymoronic situation to strategists of the 1880s and is, as such, evidence that strategy followed the needs of the politics rather than those of foreign threats. As we have seen, a cruiser must be light and fast enough to chase down any commercial ship; this speed is attained by sacrificing armor and heavy guns. Furthermore, the cost must be low enough to make it feasible for a nation to have many such ships.

The *New York* represented a dangerous series of compromises. Authorized at $3,500,000, the *New York* cost too much to ignore. By its commissioning, the navy's first armored cruiser had cost $4,346,642—approximately 1 percent of the federal government's annual revenues. With weak armament, even apologists concede that "the ship was seriously undergunned for its 7,500-ton [*sic*] displacement." While it could at times generate 21.09 knots, to travel without refueling the thousands of miles it would need to cover as a cruiser, the *New York* steamed at 10 knots.[29] In the attempt to get the armor of a battleship as well as the speed and range of a cruiser, the designers of the *New York* created an expensive ship that could provide neither.

The armor of the *New York* typifies the mixed purposes for which the armored cruiser was designed. The heavy plate that shielded the guns measured up to ten inches of nickel-steel on the barbettes, but all this would do little for a ship with only three inches of mild steel protecting the decks. Furthermore, the hull was "'soft-ended,' as approximately 90 feet of unprotected hull extended outward from the ends of the belt."[30] With ten inches of nickel-steel armor on the barbettes and virtually nothing on bow and stern, one can easily envision its pristine eight-inch guns resting on the bottom of the sea. Such was 1888's major contribution to American naval construction.

1889: Tracy Takes the Offensive

After four years, 1889 brought a return of the Republican party to the Executive Mansion, and to Congress.[31] Despite Cleveland's one hundred thousand vote plurality over Harrison, the Republican gleaned 233 electoral votes to the Democrat's 168. Secretary Tracy realized that his time in office might well be only four years. As the appropriations had already been passed by Congress for fiscal year 1890, Tracy spent his first year in office indirectly pursuing his blue-water agenda.

Long-time chief of the Bureau of Navigation, John G. Walker tried to inform incoming Secretary Tracy of the importance of the minor ships in the service. For example, he said, "The Palos is a large iron tug-boat, built upon and has a battery of light howitzers. While of no value as a fighting vessel, she is useful on the [the Asiatic] station as she can go up the rivers and into many places which a large vessel cannot."[32] Despite sagacious old navy tutoring, Tracy neglected or decommissioned such vessels. America lost a great deal of strategic flexibility by abandoning its brown-water capability. Yet, during his first year, Tracy was limited in the changes he could effect.

Before Harrison's administration had taken office, the Democrats had passed one last naval appropriations package, which continued their previous efforts to build a new navy. While authorizing a new cruiser, Congress also put up money for two new gunboats and a ram. But Secretary Tracy saw to it that the larger ships were not slighted. Tracy subverted funds for research on a submarine boat, spending it on surface ships then under construction. Doing so, he willfully misdirected $200,000 in funds allocated by Congress.[33]

Finally, at the end of the calendar year, Tracy submitted legislation that, in a modified form, shaped the navy for decades to come. His proposal was intended to commission twenty battleships within the next few years.[34] At the invitation of navalist senator Eugene Hale, Tracy proposed immediate authorization of eight such vessels (of 7,500–10,000 tons), as well as two monitors, three cruisers, and five torpedo boats. Tracy clearly wanted to build a battleship-dominated navy, as demonstrated by the fact that he called for several more of those multimillion dollar behemoths rather than for the torpedo boats, which then cost in the range of $80,000.

1890: Annus Mirabilis

In January of 1890, Secretary Tracy received a huge boost in his effort to make the United States a great naval power by the leak of Commodore W. P. McCann's Naval Policy Board report. The McCann Board called for a fantastic increase of United States naval construction (see fig. 7), totaling 497,000 tons and $281,550,000. In a curious way, this report was conservative; it proposed building ships for each type of naval defense, thereby making it possible for the navy to maintain its traditionally balanced defense. In addition to building the offensive weapons of battleships and cruisers, the McCann Board would have resuscitated the

10 "offensive" battleships
25 "defensive" capital ships
24 armored cruisers
15 light torpedo cruisers
5 China boats
10 rams
3 depot ships
100 torpedo boats

Fig. 7: McCann Policy Board Recommendations, January 1890

nation's atrophied defensive navy—its torpedo boats, rams, and monitors. Still, the scale marked a stunning departure, as it projected the United States to become the greatest naval power in the world—despite being a continent-based nation.[35] The McCann committee with its multiyear plan was undoubtedly reacting in part to the ambitious British Naval Defence Act of 1889, which planned an unprecedentedly large fleet; France and Russia had each responded with plans similar to those of McCann.

The McCann report leak could not have been better timed. Initially, the department and Tracy received an intense political haranguing, but it soon died down, leaving the nation desensitized to the relatively modest proposals of the politically astute Tracy. After a recommendation for seventy-four ships of the line, three seemed mild.

Early 1890 also brought Mahan's *Influence of Sea Power upon History, 1660–1783* to the book-seller lists, promoting the battleship philosophy that swept the great powers, starting in Britain and Germany. Yet the United States Navy still had no ships designed specifically to enact Mahan's increasingly popular notions of strategy. The *Texas* and the *Maine,* authorized back in 1886, were not commissioned until the midnineties. Even the *New York* was not ready until 1893. The policy-making elites anxiously yearned for proper battleships.

By the time the House Naval Affairs Committee came formally to investigate the options, the important decisions had already been made. Congress was left to discuss how many battleships to build, not whether to build them. The proposal called for the construction of three first-class battleships, one on each coast: Pacific, Atlantic, and the Gulf of Mexico. The ensuing debate remained temperate, probably because the major issues had been decided before the committee made its recommendations.

The Republican-dominated House Naval Affairs Committee met in January and February, hearing testimony from a self-selected group of blue-water navalists, including Secretary Tracy, the ONI chief, and officers of Union Iron Works and the Cramp shipbuilding firm. Charles Boutelle opened the testimony with Secretary Tracy, who immediately set the tone: "The point to which I wish to call the attention of the committee is whether we should continue to build cruisers, or whether we should build now some war ships. That is the only policy which the Department desires to urge upon the committee and upon Congress." The secretary of the navy thus renounced all the construction of the previous seven years. Tracy continued with a fully developed navalist argument.

The best ship in the world is the cheapest at any money—I don't care what it costs. The people of this country, in my judgement, will never approve and take pride in any second-class ship—one which is recognized from the beginning as one which will never be a source of pride to our people, but a source of humiliation.[36]

He would not have built the *Texas* or *Maine*. In effect, Tracy dismissed the cruisers and second-class battleships (as well as the monitors); he called on the nation to embrace blue-water navalism. For Tracy, the reason was clear— national pride required first-class ships.

At this point even the friendly Boutelle had to ask Tracy if the proposed first-class battleships would not also become hopelessly obsolete before entering the fleet. Tracy responded that he thought it unlikely and that the United States "would be compelled to take [its] chances or go without a Navy." Rather than take its chances, the committee reported favorably on Tracy's request for three battleships. The only vocalized dissent came from the committee Democrats who, noting the rapidly changing technology, called for only two battleships. Essentially then, the real debate concluded even before the bill left the committee. Apparently for reasons of pride and the technical ability to do so, both parties favored building battleships.[37]

Despite the fact that the substantive debate had already occurred outside the formal realm of political debate, the highly circumscribed floor discussion shows the fruition of the navalist agenda. Debate occurred because not all members concurred with the opinions of their navalist compatriots. This disputation lasted just long enough to delineate the state of navalist and antinavalist arguments in April 1890. The record of the debate clearly notes the roles that the battleship fulfilled in the political culture: as a historical icon, as an economic tool, and perhaps even as a strategic weapon.

Like its predecessors the protected and armored cruisers, the battleship was presented as everything to everyone. The battleships authorized in 1890 appeared uniquely qualified in their ability to serve the economic desires and strategic imperatives of remarkably diverse groups. Aiming to please both those groups in favor of an offensive-defense and those who called for a defensive-defense, Boutelle paradoxically introduced them as "sea-going coast-line battle-ships." Perhaps one ought not to be surprised that a Congress that had built "armored cruisers" would go on to authorize "sea-going coast-line battleships," but seagoing does generally connote a place away from the coastline. Coastline battleships were monitors of the type still championed by Senator Chandler, the former navy secretary.[38]

Many congressmen on both sides of the debate recognized the new ships as an economic windfall to the seaboard states. On that ground, Indiana's George W. Cooper opposed them, claiming, "I deny that it is a benefit to anybody except the contractors." Alabama's Joseph Wheeler candidly acknowledged a similar point from the other perspective when debating whether only two ought to be built. "If you strike out one ship, which location will lose the building of the ship? . . . I do not want the Gulf coast to lose the building of it."[39] Those who could slop at the trough would.

Those who could not, or would not, resented the others. The New Yorker Francis Spinola, a Democrat, sarcastically took to task those members so successful at wasting funds on pork-barrel construction in their home districts.

> I was interested in the statement of my friend from Pennsylvania [Charles O'Neill], who spoke as a matter of business on behalf of League Island. [Laughter] I do not object to that, and am very glad that he did something for Pennsylvania. It is right, and I would be glad to get a piece of the hog for New York. [Laughter] But I think that we have no chance of it. Therefore, I am in favor of protecting the coast. [Laughter and applause.]

The starkness of the economic interests also irked Iowa Republican freshman Daniel Kerr.

> The gentleman here from Pennsylvania [O'Neill] has insisted that the League Island navy-yard shall be considered in the matter of the construction of one of these ships. . . . Here is a gentleman representing the Gulf particularly who wants a navy-yard at Pensacola; here is another gentleman representing another section of the country who wants it; another from the Pacific coast who thinks it should be done out there.

Noting how certain members made the creation of the navy a local economic affair instead of a national strategic pursuit, Kerr fumed. "It is a great national industry that some of these gentlemen are after. It is to afford work to large sections of the people." To the somewhat idealistic freshman, Mr. Kerr, this smacked of the type of big government corruption that led to militarism and a loss of liberty.[40]

Countering Kerr's fear of oppression of the people by the republic, his opponents dragged out the old warhorse of navalist historiography—the War of 1812. William McAdoo, a Democrat and a navalist, issued the opening salvos in yet another effort to reclaim a Democratic tradition of a people armed and numerous.

> Mr. [Thomas] Jefferson, as is well known, advocated strenuously that the first step to be taken was the defense of our coasts; he held that the main line of ac-

tion for us, being not an offensive, but a defensive naval power, was to protect our 12,000 miles of seacoast [*sic*]. This is good sense now as then and sound Jeffersonian doctrine from whatever quarter it comes.

For McAdoo, the blame was not that of Jefferson, but of Congress: "Yet at such a moment as that gentlemen under this roof were inveighing fiercely against proper naval and coast defenses and the war of 1812 hastening on day by day. Phenomenal fatuity, ever repeated."[41] McAdoo called on his party to reclaim an allegedly Democratic navalist tradition by embracing the coastline battleships.

Henry Cabot Lodge, historian, navalist, and Republican from Massachusetts, returned the shots, seizing the War of 1812 for the heritage of his party.

[T]he war of 1812 settled also our naval policy. After that struggle no man argued more against the wisdom of maintaining a small but effective fighting navy of the highest type, and for fifty years this standard was maintained, and American men-of-war were admired and respected in every sea and on every station.

Men-of-war had saved the day. To assign the credit for these heroic ships, Lodge continued: "In the war of the rebellion we forged even further to the front and revolutionized naval warfare."[42] According to Professor Lodge, the secessionist-Democrats were enemies to the strength of unity of the republic.

Chairman Boutelle contributed to Lodge's claims. Boutelle pointed out that the Democrats had not built the frigates that made possible the navy's heroic actions in the second Anglo-American conflict. Rather it was the Whigs who deserved credit for them. Boutelle discussed the 1813 authorizations in glowing terms. "The enormous sum . . . was the patriotic standard adopted by the fathers of the Republic."[43] In this way, navalists relied upon the newly revised historical precedents of 1812–15.

Spinola, the freshman from New York, presented the only antibattleship response to these historical politics. Spinola rejected the new understanding of the war historiography attributing the American successes in 1812–15 to Yankee ingenuity, which allowed an ad hoc response to British naval superiority. He concluded:

During the war of 1812, when England as they claimed, sent her finest vessels to drive the American Navy from the seas, it was—

> *Then they sent their Peacock;*
> *No finer ship could swim;*
> *The Hornet took her gilding off,*
> *And Lawrence brought her in.*

Yes, sir; we can do it again, and do it on short notice.[44]

Spinola's feeble comments fell unheeded against the historiographical mastery of Boutelle, Lodge, and McAdoo. All in all, the navalists of both parties had but one tradition, and the navy won the War of 1812 once again, three generations after the last battle.

These first-term congressmen—Cooper, Spinola, and Kerr—all agreed that the naval appropriations bill for fiscal year 1891 was designed to be all things to all men. They disagreed as to its success. Still, a loose cluster of freshmen representatives (mostly from noncoastal regions) could not stop the legislative tide; only the people could do that. When the debate closed, Congress had voted in favor of the three battleships: *Indiana, Massachusetts,* and *Oregon.*[45]

The fifty-first Congress, dominated by Republicans, had made its stand on battleships. The GOP majority in each house, with Harrison's encouragement and support, easily passed through the appropriations process three first-class battleships: the largest tangible symbols of ideology of the republic since the great Civil War

Fifty-first Congress		
Republican	179	(53.9%)
Democrat	152	(45.8%)
Labor	1	(0.3%)
Fifty-second Congress		
Republican	86	(25.9%)
Democrat	238	(71.7%)
Populist	8	(2.4%)

Fig. 8: Political Makeup of the 51st and 52d Congresses

armies. Yet, the nation was still undecided about the virtue of big government. The midterm elections that followed devastatingly renounced any GOP sense of a mandate for the big government policies.[46] The Republicans lost heavily going from 179 seats to 86 (fig. 8). Losers included party regulars such as William McKinley and Joseph Cannon as well as the dissenter Robert M. LaFollette.

Joseph Wheeler (Democrat from Alabama) had noted at the end of the 1890 appropriations debate:

You may go on, but you can not go far. The people demand economy. During twenty-five years of peace you have spent $400,000,000 of the people's money for the Navy, and you have nothing to show for it. . . . [Naval] contractors and their friends have grown rich and the people have grown poor. You may battle for battle-ships, we will battle for the people.[47]

And the people spoke in 1890: time for a construction holiday.

─────────────── 1891: Temporary Setback ───────────────

The lame-duck fifty-first Congress reconvened in December 1890, thoroughly chastened by November's election. Strongly rebuffing the Republican big-government legislative agenda at the polls, voters nationwide held the big-government measures responsible for a perceived decline in the standard of living. John G. Carlisle, a Democratic senator from Kentucky, summarized the indictments: "There has never been in our history a more extravagant Congress than the present one." Carlisle claimed that the McKinley Tariff was part of a scheme "to tax the whole people for the benefit of a few" and that the big government that sponsored it further infringed on the people's rights by imposing the Federal Election of Force Bill. Even William McAdoo noted the costs, "Seventeen thousand bills were introduced in the (51-1) Congress; most of these . . . reach out to the public treasury. On the whole, expenditures are increased by about $52,000,000."[48] While it may now appear that these expenditures helped to float the nation out of the Great Depression, at the time, they seemed to many to be recklessly spendthrifty. As an early result of these apparent excesses, Democrats would not allow the GOP of 51-2 to authorize any major increases to the naval establishment.

Boutelle acknowledged this political reality, calling only for the authorization of one fast cruiser, as well as the $6,819,930.25 required for ongoing construction. The latter funds prompted considerable resentment among the Democrats who feared being saddled with years of high construction costs to pay for the GOP authorizations of 1890. When debate opened in January, the House Democrats attacked this sum from several angles, calling it: (1) another tax on the poor for the rich, or (2) money injudiciously dispersed by a poor nation, or (3) by a nation not threatened by war, and even as (4) money thrown away because all ships of war were soon to be made obsolescent by air power as projected by balloons! In the end, the House Naval Affairs Committee succeeded in pushing through its version of the bill, buttressed by the forceful arguments of such Democratic leaders as Herbert and McAdoo.[49]

The Senate, not nearly so chastened as the House by November's elections, seriously entertained the idea of authorizing funds for more cruisers than one. Other proposals would have added money for monitorlike floating batteries; the first of the new navy's double-turreted monitors—the *Miantonomoh* was at long last being commissioned in 1891.[50] In the end, however, the Senate conceded the fact of purse strings tightly drawn by the House. In early March, President Harrison signed a bill funding the *Minneapolis* and continuing the ongoing construction.

Named for the city in which the GOP convention would be held in 1892, the *Minneapolis*, as planned and built, was a fast cruiser, lightly armored with main batteries consisting of merely one eight-inch gun and two six-inch rifles. A swift ship like the *Minneapolis* was actually designed for commerce raiding—a strategy already abandoned by the navy. Yet the Naval Affairs Committees recommended its authorization, with the secretary's approbation, presumably for its political virtue—its acceptability to a chastised Congress.

1892: Strange Politics

Even while Congress paused in its buildup, the Navy Department proceeded full-speed ahead to create a modern battle force. In 1891, it had decommissioned six midcentury sailing ships, followed by three more in the following year. In 1891, it also laid down the first three battleships, three cruisers, and three gunboats, while commissioning the monitor *Miantonomoh* and the *Newark*—the first cruiser since the ABCs. Moreover, despite a temporary stay—hesitation mostly based on pecuniary concerns—Congress found itself firmly committed to a blue-water navy.

Although the new House sat with a large Democratic majority, the Senate, as well as the executive branch, remained in the control of the GOP and as such remained staunchly pro–big navy. Undoubtedly expecting opposition, the House Naval Affairs Committee introduced a bill calling for the authorization of only one ship, a *New York*–class armored cruiser and providing only $23,726,823.71 for the service, nearly $9 million less than the provisions for fiscal year 1892.[51] The House debate in early spring reflects the range of opinions, from the emerging Mahanian orthodoxy to an idealistic pacifistic position, with all stages in between.

An interesting triangular debate opened on the House floor, among those in favor of the bill (a majority of the Democrats), those opposed to it for being too small (GOP), and those disputing it for its excessive largesse (Populists and left-leaning, midwestern Democrats). The navalists, led in the House by Boutelle, pointed to the crises in which the United States involved itself in the early nineties (especially in Chile and the Bering Sea). Boutelle went into the by-then standard discourse on the lessons of 1812, as did Lodge, while proposing the substitution of two battleships and ten torpedo boats for the armored cruiser.[52]

On another side of the triangle, the "peace" party called for no new authorizations, employing a variety of arguments. Owen Scott (Democrat from Illinois), picking up on the navy's favorite historical debate, claimed that the United States had suffered no genuine invasion threat since 1814 and postulated, "The time has come when nations should cease warfare. The progress of civilization, Christianity, humanity, demands that swords shall be sheathed." Tom Watson, agrarian rebel and a Democrat from Georgia, contributed his views on the folly of war in 1812, given Britain's withdrawal of the orders in council, and opposed any new construction that might foster another pointless war.[53] However cogent their arguments, the antinavalists struggled against the current.

On the last face of the isosceles debate triangle, with the broadest base of support, was the majority position favoring the Naval Affairs Committee's *New York*-type armored cruiser and the money to continue the ongoing construction. Once again the debate focused on the question of the nation's strategic needs as informed predominately by interpretations of early national history. After Chairman Herbert's introduction, John O. Pendleton (Democrat from West Virginia) submitted one rendition: "The Navy has been extremely popular with our people since the war of 1812" and concluded that the present bill provided sustenance for the moderate navy fitting the national requirements. In the end, split opposition and arguments such as this enabled the navalists to pass the bill on to the Senate.[54]

The Republican-dominated Senate fought the meager appropriations, acceding to the House's requests only after numerous debates and intercameral conferences. Debate within the upper chamber was only two-sided: for and against increases. As in the House, the antinavalist sentiment came mostly from the Midwest. William F. Vilas (Democrat, Wisconsin), typically, opposed further construction, claiming that the navy had already proved adequate for the nation's nonaggressive needs. Francis Cockrell (Democrat, Missouri) concurred, contributing a new reinterpretation of 1812 as a case of a suitable ad hoc response to threat of invasion. Sounding "1812," however, only brought more debates on the lessons of history. John T. Morgan (Democrat, Alabama) retorted, "the mere fact that we were considered to be very weak upon the sea, [provoked the] war of 1812."[55] Most of the Senate agreed on the need to protect against another invasion. Creating a consensus on naval construction, the southern Democrats joined with the Republicans only as far as agreeing to support the creation of a coastal defense force. Significantly, the Senate did not request authorizations for any more battleships, but only for defensive ships: a coastal monitor, four river gunboats, and six harbor-based torpedo boats. The Senate, attempting to take the initiative in reformulating the national defense strategy, thus sought to reintroduce the capability for a defensive-defense.

The House majority had already abandoned any pretense of a defensive-defense, and it took three intercameral conferences finally to force the Senate to acquiesce to a solely offensive-defense formula. The conferees, navalists appointed by each house, readily agreed among themselves. In the critical second conference, the House had explicitly charged its representatives with securing funding just for one armored cruiser. The Senate, meanwhile, had instructed its conferees to authorize a monitor, four gunboats, and six torpedo boats. The navalist-dominated conference, in turn, reported in favor of one nine-thousand-ton battleship and the armored cruiser. This foreshadows Winston Churchill's statement about dreadnought authorizations some years later: the admiralty "demanded six ships: the economists offered four: and we finally compromised on eight."[56]

Herbert slid the *Iowa* into the legislation calling merely for its authorization with virtually no concomitant appropriation. This ruse allowed a cost-conscious House to authorize a $4 million-plus battleship as a less-expensive defense option than the million dollars required for the ten small boats (at approximately $100,000 apiece). With the sly addition of the largest battleship to date, the bill was reported again. The Senate approved the report essentially intact and intransigently fought the House for its approval. Finally, after a third conference, Congress authorized the construction of the *Iowa* and the *Brooklyn* on 16 July 1892.[57] Once again, only the battleship and its half sibling, the armored cruiser, were able to pass through the perilous shoals of the appropriations process, and the hardware of naval strategy moved increasingly and irreversibly toward the offensive-defense.

1893: Denouement

In November 1892, the electors of the United States returned Grover Cleveland to the Executive Mansion. As with most late nineteenth-century national elections, the popular vote was close but decisive. Soon to be replaced as secretary by his sometime ally Hilary Herbert, Tracy proposed continuing ambitious construction. He called for another *Iowa*-class battleship, several torpedo cruisers, four river gunboats, and thirty torpedo boats.[58] Despite these gestures toward a balanced fleet, Tracy acknowledged his credo that only first-class battleships should receive priority in construction.

Before the new secretary took office and before the new Congress sat, the brief second session of the fifty-second Congress considered naval appropriations for 1894. A living symbol of how close to one another the Navy Department and Congress had moved, Chairman Herbert presented his committee's report on 13 February 1893. He noted, "Our old Navy [is] now rapidly passing away." He remarked that the efforts to create a new navy were assisted by the falling prices of construction and went on to list the ships of the new navy. The one-time moderate had been converted to a belief in the value of the *guerre d'escadre*. "Congress has now provided for cruisers until, in the opinion of your committee, no others should at present be built if we are to have battleships. In battleships consists the fighting strength of a modern navy."[59]

However, given the weak state of the nation's finances (1893 brought the beginning of the depression) and the fact that armor production was two or three years behind schedule, Herbert ruefully recommended against authorizing more than one small gunboat. Debate came feebly from Boutelle who would have built at least one battleship and three gunboats. In the end, he too proved willing to concede the battleship as a lost cause for the year 1893. The Republican-controlled Senate virtually concurred, calling for four gunboats instead. Once again the resulting conference brought a larger appropriation than that recommended; this time only slightly larger: three gunboats and one torpedo boat.[60] As the session closed, both houses agreed to authorize these boats.

The Democrats of the eighties had not been the party of a big navy, but they did not oppose it in any effective way. By the nineties, they were quite willing to carry on the activities that had been set in motion by the predominately Republican navalists. As the Democrats returned to power in 1893, all the prototypical ships of the new navy were already secured. During that year, the monitor *Monterey*, the armored cruiser *New York*, the protected cruiser *Detroit*, and the gunboats *Bancroft* and *Machias* were commissioned. The *Iowa* and *Brooklyn* were laid down, and the first *Indiana* was launched. With the Republicans relinquishing control of the executive branch, the naval revolution was over—completed. Battleships would dominate the nation's defense.

CHAPTER EIGHT

— *The* —
Whole Flapdoodle Pacifist
—*and*—
Mollycoddler Outfit

In 1893 America's imperial apparatus was in place. Activist historians had established the intellectual justification. Reformers had professionalized and modernized the service. The new strategy had been designed and battleships authorized to implement it. At most points, proponents of the new navy had encountered only the slight opposition of antinavalism, a feeble movement that grew weaker with each advance by the navalists. And despite 1893's Hawaiian annexation crisis, the more broadly based opposition of anti-imperialists had not yet coalesced, and would not until 1898. Despite these limitations, the opposition to creating a new fighting navy deserves a focused inspection. Shaped like a pyramid, this chapter begins with a broad political-economic interpretation of the statistical inevitability of war, moves to a particular movement opposed to it, and concludes with the transformation of a single man as he came to fight against it.

— Economics and Empire —

The United States in the 1890s fell within the three "high risk" categories for war, according to a model proposed by political scientist Bruce Russett. The first was its rise to great power status—a position thoroughly accepted by now as applying to the nation of the early 1890s. Russett states, "great powers are, because of a combination of their capabilities and extended interests more likely to be involved in international conflict than are minor powers." If this fact alone increased the chances, the second factor certainly pushed the nation even closer to war, for "a state is more likely to engage in the threat or use of force internationally if its military establishment has been recently expanded."[1] After the first peacetime buildup, the United States qualified on this count as well.

Last, Russett notes that leaders of democratic states are much "more likely in periods of economic downturn to engage in risk-taking behavior in the international political arena."[2] The onset of the Great Depression in 1893 was not likely to do the cause of peace any good. Russett's three factors, and these are the only three he explicitly mentions, apply directly to the United States after 1893. Of course, mere statistical likelihood does not make an event happen. The United States had been experiencing some recession in prices for twenty-five years by 1898. The buildup of the 1880s has continued through today, with standstills only in the decades following major wars. And of course, the nation has been considered a great power, by various viewers, since as long ago as the first publication of Alexis de Tocqueville's *Democracy in America* of 1836.

Russett's work establishes the general politico-economic preconditions for war's increased likelihood. To explain how the United States, in particular, failed to avoid war, this study examines the cultural and military preconditions for war that had been established by 1893. Furthermore, the conditions and apparatus for preserving peace lagged far behind. Until 1893, dissent against the increasingly predominant political culture that fostered navalism and war was fragmented and impotent.

Numbers can, in part, explain the lack of impassioned antinavalism. Who could protest increasing the navy when it appeared to come at no extra cost, as was the case in the first seven years of the new navy? The seven bills including and following 1882 averaged outlays for the navy of $15.65 million, with a median of $15.28 million. The previous seven years (1875–81) averaged $16.73 million, with a $15.69 million median.[3] To most taxpayers, then, the initial appropriations for the original new navy appeared to cost slightly less than had the old.

While the unadjusted expenditures remained virtually static, the money bought considerably more material for the service. In part, these static numbers reflect falling naval costs—a boon for which the new navy's birth was particularly well timed. These falling costs are best demonstrated in terms of the lower naval expenditure price index (henceforth NEPI). The NEPI was calculated by political scientists George Modelski and William Thompson to compare the relative growth and decline of naval powers as an indicator of their respective degrees of economic and military hegemony within the international sphere. It represents the average purchasing power of the year's dollar appropriations compared to those of a base year—1913 (see fig. 9).

	in millions	NEPI	in millions (1913 pounds sterling)
1882	$15.03	106	£2.88
1883	15.28	99	3.13
1884	17.29	91	3.85
1885	16.02	84	3.87
1886	13.91	80	3.53
1887	15.14	83	3.45
1888	16.93	84	4.09
1889	21.38	79	5.49
1890	22.01	80	5.58
1891	26.11	80	6.62
1892	29.17	75	7.89
1893	30.14	76	8.05
1894	31.70	69	9.32
1895	28.80	70	8.35
1896	27.15	66	8.35
1897	34.56	67	10.46

Fig. 9: U.S. Navy Expenditures

Between 1882 and 1889, the American index fell from 106 to 84 (with 100 representing 1913 purchasing dollars).[4] Each average expenditure dollar went considerably farther.

At this point, the navy could be said to have benefited from a recession dividend. The NEPI continued to drop throughout the pre-Spanish War era—hitting 67 in the last prewar year, 1897. Naval purchases, therefore, cost 36.8 cents less per dollar in 1897 than in 1882. As most taxpayers were unlikely to expect outlays to fall during the era of increased international tensions, the navy was able to capitalize heavily on the slight annual increases in the non-adjusted dollars authorized. The effects, especially in the first seven crucial years, were propitious for building the new navy. Although gross unadjusted outlays increased only from $15.03 million in fiscal year 1882 to $16.93 in fiscal year 1888, the latter figure bought approximately 21 percent more than the former, because of the decline of the NEPI.[5] This meant that the navy could buy $20.31 million worth of 1882 expenditures in 1888, at a cost of fewer than $17 million.

In the ten remaining prewar years, the outlays doubled ($16.93 million in 1889 to $34.56 million in 1897). Meanwhile, the NEPI continued to drop from 79 in 1887 to 67 in 1897. The actual purchasing power increased dramatically. To put it another way, we learn about this increase at the purchasing power in terms of a constant unit, 1913 pounds sterling. (See right-hand column of fig. 9.) In the years 1882–88 inclusive, U.S. outlays increased from 2.88 to 4.09 million 1913 pounds, an increase of 42 percent, while the unadjusted dollar outlay increased only from $15.03 to $16.93 million, an increase of only 12.64 percent. In the nine years following, when unadjusted dollar expenditures went from $21.38 to $34.56 million (1889–97), a 61.65 percent increase, the adjusted gross purchasing in pounds went from 5.49 to 10.46 million—a 90.52 percent increase.[6]

The expenditures went much further throughout the era of the buildup, primarily because of three factors: (1) the recession bringing down the cost of raw materials and labor, (2) the rise of American industrial capacity relative to the other powers currently undergoing their own buildups, and (3) increased efficiency due to larger scale production, relatively fixed technological requirements, and sunk capitalization for naval production.[7] These factors, as well as those mentioned previously, made the buildup possible and a war statistically likely.

Peace Movements

Numbers, as well as the cultural, intellectual, and political phenomena discussed above, explain how American society embraced the buildup. But one might reasonably expect to find some vocal opposition to the creation of an imperial navy. The major problem, uncoordinated opposition, is best demonstrated with an examination of the largest peace organization of the day and its feeble, distracted efforts. Antinavalism failed because the efforts were too late and too little in opposing an item much more popularly accepted than expensive. As one historian has commented, "From 1887 to 1914, the general public in the United States showed little interest in peace questions, let alone a genuine commitment to pacifism or internationalism."[8] This section will examine the issues and reasons for such a unique shortcoming, one especially curious in the nineteenth-century political culture of dissent.

The American Peace Society (henceforth APS), founded in 1828, was the preeminent organization devoted to propagating peace and antimilitarism in the United States until the Anti-Imperialist League took the helm in 1898.

Through the 1880s, the APS, based in the city of reform movements—Boston—floundered in search of a coherent mission. Although its stated goals changed several times through the decades, the APS argued consistently in favor of increased pacifism. The APS, however, failed to take any effective measures, to make any coherent policy statements, or to combine with any other groups to oppose the growth of navalism until mid-1892 or 1893.

In part this lack of coherence can be explained by the diverse yet sparse membership and in part by the inclination to wage a positive campaign for peace rather than a negative campaign against militarism and war. As late as 1887, there were only four hundred active members in peace organizations nationwide, and even this small number could arrive at no consensus. This number could have been augmented by the numerically larger Society of Friends, but the two pacifistic groups could not agree on a policy. Through the eighties, they each concentrated their peace efforts on internal violence, such as ameliorating the conditions of the plains Indians.[9]

The fragmented membership of the APS limited the ability of the organization to derive a coherent policy and take a stance against the creation of the new American navy. The membership, based in Boston, was comprised mostly of ministers, a good portion of whom were vice presidents or directors of the society.[10] The APS constitution encouraged this narrow membership while also inviting other "Christians" to join. In addition to the ministers, it had among its officers such diverse personalities as the industrialist Peter Hewitt and Professor Francis Amasa Walker who contributed elements of divisiveness to the organization.

Hewitt and Walker also illustrate how the struggle against militarism was often far from an all-consuming enterprise. Hewitt, an iron-monger and sometime vice president of the APS, may have been as ambivalent toward the new navy as was his competitor Andrew Carnegie. Aside from the professional concerns, Hewitt shared some social views with Carnegie, including those on Social Darwinism. They both attended the testimonial dinner for Herbert Spencer at Delmonico's restaurant on 9 November 1882 at which they joined in praise for the most popular spokesman of Social Darwinism. Like other antinavalists and later anti-imperialists, Hewitt rationalized his stance based on his opinion of what would most likely strengthen the nation—concentrating on domestic development.[11] He was not alone.

Walker, a Social Darwinist and a vice president of the APS for five years until his death in 1897, was equally ambiguous in his support of the cause. He had been a politically vociferous advocate of peace since as early as 1869. He also provided some financial support for the APS. Yet he wrote books that bolstered navalist interpretations of American history. His historical works in particular drew fire for emphasizing the beneficial aspects of America's wars. The APS official organ, then called the *Advocate of Peace*, once castigated Walker for his history, which failed to note that "out of the waste, wickedness and cruelty of war, other lessons than those which glorify war may be drawn." Furthermore, Walker was an outspoken "reactionary Darwinian" who "spread a doctrine of Anglo-Saxon racial superiority and shouted warnings of 'race mongrelization.'"[12] With officers like Hewitt and Walker profiting from the buildup, the movement was not yet solidly opposed to navalism.

The movement for peace was further emasculated by editorial neglect, which, consciously or not, underutilized the enormously effective political tool of the negative campaign. In those days of brutal machine and faction politics, of sensationalist journalism and outright lying, the *Advocate of Peace* failed to take advantage of the frontal assault. While it would occasionally lambast the army, the articles and editorials throughout the era of the first peacetime naval buildup failed to question its rectitude and worth. Although the collection available is incomplete, it contained only one mention of the navy before 1892.

The editor of the *Advocate of Peace* made at least one effort to bring the campaign for peace to a broader audience. In 1886, Roland Bailey Howard, the editor and secretary of the APS, published a pamphlet *Peace and Arbitration Topic*, which included questions "suggested for essays and discussion in debating societies, schools and colleges." The work failed to gain great audiences, perhaps because of its awkward wording, which allowed only one side of the discussion: antiwar. The titles of the ten sections left no room for debate. They were (1) The Cost of War, (2) The Waste of War, (3) The Cruelty of War, (4) The Wickedness of War, (5) What Answers? (6) Remedies for War, (7) Absurdity or Reasonableness of War, (8) Christianity and War, (9) Causes of War (ambition and lust, foremost), and (10) The Warlike Spirit. Suffering from unmitigated self-righteousness, the pamphlet failed to prompt widespread debate within the educational arena.[13]

Aside from the supplement, *Advocate of Peace* concentrated, in the first ten years of the new navy, on expounding the cause of international arbitration, a particular interest after 1887's name change; the journal added to its name and became *The American Advocate of Peace and Arbitration* (henceforth *AAP&A*). In contrast to six decades' advocacy of pacifism, the five-year-long emphasis upon arbitration produced results. By the early 1890s, the United States and British governments were considering submitting the Bering fur seal fisheries dispute to arbitration. With the strong push from the APS and its political ally John Sherman, then chairman of the Senate Foreign Relations Committee, the controversy was submitted. Sherman, a one-time vice president of the APS and also of the Universal Peace Union, was able to push the petition through Congress, eventually attaining some satisfaction for each side. With this one success, arbitration gained some legitimacy.[14] Yet, as *AAP&A* readers themselves acknowledged, arbitration was not an issue that could evoke unrestrained enthusiasm.

Finally in 1892, at approximately the time that Benjamin F. Trueblood became the secretary of the APS, *AAP&A* started to acknowledge the navy as a potential threat to peace. Thus far it had only once presented a small editorial, in 1891, chastising former President Cleveland for having expressed satisfaction with recent naval progress. But the first attack on navalism came in the following year when *AAP&A* reprinted from the *Congressional Record* a speech against naval appropriations given by Representative Frederick S. White in the spring of 1892. As of late mid-1892, therefore, the *AAP&A* had failed to attack the navy as a threat to peace. Through the autumn and winter of 1892–93, the counternavalism efforts coalesced as the editor and writers attacked the navy on moral grounds as well as those political.[15]

Morally, the *AAP&A* stated, navalism was a temptation to arrogance that would lead to unjust war. It claimed that the selling of the navy encouraged the youth of the nation to "emulate the character of our great ruffian, John L. Sullivan." This arrogance would lead, history proclaimed, only to more senseless violence: "Sullivans are the men who have the most fights, and get the most severely pounded." The same, it forecasted, would hold true for nations "that make the greatest preparation for war."[16] Here Trueblood, the secretary and editor, made his first concerted effort to recapture the historiography from the navalists. In doing so, however, he overemphasized the contemporary moral issues—an approach generally less successful than cloaking them in historical tales. Thus, the *AAP&A* attacked the morality, as well as the sensibility, of the notion of preparedness—an idea that the navalists were busily boosting.

The next piece marked the beginning of *AAP&A*'s most cogent attack on the navy. As noted in chapter 3, the navy made great claims to representing the will of the nation in its buildup. For Trueblood and his advisors, the navy's claim to a popularity based upon bigness and heroism merely pandered to the nation's penchant for humbug and folderol. The writer of another 1892 piece had visited the Squadron of Evolution off Charleston, South Carolina. He noted: "The music of the bands strike up and *Anne Laurie, Dixie,* and *Yankee Doodle* enliven the air." Another writer attended the Columbian Naval Parade the next year in New York City. He too found it thrilling: "Even the most sincere peace man has hard work not to admire all this. In itself it is admirable, magnificent like a display of meteors or comets or rainbows. It was the love of display and splendor that brought the great crowds onto the shores to witness the scene." Yet he was able to step back and comment on the apparent insubstantial nature of the pyrotechnics: "But probably not one in ten cared a farthing whether we have any navy or not. The taxpayers gathered there got their money's worth of show and glitter and will probably grumble just as much as ever about taxes when they get home."[17] The peace journal and its parent organization attempted to rebut the sense of popularity and by 1892 or 1893 was in a stronger position to organize the discontent of the aforementioned nine in ten taxpayers.

In 1892 and 1893, perhaps because of the success of the arbitration movements and in response to the jingoism of the *Baltimore* and Hawaiian crises, the APS expanded its operations considerably. It organized "Committees of Correspondence" as if to emphasize and focus the revolutionary elements of antimilitarism. These groups were not, however, geographically circumscribed as their successful predecessors of the 1770s had been. Rather, they were national cells composed of members of twelve Christian denominations or groups. To complement this fragmented structure, the APS started to encourage readers to communicate and cooperate with those other peace and arbitration societies around the nation. These included national groups representing specific issues, such as the "Peace Association of Friends (Quakers) of America," to local societies, such as the "Connecticut Peace Society" based in Old Mystic. Members of such groups as these had been in part responsible for the arbitration push of the early 1890s.[18]

In the spring of 1890, many peace groups including those above but especially local meetings of Friends (Quakers), sent petitions and memorials to Congress "protesting against large expenditures and so-called coast defenses and [still] praying for the passage of the resolution relative to peace administration." The petitions represent a concerted effort mostly on the part of Quakers. These petitions, 160 in all, flowed from twenty-seven states, most heavily from the East and the Old Northwest. Despite this outpouring, the relatively conservative board of the APS held out three years before organizing any joint effort to combat militarism and navalism. The efforts and successes of these petitions must be compared to those of such groups as the Port

Townshend, Washington, Chamber of Commerce, which urged an increase in the navy.[19] And by 1890, the Quakers, if not the APS, had been actively attempting to discourage Congress from appropriating funds for a new navy.

Friends and other peace groups, in fact, provided the only popular protests to the heavily accelerating construction programs of the Tracy era.[20] The peace department of the Women's Christian Temperance Union was run by Hannah J. Bailey. She advocated peace through two monthly magazines— *Pacific Banner* and *Acorn* for children—as well as through prolific writing of pamphlets. With the support of WCTU president Francis Willard, Bailey inaugurated departments of peace in twenty-five states and the District of Columbia by 1893. Yet they remained relatively impotent to change the cultural assumptions regarding the salutary effects of war. They made a strong effort in 1892, presenting a peace memorial to President Harrison during his choleric reaction to the *Baltimore* incident. Yet historian David Sands Patterson notes that these groups remained wholly ineffective up to 1893 and even less productive after that. Only 1893 brought any cooperation—precipitated by the Hawaiian annexation crisis.

By 1893, therefore, the American Peace Society had come to recognize its natural allies within the nascent peace movement, as it encouraged its members to take an interest in and to cooperate with the other peace groups that had slowly grown in the years since the war. With the apparatus in place, they waited until the next crisis, which appeared to threaten the fundaments of republican society. In 1898 they would find common cause with other elements of the political culture, but that is another story.

Carl Schurz and Dissent

If Carl Schurz (1829–1906) was typical of anything, it was the mildness of liberal opposition to the navy in the late nineteenth century. Schurz's epimorphosis from a militant nationalism to one of tempered antimilitarism occurred over decades and coalesced only during the Hawaiian annexation crisis. Schurz had been born near Cologne and as a student at that famous old university quickly rose to fame as a radical leader in the cataclysmic uprising of 1848. He fought bravely to make his country fulfill his liberal, even whiggish, dream. Yet his forces proved inadequate and he was forced to flee his homeland for fear of being executed by the Prussian conquerors.

Arriving in America, Schurz soon reentered the fray, attempting to secure the blessings of liberalism for his adopted countrymen. With the solid political support of most German-Americans, Schurz obtained a major-generalship in the Union Army, then trying to hold together the republic. It was the perfect war for Schurz in the 1860s—a struggle to preserve the strength and unity of the republic, with the liberal effect of freeing the slaves. Each of these elements appealed to young General Schurz: militant activism, republican virtue, and democratic ideals.

Yet the war and especially the failure of radical reconstruction appear to have mellowed Schurz's convictions as to the first of these tenets. While still staunchly republican and devoted to making the nation more equitable, Schurz no longer believed that armed force would be the means to the coveted ends. He did believe in a struggle for success, having himself spoken in praise of Spencer at the 1882 Delmonico's banquet. For this effort, Schurz traded his sword for a pen. As an editor and writer, Schurz earned his most enduring fame. He started writing anonymous feature articles for *Harper's Weekly* in 1892. He was, by then, clearly opposed to the type of excessive nationalism that led to wars of conquest. In fact, just this point of conscience forced him to resign his position at *Harper's* in 1898 because of "his refusal to support the drift to war with Spain."[21] Through the midnineties, however, Schurz was still reminding *Harper's* readers of the virtues of liberal republicanism.

By 1893, Carl Schurz had already decided that a large navy threatened liberty in America, by encouraging a resurgence of the expansionist spirit connoted in "manifest destiny." Precipitated by the Hawaii annexation crisis of 1893, Carl Schurz's broadside against navalism and manifest destiny marked the beginning of the modern coherent battle against an empire. Schurz's article summarized all the important elements of the anti-imperialist arguments that emerged in 1898. In its course, he attacked expansionism on moral, historical, and strategic grounds, starting with the first by establishing the corrupt origins of manifest destiny in the extension of slavery. Manifest destiny, for Schurz, had caused the Civil War. The war, in turn, ended the causes of its precipitant, temporarily, by halting slavery and encouraging contemplation of the evils of war.[22]

The efforts of expansionists to bring Hawaii into the Union, however, brought a return of the manifest destiny spirit and an evil partner—navalism. Schurz's argument against this lobby was twofold. First, he held that navalism was the will of a noxious minority, and second, that it threatened the destruction of the republic. The navalists, according to Schurz, consisted of three self-interested groups who would impose a tyranny of their minority upon the otherwise righteous nation. The three were: (1) businessmen hoping for gain in international commerce, (2) ardent nationalist-internationalists, and (3) the "navy interest—officers of the navy and others taking especial pride in the development of our naval force." Schurz rejected their hubris and condemned their arguments; for "the patriotic ardor of those who would urge this republic into the course of indiscriminate territorial aggrandizement to make it the greatest of the great powers of the world deserves more serious consideration." Under that consideration, Schurz decided that the accretion of lands with people of vastly different cultures would be more than the republic could successfully assimilate.

After Hawaii, Schurz claimed, the United States would be forced down the slippery slope of hemispheric conquest: taking Mexico, Cuba, Santo Domingo, Haiti, Puerto Rico, Jamaica, and then Central America. Not explicitly racist, Schurz eschewed this train of events because of an impression of the decadence inherent to these regions. There is not, he claimed, "a single instance of the growth of a strong Anglo-Saxon democracy in tropical latitudes." With these decadent accretions, therefore, the republic's democracy would be undermined by "dozens of Senators and scores of Representatives" who were inexorably undemocratic. Then, hinting at undeniable evils of miscegenation, Schurz asked, "What kind of people are those we take in as . . . members of our national household, our family circle?"[23] Turning from the social and political arguments, Schurz trained his acid pen on the strategic inefficacy of annexing Hawaii.

Schurz's strategic arguments against annexing Hawaii essentially comprised a diatribe against the new offensive navy. Schurz noted America's naturally strong defensive situation,

> one that is not threatened in any of its points by powerful neighbors; the only one not under any necessity of keeping up a large armament either on land or water for the security of its possessions; the only one that can turn all the energies of its population to productive employment.

Schurz pointed to America's natural security. His reckoning, if not his conclusions, foreshadow Karl Haushofer's understanding of the "heartland": "Our territory is large but our means to interior communication is such as to minimize the inconveniences of distance." Schurz knew something of which he spoke, given his Civil War strategic experiences and his practical peacetime knowledge of the country, especially during his tenure as secretary of interior (1877–81). He could, with considerable authority, conclude, "in our compact continental stronghold, we are substantially unassailable."[24]

Not content to show the strategic folly of a "large" policy, Schurz attacked the notion that a navy could possibly do the nation any good. He pointed out the safety of international waters in peacetime and the futility of building for a war at the time when technology was changing so quickly as to make ships not yet commissioned obsolete. Rather than building a navy that would go out of its way to create a role for itself in international crises, Schurz advocated return to the traditional mixed strategy with a flotilla of a "moderate number of swift cruisers capable of doing high police duty, and with some floating batteries and a good supply of torpedo-boats, and other contrivances for coast defense."[25] Thus Schurz's words typified the discourse of the anti–big navy debate as it had coalesced between 1882 and 1893. Schurz and his allies, however, lacked popular support for their mugwump agenda.

Perhaps the peace movement was bound to fail, given international economics, politics, and military strategy. But to understand its failure, we must also understand its efforts. On the whole, the pacifists (although not actually flapdoodles) lacked organization and drive, while the moderates mollycoddled mostly to the more militant elements. The efforts for peace before the major crises of the nineties were too diffuse to be effective.

CHAPTER NINE

The Triumph
of
Navalism

A new aggressive American naval strategy emerged in the 1880s and nineties as the product of a distinct political agenda formulated and effected by a small group of energetic, progressive, intellectual timocrats. Although the navalists provided the catalyst for the new navy, the process of its creation required popular support. The general public, as well as the political and intellectual elites, determined the shape and consequently the strategy of the new navy. Together, they created an imperial service.

The nation's first peacetime buildup was executed with remarkable speed and thoroughness, due mainly to the extraordinarily wide-ranging efforts of the navalists. These men knew that to effect a new grand strategy they had to generate support for a new political discourse, which in turn would engender the strategy. Although it changed through the years, the navalist strategic vision called essentially for a fleet-in-being composed of first-rate ships combined to implement American policies abroad through a concerted force capable of dealing a lethal blow to the enemy on the high seas. This military strategy accompanied a less clearly defined grand strategy in which the United States would claim its place among the great, or even greatest, powers.

Politically engaged intellectuals in the early 1880s cleared the path for these visions by providing historical and concomitant strategic justifications for building a powerful navy. Most effectively in their revision of the historiography of the War of 1812, navalist authors including Theodore Roosevelt and James Russell Soley and, later, Alfred Thayer Mahan fundamentally altered contemporary understanding about the importance of sea power in creating and sustaining the American republic. The American Revolution had not secured, in their opinions, the nation's full birthright including freedom of the seas. Only the War of 1812, feebly fought a generation too late, eventually secured this freedom. To push the nation into a more aggressive nationalist position, the navalist historians wrote in a more expansive notion of freedom—now including an absolute right to trade, even with belligerents. "Free Bottoms, Free Goods," however, contradicted the Union position taken during the time of the Civil War's leaky blockade. This in part explains why the small-scale War of 1812 better served the purposes of the navalists than did the cataclysmic war of 1861–65. The wounds of the earlier war had generally healed, and the issues were open to relatively dispassionate discussion, by both the North and South.

The War of 1812, then, provided fertile ground for discussion of America's foreign policy. To support their new interpretation of prerogatives, the navalist historians emphasized first the mistakes of the leaders and second the penalties for neglecting national rights. The chief culprit proved to be Thomas Jefferson for his notorious failure to prepare the nation adequately for war and in particular for war at sea. Only the valor and extreme efforts of the officers and men of the navy bestowed upon the United States its de facto freedom. These interpretations quickly came to dominate not only navalist history, but popular discourse as well.

Within this framework, Jefferson's "embargo" became a watchword, a craven and dangerous occasion of appeasement. The navalist historians used their new-formed historical lessons to rail against similarly treacherous cowardice in the late nineteenth century. They called on the nation to build a strong navy able to preserve American integrity and rights, as it should have been able to do in the era of the early national republic. These lessons quickly spread to the works of more general authors, into popular histories and even schoolbooks. In this way, the reading public was soon generally introduced to the importance of sea power to American freedom.

While historians were laying an intellectual framework for the new navy, they and other navalists were doing everything they could to popularize the service, employing a remarkable array of media. In addition to histories, navalists wrote pronavy pieces for fictional, journalistic, and even technical media. In the mideighties and especially the nineties, the entire spectrum of American publications allowed a growing group of navalist authors to describe and discuss the merits of the navy for the reading public. While the elite magazines offered space to navalist writers, the more popular publications were even more enthusiastic. The yellow press, always on the verge of demagoguery, picked up the cause of the navy with at least as much fervor as had such self-consciously elite journals as the *North American Review*. Editors across the spectrum increasingly offered space to navy secretaries and officers or amateur enthusiasts, space to explain the necessity of naval preparedness and the virtues of its heroism. Boys' magazines, for instance, used navy stories to portray the paradigm of the modern boy—brash, adventurous, and honorable. For the literate adult public, officers produced discourse on *machtpolitik* as well as stories of brave deeds and gallant leaders. Beyond their highly successful literary efforts, the navalists succeeded in marketing the service via parades, exhibitions, and expositions.

These grand events appealed to the public fascination with heroes and the gee-whiz technology of great machines. The full-scale battleship constructed in Lake Michigan, for the 1893 Columbian Exposition, allowed hundreds of thousands of Americans to step on board and experience the wonders of the electric lights, massive engines, and great guns. At the same time, the navy treated its visitors to the staged heroics of mock sea rescues regularly performed by the crew of the USS *Illinois*. These demonstrations, as well as reenactments, parades, and commissionings, encouraged the public to participate in the excitement of the new navy. Also in this era, the music of John Philip Sousa and his United States Marine Corps Band entertained millions, encouraging their support for the brightwork of the navy. Through many trials and few errors, the navy sold itself to the nation.

The navalists "polished up that handle so carefully" to ensure support for the advancement of their political agenda. This work brought great changes to the actual condition of the navy as well. Men and officers were taught to think professionally about how to organize their efforts in the management of violence. Stephen Luce, the preeminent leader in the reorganization of the naval education system, provided training programs for youths, for sailors and, most notably, for officers. His Naval War College quickly gave to the service not only a professional veneer—a professional military direction for the navy and the concept of a professional education for senior officers—but also a new strategy that grew out the efforts to validate strategy with historically proven tradition.

The most perceptible outcome of Luce's Naval War College—the battleship philosophy—not only set the tone for America's naval strategy, but also reflected the new American way of doing business. The concentration of battleships into fleets appeared at the same time that the concentration of industrial and commercial might was just beginning to become the standard American business practice.[1] It is not surprising that the trusts developed in the 1880s were followed by analogous concentrations of force in the military. Since before the Civil War, as the historian Alfred D. Chandler points out, the military had been cooperating with big business, sharing production techniques and logistical skills. Furthermore, it should be noted that the two most influential secretaries of the new navy, Benjamin F. Tracy and William C. Whitney, had previously worked as corporate lawyers. (In fact, all of the secretaries of the emerging new navy had been trained as lawyers.) Luce's reforms, then, were not *sui generis* but arose and succeeded in part because they reflected current organizational practices. Reorganizing inefficient yards, halting excessive repairs, retiring alcoholic or incompetent officers, and opening up the bidding-contracting system were among the secretaries' most important efforts to create efficient land and personnel establishments.

Complementing the new land establishment, the navy developed a new mentality—a vision most clearly expressed in relation to the Pacific Ocean. The officers of the old navy had viewed their work almost as providing a police service for far-flung American enterprise. The work was dangerous but worth the effort for the excitement of travel and the potential for heroics. On the Pacific Ocean, especially, an officer could make his name fighting dangerous natives and braving the perilous elements. Robert Shufeldt personified the best of the old navy experiences on the Pacific. A good sailor and officer, Shufeldt enjoyed his tours of duty, going far beyond the routine patrolling to engage in creative and competent diplomatic relations with the people of the Pacific, in Indonesia, China, and most notably Korea, which he "opened." At home on the sea, Shufeldt expressed the perspectives that personified the old navy. But by the late eighties, new steel ships, coal-driven engines, and a professionalized service created a new set of values.

On the whole, officers of the new navy held different perspectives of a different Pacific, an ocean upon which they could express their new idealized vision of their roles as warriors fighting for a sense of honor, which they believed to have derived from an earlier, more perfect era. One finds this type of urge across the centuries, most clearly perhaps at the close of another epoch, the late Middle Ages. The ritualized jousting tournaments of early modern Europe had allowed knights to pretend that they were still important on battle-fields, which were, by then, actually dominated by longbows. These atavistic warriors rode early fourteenth-century equivalents of armored battle cruisers into carefully cordoned-off grounds—their own versions of Mahan's idealized Pacific. Each of these warriors, early and late modern, was heavily armed and armored, yet extremely vulnerable. They fought not deadly campaigns with lo-gistical problems, pestilential suffering, and suffocating death, but rather cleaned-up, formalized war games, with logical and predictable outcomes.

Where early modern warriors read romances about Paladin and manuals of courtly behavior, late modern warriors waxed equally nostalgic for great battle, empire, and the laws that allegedly ruled them. They also entered tournaments called war games—which they had taken from the German *kriegspiel* in 1887, itself a descendant of chess, which had formalized warfare for gaming centuries before.[2] The officers of the new navy valued the Pacific as a place on which to play their war games and test the immutable laws of world strategy. This compulsion for order left out those people who did not understand the rules. This notion reduced the peoples of the Pacific to mere shadows. It sub-sumed local interests into those of the great powers. Alfred Thayer Mahan, the officer, typified this alienation and desperate need for order, which caused him to reevaluate the ocean. Mahan, the writer, reflected these concerns, couching them in a historical discourse that had been laid out by his predecessor naval-ist historians.

The development of a new navy mentality complemented the increasing dis-crepancy between the nation's perceived and actual defense needs. Navalists in the defense establishment called increasingly for the largest possible ships, which in the early eighties meant protected cruisers and then armored cruis-ers. Unarmored cruisers already had a place within the mixed strategy of the seventies and early eighties; as the sole offensive component of the national defense, they would chase and sink enemy merchant shipping during time of war. Where lightly protected cruisers held a place in the traditionally defined and proven national defense policy, the armored ships had no established jus-tification.

Armored cruisers sacrificed the speed that was the essence of cruisers in favor of heavy plate and guns that would allow them to engage enemy war-ships. Trying to do too much, armored cruisers did little in themselves to enhance the nation's defense capacity. Indeed, they turned out to be mere stepping stones to the construction of battleships. They had not truly been authorized as technological experiments, however. Politician-strategists, especially Secretary Tracy, had created a need for them when it became apparent that they could, politically, be constructed. The politics that created armored cruisers reflected domestic agendas and apparently illogical compromises between defensive and offensive defense strategies.

Chapters 6 and 7 on defense and offense demonstrate how politics created strategy in the late nineteenth century; navalists were able to alter the political discourse sufficiently to create an offensive navy, the embodiment of their aggressive agenda. Historically, two schools have vied to explain America's increasingly aggressive role in world affairs. Internalists, who tend to come from the political left with an overt anti-interventionist agenda, generally find the roots of "American empire" in the selfish search for economic gain. Externalists, on the other hand, coming from the center or the right, explain "liberal internationalism" as derived in reaction to foreign aggression.[3] The truth lies somewhere in between. There will always be opportunities for intervention, for example, a Cuban revolution to aid (1873–98) or thwart (1959–present); a Chilean civil war to encourage (1891) or subvert (1973); or an oppressed and apparently fragmented China in which to intervene (1900) or not (1989).

The navalists understood this fact and confidently believed that America's proper role was to take part in foreign affairs by using sea power to influence other nations and thereby to help the people of the United States and other nations. They had no dreams of creating a formal empire but still set out to write their self-confident vision on their home and foreign lands. In their sincere efforts to encourage America to take its allegedly rightful place as the leader among nations, the navalists conceived of an agenda that allowed the best and brightest to lead the new nation. The self-assuredness of navalism was based on a belief in rationalization and professionalization. For three reasons it succeeded. First, foreign crises granted reprieves from domestic travails. As Paul Kennedy writes, "The emperors, kings, prime ministers and presidents of great powers have always preferred the heady world of diplomacy, war and international affairs to the unglamourous realm of fiscal reform, educational change, and renewal."[4] Second, comprehensiveness and cohesiveness of navalist efforts made for an overwhelming movement. They fought for a large navy by creating historical and strategic justifications, by reorganizing and professionalizing the service, and by marketing it based on the widespread appeal of the big and heroic. Last, it succeeded quickly because it faced immature and splintered opposition.

The final chapter of this work examines the opponents, those people derided by Roosevelt as "flapdoodle pacifists and mollycoddlers." Like the anti-anticommunists of the Cold War, antinavalists were sometimes branded traitors. Actually they were merely expressing their different visions of America's destiny. Some were pacifists from the cash-poor Midwest or South who held economic or religious perspectives that opposed war. Some were politicians who wanted to save, or at least to appear to save, money. Others, like Carl Schurz, wanted to avoid foreign entanglements precisely because they diffused efforts to improve the domestic situation. Schurz, a "forty-eighter," had watched as his native Germany's rulers used the strains of an aggressive foreign policy as a pretense to stifle domestic reform and progress. Perhaps the most confusing antinavalists were men working both sides of the issue, such as Francis A. Walker, whose historical writing helped popularize the navy, and Andrew Carnegie, who personally negotiated large contracts for armor plate; both of these men were professed anti-imperialists by the late 1890s. All in all, antinavalism was unable to coalesce until the more visible imperial crisis of 1898.

Surprisingly little literature, American or other, documents the anti-imperialist efforts during the era of new imperialism. This dearth accurately reflects the comparatively small size and fragmented nature of the respective movements and the breadth of the sources. The campaign, for example, to build a great American navy can be documented through sources in fictional and nonfictional literature, exhibitions, monuments, and even music, as well as in an understanding of the changing economic and political situations. Investigating those opposed to the buildup, however, pointed more often to what they were not, and resources or arguments they failed to use. This absence is, in part, explained by falling costs and increased efficiency. During the dozen years examined by this work, the purchasing power of naval expenditures increased extremely rapidly. The naval expenditure price index decreased between 1882 and 1893, from 106 to 76—indicating a drop in real costs of close to 30 percent. The big new navy, as a consequence of this and cut waste, cost only $15 million more per year than had the old. In the days of great trusts and, for part of the time, even a considerable treasury surplus, few people begrudged these paltry sums.

This book, then, is not merely the story of the first American peacetime buildup. The revolution initiated by navalists in approximately 1882 altered the course of American politics in the late nineteenth century. This movement affected and reflected the nation's changing politics, economy, and culture. Most clearly and thoroughly, it altered the nation's destiny. The rise of American sea power, more than any other innovation of the late nineteenth century, influenced the course of the emerging great power.

Postscript

Navalism at Work

─────── Honolulu, Hawaii, in January 1893 ───────

On the sixteenth of January 1893, Hawaii was on the verge of revolution. Queen Lili'uokalani was attempting to amend the constitution and push the *haole* elite out in the cold. Reclaiming the right to dissolve governments and to chose her own ministers, the queen's actions betrayed her will to govern—a monarchical right ceded by her brother-predecessor. Anticipating turmoil and hoping to be the agent of annexation, U.S. envoy extraordinary and minister plenipotentiary John S. Stevens had requested orders nearly a year before.

> Should a revolutionary attempt . . . be made, there are strong reasons to presume that it would begin with the seizure of the police station, with its arms and ammunition, and this accomplished, the Royal Palace and the Government building, containing the cabinet offices and archives would very soon be captured, the latter building being about one-third of a mile from the police station. In such contingencies would it be justifiable to use the United States forces here to restore the Government buildings to the displaced officials?"[1]

At that point, Stevens had not yet set his mind against the queen, and the response from the Harrison administration has not been recorded. But by the following January, Stevens envisioned a different role for American forces.

By 16 January, Stevens had not only changed his mind but had also formulated plans for such an intervention while on the protected cruiser USS *Boston* cruising to Hilo and back earlier that month. The first ship of the new navy, the 3,189-ton *Boston,* may not have inspired terror among the great powers, but in Pearl Harbor it earned respect. Its two eight-inch and six six-inch guns would not have made the slightest impression on a Gibraltar, but they did have moral power in Honolulu. And its thickest armor—two inches around the guns and conning tower—would not have lasted ten minutes in a duel with the new British cruisers with their 9.2-inch main guns, let alone with the *Majestic* class of modern battleships just then being laid down in Portsmouth; yet it could easily have repelled the rifle shot of angry Hawaiians. Rigged to carry over ten thousand square feet of sail (as well as being underpowered with a 4,030-horsepower engine), the *Boston* would have looked like a relic at Spithead or Marseilles, but halfway around the globe and in no hurry, it seemed quite sensible to be independent of local coal.[2] In January 1893, therefore, the new navy's *Boston* represented unassailable might. To maintain her own power, the queen would have to act quickly and deftly to avoid conflict with such a magnificent force.

On the fourteenth, Lili`uokalani prorogued the legislature, making her play for power. Much of Honolulu's white population gathered in the music hall to plot its reaction. At this point, and according to plans previously made, Stevens wrote the *Boston*'s Captain Gilbert C. Wiltse:

> Sir: In view of the existing critical circumstances in Honolulu, including an inadequate legal force, I request you to land marines and sailors from the ship under your command for the protection of the United States legation and United States consulate, and to secure the safety of American life and property.[3]

Wiltse, a thirty-six year veteran, remained calm and unruffled by the request, complying immediately by landing 162 men and officers under Lieutenant Commander William T. Swinburne in the late afternoon. He wrote to Tracy, "One detachment of marines was placed at the legation and one at the consulate, while the main body of men, with pieces of artillery, were quartered in a hall of central location near the government building."[4]

Approximately thirty marines guarded the American consulate and legation, which were never even threatened. Swinburne posted the others at Arion Hall, "a small wooden building about eighty feet west of [just across the street from] the Government building."[5] The Hawaiian government and representatives of other nations protested, but the small city remained quiet.[6]

The men of the *Boston* had landed to protect American property and lives in Honolulu during a time of instability. And yet, less than a fifth of those men were on or near American property; the others encamped only feet from the government building and the palace. Nor were they idle long. Minister Stevens was preparing to make them busy as he plotted with the would-be annexationists.

Soon after lunch on the next day, the "Committee of Public Safety," comprising thirteen white men (some only recently moved to Hawaii), "read a proclamation deposing the Queen and establishing a 'Provisional Government.'" They did so right in front of the American troops, who were indeed protecting what Minister Stevens and Captain Wiltse had deemed to be American interests.[7] Stevens, who had apparently helped choreograph the coup and arranged for the Americans' landing, immediately recognized the new government. But the revolution was not over; it had only just begun. Nor was annexation a foregone conclusion, with the anti-imperialist Grover Cleveland having recently been voted back into the Executive Mansion. The Republic of Hawaii would last five years until "military necessity" forced Cleveland's successor, William McKinley, to annex the islands to the United States. Nor was the story of the revolution even one principally about the navy; but the "timely" intervention of Captain Wiltse and his men had made it possible.

Notes

Introduction

1. Craig L. Symonds, *The Navalists and Anti-Navalists: The Naval Policy Debate in the United States, 1785–1827* (Newark: University of Delaware Press, 1980), introduction.

2. Martin van Creveld, *Technology and War: From 2000 B.C. to the Present* (New York: Free Press, 1991), esp. 285–310.

3. See Jon T. Sumida, *In Defence of Naval Supremacy: Finance, Technology, and British Naval Policy, 1889–1914* (Boston: Unwin Hyman, 1988), and Nicholas A. Lambert, "The Influence of the Submarine upon Naval Strategy, 1898–1914" (Ph.D. dissertation, University of Cambridge, 1992).

4. Edward Rhodes suggested the term "ideational explanation" in "U.S. Strategic Adjustment in the 1890s" (paper presented to the SSRC/MacArthur workshop on strategic readjustment at the University of Texas, Austin, April 1994) 3/ff. Rhodes's paper contains an argument similar in structure to that presented in the preceding two pages.

Chapter 1

THE INFLUENCE OF HISTORY UPON SEA POWER

1. John Lewis Thomson, *History of the Second War between the United States and Great Britain* (Philadelphia: Hogan & Thompson, 1848); originally published soon after

the 1815 peace, this edition was issued with addenda on the Black Hawk War, Seminole wars, and the Mexican War.

Much of this chapter has appeared as "The Influence of History upon Mahan: The Navalist Reinterpretation of the War of 1812," in *The Journal of Military History,* April 1992, 183–206. It has benefited from comments and suggestions by Peter Karsten, Michael Palmer, and Ronald Spector.

To see how typical these works were, I have also consulted numerous other pre-1882 works including: W. H. Bartlett and B. B. Woodward, *The History of the United States of North America,* 3 vols. (New York: George Virtue & Co., n.d.); H. M. Brackenridge, *History of the Late War* (Philadelphia: James Kay, jun. & Brother, 1836); Paris M. Davis, *An Authentic History of the Late War* (New York: Ebenezer F. Baker, 1836); Abel Bowen, *The Naval Monument* (Boston: George Clark, 1842); Charles J. Ingersoll, *Historical Sketch of the Second War between the United States and Great Britain,* 3 vols. (Philadelphia: Lea & Blanchard, 1845); J. Fenimore Cooper, *History of the United States of America* (New York: G.P. Putnam & Co., 1853, 1856); Marcus Willson, *American History, Compromising. . . .* (New York: Newman & Luison, 1853), which devoted forty-eight paragraphs to the army/militia compared to eighteen for the navy; George Eoggeshall, *History of American Privateers* (New York: n.p. 1856); John S. Williams, *History of the Invasion and Capture of Washington. . . .* (New York: Harper & Brothers, 1857); Benson J. Lossing, *Our Country: A Household History for All Readers from the Discovery of America to the Present Time* (New York: Henry J. Johnson, 1877), vol. 2.

As far as I am aware, the historiographical revisions of the War of 1812 have not yet been explicitly documented, although there have been a couple of hints at them. In the preface to Harry L. Coles, *The War of 1812* (Chicago: University of Chicago Press, 1965), series editor Daniel J. Boorstin noted: "Henry Adams, Admiral Mahan, and Theodore Roosevelt had made the war a parable of American policy even before the specialists of the new profession of American historian had begun its more academic debates. . . . we are seeing how the American past itself, in the hands of historians, becomes an instrument for shaping the present" (viii). Boorstin's point has never been expounded; the subsequent interpretations regard navalists' works simply for their insights into the early national period. For one of many recent books, see Donald R. Hickey, *The War of 1812: A Forgotten Conflict* (Urbana: University of Illinois Press, 1989), 321. The only sustained interpretation of these works as political activities can be found in Peter Karsten, "The Nature of 'Influence': Roosevelt, Mahan and the Concept of Sea Power," *American Quarterly,* October 1971, which established Roosevelt's intellectual influence over Mahan. Karsten asked, "is this not the same Roosevelt who wrote *The Naval War of 1812* and demanded naval reform and expansion years before meeting the Captain?" (591).

2. This book did not present detailed discussions of the financing, organization, politics, social climate, logistics, or other nonmilitary facets of the war. *History of the Second War* was purely an operational history.

3. J. H. Patton, *The History of the United States of America . . . ,* (New York: D. Appleton & Co., 1862), 584.

4. Patton, *History,* 588–89.

5. Ibid. 588–98. Army and militia were mentioned in sixty-one paragraphs; navy was mentioned in twenty-seven.

6. John Clark Ridpath, *A Popular History of the United States of America from the Original Times to the Present Day* . . . . (New York: Phillips & Hunt, 1882), ii, dated 1 January 1881.

7. Ridpath, *Popular,* 389–90, 415.

8. Ibid. 392/ff. Land forces are mentioned in thirty-five paragraphs and navy in thirteen.

9. Elia W. Peattie, *The Story of America.* . . . (Chicago: R. S. King Publishing Co., 1889), 454–55, and Patton, *History,* 588.

10. Peattie, *Story,* 455.

11. Theodore Roosevelt, *The Naval War of 1812* (New York: G. P. Putnam's Sons, 1882). Roosevelt brought out the work just as J. R. Soley was independently publishing his own preliminary version of the war ("The Naval Campaign of 1812," U.S. Naval Institute *Proceedings,* no. 3, whole no. 17 [1881]: 297–324), which shared with Roosevelt both the emphasis on the naval aspects, and the notions of preparedness and national vigor. This demonstrates the idea that the mood of the times was a factor in the reshaping of the view of history, as Roosevelt and Soley had not been in communication. See preface of Roosevelt, *1812.* Soley's work also reflects the common intellectual debt that both authors owed to a previous generation of navalists and to Fenimore Cooper in particular.

12. Roosevelt, *1812* (1882 ed.), v.

13. Theodore Roosevelt and Henry Cabot Lodge, *Hero Tales from American History* (New York: The Century Co., 1895; 2d ed., 1902), ix. These ideas were new to the American political dialogue of the 1880s.

14. Roosevelt, *1812,* 26–27; Roosevelt and Lodge, *Hero Tales,* ix.

15. Roosevelt, *1812,* 199. Roosevelt was a Republican and certainly believed, growing up in the postwar era, that states should be subordinate to the federal government. According to contemporary historiography, Jefferson was the greatest defender of states' rights until John C. Calhoun, and was, therefore, culpable for the sins of small government.

16. Roosevelt, *1812,* 3d ed. (New York: G. P. Putnam's Sons, 1894), 455. Completely consistent, this is how Roosevelt judged his own presidency two decades later. See *Theodore Roosevelt, An Autobiography* (1913; reprint, New York: DaCapo Press, 1985), 563–65.

17. James Barnes, *Naval Actions of the War of 1812* (New York: Harper and Brothers, 1896), p. 10. Barnes, the son of an Annapolis graduate, was considered to have inherited an interest in naval matters, which he expressed in his books for children and general audiences. See *National Cyclopedia of American Biography* (New York: James T. White & Co., 1917), xiv, 437.

18. Barnes, *Naval Actions,* 1; Lodge and Roosevelt, *Hero Tales,* ix.

19. Rossiter Johnson (born 1840 in Rochester, New York) graduated from the University of Rochester in 1863, was a journalist, author, and editor of numerous standard histories of the United States, as well as collections of poetry and of classical literature. As editor of Appleton's *Annual Cyclopedia* and author of numerous history books and biographies, Johnson was among the foremost historians in the 1880s and 1890s. See the *National Cyclopedia,* vol. 2 (New York: James T. White & Co., 1921), 63–64.

20. Rossiter Johnson, *A History of the War of 1812–1815* (New York: Dodd, Mead, & Co., 1882), 23.

21. In defense of the administration, Peattie (*q.v.*) noted correctly that the Royal Navy had one thousand vessels and 144,000 sailors (Peattie, *The Story of America,* 457).

22. Johnson, *History,* 23.

23. Roosevelt, *1812,* 26, 29; *Atlantic Monthly,* "American Sea Songs," 69 (April 1892): 495; a lengthy anonymous review of a work by Alfred M. Williams.

24. Perry's victory is now better known as the Battle of Lake Erie (1813). Roosevelt, *1812,* 270 ff., 279 (his emphasis).

25. Roosevelt, *1812* (1894), preface.

26. Roosevelt, *1812* (1882), preface.

27. Roosevelt, *1812* (1894), preface.

28. Noted in appendix C of Roosevelt, *1812* (1882), regarding Soley, "Naval Campaign of 1812."

29. J. R. Soley, "The Wars of the United States, 1789–1850," in Justin Winsor, ed., *Narrative and Critical History of America,* vol. 7 (New York: Houghton Mifflin & Co., 1888). It was a detailed effort to write the entire history of America, with historiography and supporting documents included. Only the year before, Soley brought out his *The Boys of 1812 and Other Naval Heroes* (Boston: Little, Brown, and Co., 1887), another major history. Inclusion in *Critical* was regarded as authoritative by the "leading historical arbiter of the time, Justin Winsor," according to Jerald A. Combs, *American Diplomatic History, Two Centuries of Changing Interpretations* (Berkeley: University of California Press, 1983), p. 46; Soley, "Wars," 377–405, for 1812 study. It is also interesting to note that Soley, decidedly a navy and naval historian, was chosen instead of an army historian, given the army's greater share of the military operations in the War of 1812.

30. Soley, "Wars," 360. The first authorization was in 1794 for 1795, and the Department of the Navy was founded in 1798.

31. Soley, "Wars," 378–79.

32. Roosevelt, *1812* (1894), chapter 10, "Battle of New Orleans," 455/ff. Furthermore, Roosevelt credits this victory to the irregulars and militia, not to Maj. Gen. Andrew Jackson's regular army or even to British incompetence.

33. Soley, "Wars," 377–78, 382, 392.

34. Johnson, *History,* 25–26.

35. Francis A. Walker, *The Making of the Nation* (New York: Charles Scribner's Sons, 1895). Walker, born 1840, graduated from Amherst College in 1860, serving as lieutenant in the army, working his way up the grades to brevet brigadier general when injuries forced him to leave the service in January of 1865. Eight years later he was a professor at Yale, serving for eight years before ascending to the presidency of Massachusetts Institute of Technology, the post at which he died in 1897. Also a statistician, Walker superintended the famously successful ninth and tenth censuses of 1870 and 1880. Analysis of Walker's statistical works can be found in Margo A. Cork, *The United States Census and Labor Force Change: A History of Occupational Statistics 1870–1940* (Ann Arbor: University Microfilms International, 1987), as well as *National Cyclopedia of American Biography,* vol. 5, 401–2.

36. Walker, *Making,* 293–97.

37. Jefferson repealed the embargo at the end of his second term (Ibid., 202); see also 202–7 for further derision of Jefferson.

38. Ibid., 221–22, 230–40; each is mentioned in six paragraphs.

39. Horace E. Scudder, *A History of the United States of America . . . for the Use of Schools and Academies* (New York: Sheldon & Co., 1884). Twenty-four paragraphs were given to land operations versus ten to the navy. See especially 289–300; Allen C. Thomas, *A History of the United States* (Lexington, MA: D. C. Heath & Co., 1893); the 1897 edition has no changes in this section, 172–80; each is mentioned in four chapters.

40. Henry Adams, *Life of Albert Gallatin* (Philadelphia: J. B. Lippincott & Co., 1880); *History of the United States of America . . . ,* 8 vols. (New York: Scribner's, 1889–1891).

41. Adams, *Gallatin,* 170.

42. Ibid., 170–71.

43. Ibid., 172. Adams became completely disaffected by the government's ability to improve the human condition, while at the same time he suffered the suicide of his wife. See *The Education of Henry Adams* (Boston: Massachusetts Historical Society, 1918) for the former problem and Marcus Cunliffe and Robin Winks, *Pastmasters* (New Haven: Yale University Press, 1965), chapter 2, for a hint of both.

44. See Adams, *Education,* chapters "Chicago" and "The Virgin and the Dynamo." Great-grandfather John Adams had been vice president until 1797, and then president until 1801. Grandfather John Quincy Adams had served as secretary of state under Monroe (1817–25) and as president during the following term.

45. Adams, *History,* vol. 1, 223, 242.

46. Ibid., vol. 6, 113.

47. Ibid., 289, 363.

48. Adams, *Education,* 327.

Chapter 2

CLEANING UP THE ACT

1. William H. Hunt (1823–83), a man of modest southern background, was a long-time Republican appointed to his post mostly to round out the geographical needs of cabinet making. For a varnished view of Hunt see his son's biography: Thomas Hunt, *The Life of William H. Hunt* (Brattleboro, VT: E. L. Hildreth & Co., 1922).

For "high-water," see Robert G. Albion, *Makers of Naval Policy,* 1798–1947, ed. Rowena Reed (Annapolis: Naval Institute Press, 1980), 207.

2. For more detail, see M. R. Shulman, "Hilary Abner Herbert," *American National Biography* (New York: Oxford University Press, forthcoming) or Hugh B. Hammett, *Hilary Abner Herbert: A Southerner Returns to the Union* (Philadelphia: The American Philosophical Society, 1976).

3. Stephen B. Luce, *The Writings of Stephen B. Luce,* ed. John D. Hayes and John B. Hattendorf (Newport: Naval War College Press, 1975), p. 16. This work also provides the most extensive published biography of Luce since Albert Gleaves, *The Life and Letters of Stephen B. Luce* (New York: G. P. Putnam's, 1925).

4. It was not beyond Soley to exploit his Harvard connections either; they helped bring him together with Henry Cabot Lodge and Theodore Roosevelt.

5. Congress had abolished the ranks of admiral and vice admiral with the deaths of Civil War heroes David Dixon Porter and Steven Rowan in 1891 and 1890 respectively.

Efforts to redivide the department into a mere three bureaus failed to gain the approval of the Naval Affairs Committees of Congress. See *Congressional Record,* 49th Cong., 1st sess., 1462, 1469. The bureaus remained as follows: yards and docks, ordnance, construction and repair, medicine and surgery, provisions and clothing, navigation, steam engineering, and equipment and recruitment.

6. See the *Annual Report of the Secretary of the Navy, 1884* (Washington, DC: Government Printing Office, 1885) as well as the *New York Times,* 2 October 1884. Peter Karsten, *The Naval Aristocracy: The Golden Age of Annapolis and the Emergence of Modern American Navalism* (New York: Free Press, 1972), 6/ff., points out that officers of the old school had often to be politically connected just to obtain their appointment as midshipmen. He mentions Walker and Schley in particular as having used connections. Albion also mentions Walker's sway (*Makers,* 72); and see Daniel Howard Wicks, *New Navy and New Empire: The Life and Time of John Grimes Walker* (Ph.D. diss., University of California at Berkeley, 1979).

Sicard was powerful enough to regain his commission after his retirement so that he might serve in the Spanish war; see Karsten, *Naval Aristocracy,* 135. Chandler, the consummate politician, probably created this board to keep officers from going over his head to Congress for details. He could control membership of the board, thereby keeping some of the power to himself. As chapter 6 indicates, Chandler succeeded in this effort, at least as long as his term of office.

7. Secretary of the Navy, *General Orders* 292, 23 March 1882. See Charles C. Rogers, "Naval Intelligence," U.S. Naval Institute *Proceedings* 9, no. 5, whole no. 27 (1887): 659–92. See also Jeffrey Dorwart, *Office of Naval Intelligence* (Annapolis: Naval Institute Press, 1979). Or see the article upon which much of this analysis is based, M. R. Shulman, "The Rise and Fall of American Naval Intelligence, 1882–1917," *Intelligence and National Security,* April 1993, 214–26.

8. See Dorwart, *ONI,* 28, for details. In many ways, ONI influenced other intelligence organizations as well. For instance, Col. William Donovan had worked with ONI and Assistant Navy Secretary Franklin Roosevelt during World War I, years before FDR asked to develop the organization that became the Office of Strategic Services (OSS) and then the CIA.

The Naval Records Office and Library has also had considerable influence, mostly through its successor—the Naval Historical Center. Soley played crucial roles in the founding of each of these institutions, reflecting and reinforcing the navy's traditionally strong intellectual reliance upon the study of history.

9. For the Greely expedition and its public relations successes, see chapter 3, "Selling the Navy." Also see Office of Naval Intelligence, "International Columbian Naval Rendez-Vous and Review of 1893 and Naval Maneuvers of 1892" (Washington, DC: Government Printing Office, 1893), the original of which can be found in NARA RG 38, item 141, appendix 7, volume 12.

10. Chandler to T. B. M. Mason, 25 July 1882, NARA RG 45, "Letters to Officers," v. 12. Cited also in Dorwart, *ONI*, 15.

For more on Sims, see Elting E. Morison, *Admiral Sims and the Modern American Navy* (New York: Houghton Mifflin Company, 1942); Robert O'Connell, *Sacred Vessels: The Cult of the Battleship and the Rise of the U.S. Navy* (Boulder: Westview, 1991); James Bradford, *Admirals of the New Steam Navy: Makers of the American Naval Tradition, 1880–1930* (Annapolis: Naval Institute Press, 1990); M. R. Shulman, "William Sowden Sims," *American National Biography* (New York: Oxford University Press, forthcoming).

11. *The Annual Report of the Secretary of the Navy* (ARSN) consisted of letters to Congress from the secretary, the admiral, each bureau chief, and the commanders of land bases, detailing the accomplishments, goals, and costs for each year. In one or two volumes, they detailed most of the service's operations and administration.

12. Cited in Paolo Coletta and K. Jack Bauer, eds., *United States Navy and Marine Corps Bases, Domestic* (Westport, CT: Greenwood Press, 1985), 482.

13. *Annual Report of the Secretary, 1882*. See also Albion, *Makers,* 65, 208. See also *Congressional Record,* 47th Cong. Sess. 1, ch. 391, 5 August 1882, 291. "Bureau of Construction and Repair" included the provisions that greater repairs could be authorized for ships "stranded in foreign waters or on the high seas, so far as may be necessary to bring them home."

Adm. David Dixon Porter, the perennial arbiter of status quo, objected to this rule, noting that 40 percent "would be a more reasonable limit, and by adopting it, many vessels might be saved to the service until we are able to build a real navy." *Annual Report of the Secretary, 1883,* no. 19, "Report of the Admiral," 394.

14. *Congressional Record,* 24 July 1886, 7488. Ironically, pronavy newspapers and almanacs, like the *New York World,* published these lists to show how rapidly the navy was decaying.

15. Most of this material comes from reports in the *New York Times,* especially 22 May 1885, 1 June 1885, 3 August 1885. Whitney, a Democrat, had recently assumed office from Chandler, whose reforms only went so far as to create the laws for reform. It took a change of party to effect the major reforms. The work on the *Mohican* and the "certain foremen" had provided considerable support for the GOP in the Bay Area. No one was indicted, least of all Commodore Russell, who had already served forty-one years and was very close to collecting his pension.

16. Coletta and Bauer, *Bases, Domestic,* 59.

17. See the navy *Register* of any year and A. Hunter Dupree, *Science in the Federal Government* (Cambridge: Harvard University Press, 1957), chapter 9.

18. Ibid., 186.

19. Seaton Schroeder of the *Benicia* in *My Half Century of Naval Service* (New York: D. Appleton, 1922), 29–30. He went on to describe the beauty of the guns, as well. The *Algoma,* an *Alaska*-class wooden screwsloop launched in 1868, was renamed *Benicia* and served only until 1875.

For more on the steel question, see Dean Allard, "The Influence of the U.S. Navy upon the American Steel Industry" (M.A. thesis, Georgetown University, 1959) and Walter

Brandt, "Steel and the New Navy, 1882–1895" (Ph.D. diss., University of Wisconsin, 1920).

20. The editors neglected to note that "Chicago" is also a word of American Indian origin: "Chigagou" or "the wild-garlic place." (*New York Times*, 3 May 1883).

21. See chapter 3 and "Handbook of the Philadelphia Centennial Exposition" (Philadelphia: n.p., 1876).

22. Luce, "The Manning of Our Navy and Mercantile Marine," U.S. Naval Institute *Proceedings* 1, no. 1, whole no. 1 (1874): 17–37. See also Henry Glass, "Some Suggestions for Manning our Future Naval Vessels," U.S. Naval Institute *Proceedings,* 12, no. 1, whole no. 37 (1886): 41–52.

Frederick Harrod, *Manning the New Navy: The Development of a Modern Naval Enlisted Force, 1899–1940* (Westport, CT: Greenwood Press, 1978), p. 34, citing *Tribune* 23 September 1897, 7. Sims's letter to Richardson Clover in W. S. Sims Collection, Library of Congress, box 12 (3 January 1898). This sentiment has been echoed frequently, most recently by John Hattendorf in "The Anglo-American Way in Maritime Strategy," *Naval War College Review* 43, no. 1, seq. 329 (1990): esp. 96.

23. See A. P. Cooke, "Our Naval Reserve and the Necessity of Its Organization," U.S. Naval Institute *Proceedings* 14, no. 1, whole no. 44 (1888): 169–234. See also Kevin R. Hart, "Towards a Citizen Sailor: The History of the Naval Militia Movement, 1888–1898," *The American Neptune,* October 1973, 33.

For figures see Allan R. Millett and Peter Maslowski, *For the Common Defense* (New York: Free Press, 1984), 263, and Kenneth J. Hagan, *American Gunboat Diplomacy and the Old Navy* (Westport, CT: Greenwood Press, 1973), 53. And see for examples of actions in war by the auxiliary cruisers *Yale, Harvard,* and *St. Louis* G. J. A. O'Toole, *The Spanish War: An American Epic—1898* (New York: Norton, 1984), 209 and 219.

24. Luce, "The Manning of Our Navy and Mercantile Marine," and "United States Naval Training Ships," *United Service,* 1 (July 1879): 423–43. See also "Manning and Improvement of the Navy: An Address Delivered at the United States Naval Academy" (n.d., n.p.) reproduced in Luce, *Writings.* Cdr. French Ensor Chadwick agreed and publicized the training of youths also in "Training of Seamen," *Public Service Review,* 16 June 1887, 100.

25. See Luce, "How Shall We Man Our Ships?" *North American Review* 152, no. 410 (1891): 64–69. Harrod details this story (*Manning,* 19–21). For retention rates, see Karsten, *Naval Aristocracy,* 89, and John Alden, *American Steel Navy: A Photographic History of the U.S. Navy from the Introduction of the Steel Hull in 1883 to the Cruise of the Great White Fleet, 1907–1909* (Annapolis: Naval Institute Press, 1972), 265.

26. Harrod, *Manning,* 16–17, citing Frank Bennett, "American Men for the Navy," *United Service Review,* 2d ser., 11 (1894): 101–5. See also Luce, "United States Naval Training Ships." Also note, the *Philadelphia* had, by 1895, a complement of 232 men, 159 (68.5 percent) of whom were native-born Americans, in addition to 39 (17 percent) naturalized citizens (NARA RG 45, United States Navy, "Old Subject File," box 465, file 2). Whether or not they were American citizens, Tracy's goal was to rid the service of those not born in the United States.

27. Typical of the Progressive spirit of progress theory and rationalization was the ordering of the races. Increasingly viewed as inferior on land in the late nineteenth century,

blacks were rationalized out of their best jobs at sea as well. A typical service opinion editorialized on the increase of lynching in the South "indicating the growth of popular impatience with delay and uncertainty of the administration of criminal law," in *Public Service Review*, 21 July 1888, 87. See Harrod, *Manning*, 10–11, and Dennis Denmark Nelson, *Integration of the Negro into the U.S. Navy* (New York: Farrar, Straus & Young, 1951).

A concerted effort to eradicate homosexuals from the navy appears only to have come about at the end of the Progressive Era, during the First World War. I found such no court-martial proceedings before then, although the process could easily have taken other forms. See also Randy Shilts, *Conduct Unbecoming: Lesbians and Gays in the U.S. Military* (New York: St. Martin's, 1993), 16.

28. Harrod, *Manning*, 18, citing Higginson to chief, Bureau of Equipment, 23 March 1889, NR-Recruiting and Enlistment, Subject File, RG 45, NARA. See chapter 3, "Selling the Navy," for more detail.

29. For corporal punishment, see Secretary Hunt, *General Orders* no. 287 of 1882. Although de-emphasized, corporal punishment certainly remained an option sometimes abused by officers. Sailors had few inalienable rights. See Karsten, *Naval Aristocracy*, 210, for some discussion.

For a first-hand account of the boat races, see Albert Bergman, *The Eclipse Expedition to the West Coast of Africa* (New York: n.p., 1890), 66.

Commander Evans bemoaned the loss of "iron men" but not the loss of "wooden ships" in his testimony to the House Naval Affairs Committee on 1 February 1882 while discussing the creation of a new steam navy (*Congressional Record*, 47th Cong., 1st sess., *House Report 653*, 63). See Harrod, *Manning*, 114, for details of Evans's efforts to orga- nize sports for the men.

30. To many sailors, the bad food was especially significant, as they were generally fed "dandy funk," or gruel. Other complaints, such as being away from loved ones, were virtu- ally irremediable. See Harrod, *Manning*, 149. See also Daniel Delehanly, "A Proposed System for Messing Our Men-of-War," U.S. Naval Institute *Proceedings*, 14, no. 4, whole no. 47 (1888): 739–50.

31. Harrod, *Manning*, 98–99.

32. The navy averaged one thousand desertions each year from its eight thousand men, according to Millett and Maslowski (*For the Common Defense*, 261). Harrod cites the act of 26 July 1894, U.S. *Statutes at Large*, 28:124 in *Manning*, 15–17. See also Charles H. Stockton, "The Naval Asylum and Service Pensions for Enlisted Men," U.S. Naval Institute *Proceedings*, 12, no. 2, whole no. 37 (1886): 53–68.

33. Indeed, it is with good reason that Ronald Spector wrote of "The Triumph of Professional Ideology: The U.S. Navy in the 1890s" in Kenneth J. Hagan, *In Peace and War: Interpretations of American Naval History, 1775–1984*, 2d ed. (Westport: CT: Greenwood Press, 1984). For quotation, see *New York Times*, 14 July 1884.

34. *New York Times*, 6 October 1884, as well the report that is printed in the *Annual Report of the Secretary of the Navy, 1884*. Compare to the reforms of the Indian Civil Service, which was open to Indians after 1857, but the exam for which was only given in London into the twentieth century. In the navy's case, the government truly wanted to ex-

pand the general representation in the service, and the reforms went through much faster. For figures, see Karsten, *Naval Aristocracy,* 284.

35. For Michelson, see Bernard Jaffe, *Michelson and the Speed of Light* (Garden City, NJ: Doubleday, 1960); Dorothy M. Livingston, *The Master of Light: A Biography of Albert A. Michelson* (New York: Scribner, 1973). For Fiske, see Paolo Coletta, *Admiral Bradley A. Fiske and the American Navy* (Lawrence: The Regents Press of Kansas, 1979); Fiske, *From Midshipman to Rear-Admiral* (New York: Century, 1919).

36. See Lawrence C. Allin, *The United States Naval Institute: Intellectual Forum of the New Navy: 1873–1889* (Manhattan, KS: Military Affairs/Aerospace Historian Pubs., 1978) and Albion, *Makers,* 72–73.

37. Quoted in Millett and Maslowski, *Common Defense,* 259. See also Luce, "The United States Naval War College," *United Service Review,* 12, no. 1 (1885): 79–90. Also see Ronald Spector, *Professors of War* (Newport: Naval War College Press, 1977) and John B. Hattendorf et al., *Centennial History of the Naval War College* (Newport: Naval War College Press, 1984).

38. *New York Times,* 14 October 1884, editorial. And see William McBride, "The Rise and Fall of Strategic Technology: The American Battleship from Santiago Bay to Pearl Harbor, 1898–1941" (Ph.D. Diss., The Johns Hopkins University, 1989), chapter 1.

39. See Nathan Prefer, "Uncertain Mission, the United States Marine Corps in National Defense" (Ph.D. diss., City University of New York, 1983).

40. Cited in William Still, *American Sea Power in the Old World* (Westport, CT: Greenwood, 1980), 13, quoting from Robert G. Albion, "Communications and Remote Control," U.S. Naval Institute *Proceedings,* 82, no. 8, whole no. 642 (1956): 832–35.

41. These numbers are from Karsten, *Naval Aristocracy,* 359; George T. Davis claims that there were 1,451 in 1897, not including the 74 Marine Corps officers (*A Navy Second To None* [New York: Harcourt, Brace & Co., 1940], 469). In any case, there were obviously fewer officers in the growing new navy. See also 49th Cong., 1st sess., H. R. Bill 96, "Retirement of Officers."

Chapter 3

SELLING THE NAVY

1. Most early historical treatments unabashedly welcomed navalism and Mahan's role in its formation. Examples include Dudley Knox, *History of the United States Navy* (New York: Van Rees Press, 1936); Harold Sprout and Margaret Sprout, *The Rise of American Naval Power, 1776–1918* (Princeton: Princeton University Press, 1939). Charles A. Beard, believing that the nation had been dragged into the First World War for economic gain, wrote the only major historical piece to question the navy's impact on the nation, *The Navy, Defense or Portent?* (New York: Harper and Brothers, 1932); George Davis in *A Navy Second to None: The Development of Modern American Naval Policy* (New York: Harcourt Brace, 1940) points to some of the costs of navalism, mostly in terms of creating an imbalanced fleet.

The New Left, echoing Beard, in its 1960s revisions presented the first major historical questions as to the impact of navalism on America's international relations. Walter

LaFeber, *New Empire: An Interpretation of American Expansion* (Ithaca: Cornell University Press, 1963) and Peter Karsten, *Naval Aristocracy* (New York: Free Press, 1972) provide authoritative examples. More recently the questions have been touched upon in broader studies such as Michael Hunt, *Ideology and US Foreign Policy* (New Haven: Yale University Press, 1987), Kenneth J. Hagan, *In War and Peace: Interpretations of American Naval History, 1775–1878* (Westport, CT: Greenwood Press, 1978) and Hagan's indispensable survey, *This People's Navy: The Making of American Sea Power* (New York: The Free Press, 1991).

See also Mark R. Shulman, "The Influence of Mahan upon History" in *Reviews in American History* (December 1991), and Hagan and Shulman, "Mahan Plus One Hundred: The Current State of American Naval History," in John B. Hattendorf, ed., *Ubi Sumus: The State of Naval and Maritime History* (Newport: Naval War College Press, 1994). These and other recent works have brought the field to a situation in which most agree on the limitations of Mahan's work and his contemporary influence; most definitively, see John B. Hattendorf, ed., *The Influence of History upon Mahan* (Newport: Naval War College Press, 1991) and especially contributions by Hattendorf, Barry Gough, John Maurer, and George Baer.

2. *Youth's Companion* ranked among the four best-selling magazines in the United States throughout the 1880s and 1890s, with a monthly circulation of around 500,000 copies. The other consistent leaders were *Comfort* and *Ladies' Home Journal.* The research for this chapter covers every edition of all three magazines between 1882 and 1899. Fifty percent of all journals and magazines founded between 1885 and 1905 also closed within that era. In 1885, there were only 3,000 magazines in the United States, but some 7,300 were opened in the following twenty years, with nearly 3,700 failing. The following is based on a reading of nearly two decades of *Youth's Companion.* All figures on publishing are from Frank Luther Mott, *History of American Magazines* (Cambridge: Harvard University Press, 1957), esp. 11, 16/ff.

3. Luce, "Just the Boy That's Worked for the Navy," *Youth's Companion* 62 (3 May 1889); "The Powder Monkey," *Youth's Companion* 64 (23 April 1891): 248; "The Caravels of Columbus," *Youth's Companion* 65 (21 June 1892): 281–82; and "My First Ship," *Youth's Companion* 65 (22 December 1892): 673–74. Luce wrote prolifically and with success to popularize the navy. See Albert Gleaves, *The Life and Letters of Stephen B. Luce* (New York: Putnam's, 1925); John Hattendorf and John Hayes, ed., *The Writings of Stephen B. Luce* (Newport: Naval War College, 1977).

4. *Ladies' Home Journal* rivaled *Youth's Companion* for America's greatest circulation through much of this era, and its advertisements, especially through the 1890s, demonstrated the great marketability of sailors' suits.

On readership, approximately 1 in 6.6 white boys read *Youth's Companion* on a regular basis. I have calculated this figure based upon two readers per issue and approximately 6,660,000 nonblack boys between the ages of five and fifteen at the 1890 census (*Historical Statistics of the United States* [Washington, DC: Government Printing Office, 1975], series 91–93, 119, 121–22).

5. In the second half of 1889, there were no articles on the navy in *Harper's New Monthly* magazine, but by late 1896-early 1897, 3.3 percent of the articles discussed it by

name. From autumn 1889 to winter 1896–97, *Century's* percentage increased from 4.8 percent to 5.8 percent. The *North American Review* increased its share from 3.2 percent in the fall of 1889 to 8 percent in the winter of 1896–97.

6. The *North American Review* shared at least one editor with *Youth's Companion.*

7. The *North American Review* also gave space to proponents of expansionist policy, such as those who were procanal or those favoring the annexation of Hawaii in 1893. These findings are based on my survey of each issue of the *North American Review* in the 1880s.

8. Luce, "Benefits of War," *North American Review,* December 1891.

9. This statement is derived from publishing house advertisements in various magazines.

10. Based on a reading of the *New York World Almanac* annual issues of 1890–1899, with circulation figures published on the cover of each (quotations from *World Almanac,* 1892, 251).

11. *World Almanac,* 1892, 251–52. The *World* was not alone in this type of scare tactic. For example, Henry Cabot Lodge preceded a call for an offense-capable Navy by voicing his own war-scare story of the Royal Navy bombarding New York ("Congressional Record" 51st Cong., 1st sess. [8 April 1890] 21, 3169–70). Here the *World* appeared to be following a jingo, not creating one.

This type of tactic only works if one considers capability the relevant factor in threat assessment. Until the late 1880s, most Americans appear to have believed intentions more important in this calculation. This change is also reflected in the changing nature of naval intelligence, which, as noted above, shifted from gathering political information to counting ships.

12. *World Almanac,* 1892, 253.

13. During the Progressive Era, this obelisk was renamed the "Peace Monument" and remains as such today. Short of visiting the monuments, see James M. Goode, *Outdoor Sculpture of Washington D.C.* (Washington, DC: Smithsonian Institution, 1974).

14. To demonstrate the lasting effect of the Civil War naval hero worship, Congress continued to erect statues into the twentieth century. For example, just after the turn of the century, Samuel F. DuPont, the hero of Port Royal, received a huge statue and circle in Washington; John Ericsson, the Union's favorite naval architect (now all but forgotten) was commemorated with a granite allegory on the Polo Ground near the Lincoln Memorial.

15. Seventy-five thousand people arrived in New Haven that day, and twenty thousand participated in the parade up Orange Street, according to the New Haven *Evening Register,* 17 June 1887, and *Public Service Review,* 2 June 1887.

16. *Public Service Review,* 2 June 1887, and see Sean D. Cashman, *America in the Gilded Age* (New York: New York University Press, 1988), 183.

17. Orders from Luce to commanders of fleet, in National Archives and Records Administration Record Group 45, old subject file "OO," box 460, file 05/06—28 October 1886.

18. For this distrust see Samuel Huntington, *The Soldier and the State* (Cambridge: Harvard University Press, 1957), esp. 97, 151–55, 166–75. See also Allan R. Millett, *Semper Fidelis: The History of the United States Marine Corps* (New York: Macmillan, 1980).

19. The Naval Academy Band also enjoyed great popularity, especially under the direction of Charles A. Zimmermann from 1884 until his death in 1916. Zimmermann composed many famous navy songs, including "Anchors Aweigh," according to W. C. White, *History of Military Music in America,* chap. 15. When the navy bands could not be present, their sheet music was widely available, as well as the various compilations of navy music published in this era, including a book of sea chanties edited by Luce, *Naval Songs: A Collection of Original Selected and Traditional Sea Songs* (New York: Pond, 1883) and the yearly albums put out by the candidates at the Naval Academy, for example, *Lucky Bag* (Annapolis: n.p., editions of 1887, 1894, 1895).

20. Amherst professor D. P. Todd took several expeditions abroad in the late nineteenth century, at least one to the west coast of Africa on the *Pensacola* (Todd papers, Yale Manuscripts and Archives Library and Mark R. Shulman "David Peck Todd: Public Astronomer" [B.A. thesis, Yale University, 1985]).

The *Jeannette* was a ship inadequate for Arctic exploration, and Senate investigations later faulted the navy for sending it through the Bering Strait. The mistake of using an inferior tool for a big job would not be forgotten by the rebuilding navy of the following two decades. The expedition had set out in 1879, only to be caught in the closing ice, too slow to escape its advance. Stuck in the ice for most of two years, the crew escaped when the bulkheads started to give on 12/13 June 1881. Three boats set out, but the crew of only one boat survived; the others perished from starvation, hypothermia, and other distresses.

21. Lt. John Danenhower concurred and George Melville disagreed: "Men are being born every day to die." Why not for knowledge? he wondered (U.S. Naval Institute *Proceedings,* 11, no. 4, whole no. 35 [1885]: 685). R. W. Bliss anticipated Danenhower's opinions when he entitled his book on the (still lost) *Jeannette* expedition *Our Last Explorers* (Hartford: n.p., 1882). See also John E. Caswell, *Arctic Frontiers: United States Explorations in the Far North* (Norman: University of Oklahoma Press, 1956) and especially William H. Goetzmann, *New Lands, New Men: America and the Second Great Age of Discovery* (New York: Penguin, 1986), chap. 11. Also see George W. De Long, *The Voyage of the Jeannette: The Ship and Ice Journals of George W. De Long, Lieutenant-Commander U.S.N. and Commander of the Polar Expedition of 1879–1883,* 2 vols. (Boston: Houghton Mifflin, 1883).

22. A. Todd, *Abandoned* (New York: McGraw Hill, 1961), p. 73. "President Arthur . . . ." 48th Cong. 1st sess., H. Exec. Doc. 112.

23. John Lowe Diary, Library of Congress, Manuscripts Division, 24 April 1884, and see Todd, *Abandoned,* 217

24. According to Chandler, in William A. McGinley, *Reception of Lt. A. W. Greely* (Washington, DC: Government Printing Office, 1884).

25. Portsmouth was also the navy yard farthest north.

26. McGinley, *Reception,* 26. In 1885, Greely published his own account, but it remained generally ignored, being largely a discussion of the scientific aspects of the expedition (A. W. Greely, *Lady Franklin Bay Expedition* [Washington, DC: Government Printing Office, 1885]).

27. Printed originally as "Report of Winfield Scott Schley, Commander USN Commanding Greely Relief Expedition of 1884," 49th Cong. 2d Sess. H.Misc. Doc. 157, the

report was reprinted by Schley, in a first run of five thousand copies. Also see *Public Service Review,* 9 June 1887.

28. Nonetheless, Elison did not survive the voyage home, but the other six lived.

29. For context, see Richard W. Rydell, *All the World's a Fair: Visions of Empire at American International Expositions, 1876–1916* (Chicago: University of Chicago Press, 1984), esp. chaps. 1 and 2.

30. "Handbook of the Philadelphia Centennial Exposition," (Philadelphia: n.p. 1876).

31. The *World* was literally correct, as the navy had no battleships at that date. The so-called second-class battleships *Maine* and *Texas* were really armored cruisers and were reclassified as such soon after the *Oregon* was launched. The *World's* circulation was 370,000 daily, in April 1893. The exposition drew twenty million different visitors in 1893 when the population of the United States was 66,970,000.

32. For further description, see Bureau of Navigation, Office of Naval Intelligence, "International Columbian Naval Rendez-vous and Review of 1893 and Naval Maneuvers of 1892" (Washington, DC: n.p. 1893), original in NARA r.g. 38, item 141, appendix 7, v. 12. The major newspapers of New York devoted most of the front pages for the week, as well as special photo supplements, to the review and parade. The *Times,* for example, devoted much of the week's news space to the review, as did the *World,* which also devoted the entire first page on 27 April 1893.

33. China had 69, Holland 34, Denmark 34, and Brazil 16, according to the *New York Times* (4 October 1892). The French "Young School" brought the deployment of torpedo boats to the fore of strategic discussion in Europe. See Z. Montechant and M. Montechant, *Les Guerres de Demain* (Paris: n.p., 1892), and also Theodore Ropp, "Continental Doctrines of Sea Power," in Edward Mead Earle, *Makers of Modern Strategy: Military Thought from Machiavelli to Hitler* (Princeton: Princeton University Press, 1943), chap. 18.

34. J. D. J. Kelley, *Our Navy: Its Growth and Achievements* (Hartford: American Publishing Company, 1897), 47. Following up on the public relations successes of the rendez-vous, the navy gave a great deal of attention to preparing for the following year's exhibit at Chicago. The *Constellation* went to Naples to collect that city's exhibitions, while Lt. Mason Shufeldt (Rear Adm. Robert W. Shufeldt's son) went to South Africa to negotiate for pygmies. Young Shufeldt succumbed to yellow fever before he succeeded. Relevant papers are in the R. W. Shufeldt papers of the Library of Congress, Manuscript Division. See also, Homer Poundstone (Lieutenant, United States Navy) "Catalogue of the Exhibit of the United States Navy Department's World's Columbian Exposition" (Chicago: n.p., 1893).

Alex Roland's *Underwater Warfare in the Age of Sail* (Bloomington: Indiana University Press, 1977) and Robert O'Connell's *Sacred Vessels: The Cult of the Battleship and the Rise of the U.S. Navy* (Boulder: Westview Press, 1991) provide and build upon the David-Goliath metaphor, the first constructively and the second at the expense of useful technological or strategic analysis.

35. See Rydell, *All the World's a Fair,* 40, and "Constitution of the Naval Veterans Association," 8.

36. Membership figures from *World Almanac,* 1892.

Chapter 4

THE OLD NAVY'S PACIFIC

1. Figures derived from Tyler Dennett, *Americans in Eastern Asia: A Critical Study of the Policy of the United States with Reference to China, Japan and Korea in the 19th Century* (New York: Macmillan, 1922), 581, which Dennett had adapted from *Monthly Summary of Commerce and Finance* (September 1904), 1211.

Many American historians (like their British counterparts) have traditionally referred to this era as one of informal empire. They include William Appleman Williams, Walter LaFeber, Frederick Drake, and Stephen Roberts, the last in "An Indicator of Informal Empire: Patterns of U.S. Navy Cruising on Overseas Stations, 1869–1897," in C. L. Symonds, ed., *New Aspects of Naval History* (1979). Instead, I would suggest that there were too many competitors in the scramble for the Pacific for any one to establish an informal empire, including especially Great Britain, the United States, Germany, Russia, Japan, France, and China—each of whom had Pacific conquests in the late nineteenth century. Even such minor Pacific powers as Chile, Australia, New Zealand, and Cochin Indochina attempted to follow the dictum of "trade where possible; rule where necessary." The "pattern" that emerges is that nations were each attempting to support those interests that they deemed vital and defendable, as all the while notions of policed laissez-faire international trade became increasingly accepted among even the most remote of societies.

2. After 1883, the Asiatic covered five regions: south Asia, southeast Asia, China, Japan, and Korea, the last three of which saw an almost continuous presence by the Americans; see Roberts "Indicator," 259. See also Robert E. Johnson, *Far China Station: the United States Navy in Asian Waters, 1800–1898* (Annapolis: Naval Institute Press, 1980); Edwin P. Hoyt, *Lonely Ships: The Life and Death of the U.S. Asiatic Fleet* (New York: McKay, 1976); Richard Challener, *Admirals, Generals, and American Foreign Policy* (Princeton: Princeton University Press, 1973) and especially William Reynolds Braisted, *The United States Navy in the Pacific, 1897–1909* (Austin: University of Texas Press, 1958).

For yards, see Coletta and Bauer, *United States Navy and United States Marine Corps Bases* in two volumes: *Domestic* and *Overseas*. See also 48th Cong., 1st Sess., "Report of the Commission of the Navy-Yards" 1 December 1883, Senate Executive Document No. 55 (Washington, DC: Government Printing Office, 1884).

3. In addition, the navy operated a special service fleet that cruised for several years in the early 1890s, in the effort to keep the Canadians from completely destroying the Pribilof seal population. See James Thomas Gay, *American Fur Seal Diplomacy* (New York: P. Lang, 1987) for the immediate context and C. J. Campbell, "The Anglo-American Crisis in the Bering Sea 1890–1891," *Mississippi Valley Historical Review* [*Journal of American History*] 48 (December 1961): 393–414, and Robley D. Evans, *A Sailor's Log* (New York: D. Appleton & Co., 1901).

4. See David F. Long, *Gold Braid and Foreign Relations* (Annapolis: Naval Institute Press, 1988), 230–34, and J. Spence, *The Search for Modern China* (New York: W. W. Norton & Co., 1990), 181.

Americans carried on this belief; see Albert Barker, *Everyday Life in the Navy* (Boston: R. Dedger Publisher, 1928) for his toast to the queen (81). See also Asiatic Commander in Chief Ralph Chandler to the secretary of the navy, reporting on the fleet's participation in a jubilee for the fiftieth anniversary of Victoria's rule, in NARA RG 45, "Old Subject File OO," box 469, file 14/01, of 20 June 1887.

For a broader account of Anglo-American naval rapport see the section by that name in Peter Karsten, *Naval Aristocracy,* 107–16.

5. For example, consider the problems caused by the telegraphic delays from Santiago de Chile during the *Baltimore* crisis, in which the United States consul (Patrick Egan) and the *Baltimore* captain (W. S. Schley) were left virtually without orders despite the fact that Santiago was indirectly connected to Washington by cables. The American cable network was feeble compared to that of Great Britain and remained so into the twentieth century; see Paul Kennedy, "Imperial Cable Communications and Strategy, 1890–1914," *English Historical Review* 76 (1971).

6. Walter LaFeber in *New Empire* (Ithaca: Cornell University Press, 1963) referred to Shufeldt as imperialist and shared this notion with his student Frederick Drake, whose otherwise exemplary biography of Shufeldt is cited below. Lafeber iterates this interpretation in *The American Age* (New York: W. W. Norton & Co., 1989), in which he refers to Shufeldt as "an ardent expansionist" by quoting from the Sargent letter, 172. Shufeldt intended to expand trade but not rule, an essential distinction in the story of the creation of an empire. See Drake, *Empire of the Seas* (Honolulu: University of Hawaii Press, 1984) and Kenneth J. Hagan, *American Gunboat Diplomacy and the Old Navy, 1877–1889* (Westport: Greenwood Press, 1973).

For an introduction to the history of orientalism, see Edward Said, *Orientalism* (New York: Praeger, 1977). Said defines it essentially as the way Western scholars have pseudo-scientifically conceptualized Asia and Asians, with the often unstated goal of furthering their own nation's imperialist agenda. The categorization of the Asians generally included two types of people, the effete, lazy, inscrutable sort and the vigorous, plucky warriors. Neither was viewed positively, although the latter was usually more convenient.

7. John A. Hobson, *Imperialism* (London, 1901) claimed that the limited markets led invariably to a military competition.

8. Numerous historians have attempted to explain the scramble for Africa that occurred between 1884 and 1897, but the literature on the contemporary scramble for the Pacific is considerably more sparse. For Africa, the leading books include Ronald Robinson, Jack Gallagher, and Alice Denny, *Africa and the Victorians* (Cambridge: Cambridge University Press, 1961), Roland Oliver and G. N. Sanderson, eds., *Cambridge History of Africa,* vol. 6 (Cambridge: Cambridge University Press, 1985), and Thomas Packenham, *The Scramble for Africa, 1876–1912* (New York: Random House, 1991). No integrated monograph on the scramble for the Pacific yet exists.

9. The *Ticonderoga* was an antiquated ship with smooth-bore cannon and a handful of Parrott guns. This trip has been discussed in Hagan, *American Gunboat,* Drake, *Empire,* and Long, *Gold Braid,* as well as in Charles O. Paullin, *Diplomatic Negotiations of American Naval Officers, 1778–1883* (Baltimore: The Johns Hopkins University Press, 1912). The log of the *Ticonderoga* as well as the manuscript that Shufeldt prepared from

it, are currently available only in the National Archives (NARA, RG 45, Naval Records Collections of the Office of Naval Records and Library, Appendix A, Entry 25, "Letters from Officers Commanding Expeditions, Jan. 1818–Dec. 1885," series entry 11 and his letters to secretary of the navy (Robert Thompson) are RG 45, Entry 464, Subject File, Box 351, "OC Cruises and Voyages [Special], 1878–1884") and the Shufeldt papers. Also see George L. Allen, *The Pilgrimage of the Ticonderoga* (San Francisco: n.p., 1880).

For another perspective, Mahan euphemistically called the new imperialism of the late nineteenth century "a restlessness in the world at large," in the "The United States Looking Outward" in *The Importance of Sea Power for America* (New York: Harper's, 1897), 7.

The canal appeared increasingly important after Ferdinand de Lessups, the French financier who had built the Suez Canal, contracted to build one in Nicaragua in 1879, starting work in 1883. See David McCullough, *The Path between the Seas: The Creation of the Panama Canal, 1870–1914,* (New York: Simon and Schuster, 1977).

10. By grand strategy I mean the integration of political, economic, and military policies to shape the international status of the nation. The nature of the United States government has never allowed for such integrated policy to be enacted although strategic theorists such as Shufeldt, Mahan, and Theodore Roosevelt certainly tried. Only with the great crises of the twentieth century can America be said to have had anything like a grand strategy.

11. R. W. Shufeldt, "The American Navy, a Criticism of Our Naval Critics" *Sunday Chronicle,* 6 November 1887, from a letter written in Japan on 3 October 1887. Clipping in R. W. Shufeldt collection at Library of Congress. That the navy of this period suited the needs of the nation has been best argued in this century by Lance Buhl in "Maintaining 'An American Navy,' 1865–1889," in Hagan, *In Peace and War: Interpretations of American Naval History, 1775–1984* (Westport: Greenwood Press, 1984) as well as in his "Smooth Water Navy: American Naval Policy and Politics, 1865–1976" (Ph.D. diss., Harvard, 1968) and in Hagan's own *This People's Navy* (New York: Free Press, 1991).

12. Karsten discussed this appointment hump and some of its demographic implications, indicating that it provided much of the impetus for the reforms that created the new navy (Karsten, *Aristocracy,* especially chapter "Career Anxiety and the 'New Navy': The 1880s," 277–325). Shufeldt himself, it must be noted, was aware of the slow rate of promotion. The Shufeldt collection in the Library of Congress contains the Navy register for the year 1882 in which the top 49 numbers, that is, the admirals and captains, had each served over forty years. See box 32 for Shufeldt's personal copy of U.S. Navy, *Register* (Washington, DC, 1882).

13. This special service squadron like the Bering Sea Fleet of the early 1890s was detailed specifically to halt illegal trade—the type of service a brown-water navy could perform.

14. For example, see Als from Shufeldt to Senator John A. Quitman dated 15 July 1857 in Houghton Library, Harvard, obsequiously requesting his first consular post at Trinidad de Cuba.

15. For Shufeldt's role in the *Trent* affair, see Drake, *Empire,* 33–34. For context see Long, *Gold Braid,* 322–28, or Gordon H. Warren, *Fountain of Discontent: The Trent Affair and Freedom of the Seas* (Boston: Northeastern University Press, 1981).

16. September 1863, in Drake, *Empire*, 75–76, 89. He also said "I love the sea . . . because it brings into play that part of being nearest akin to power" (Karsten, *Aristocracy*, 52, quoting from F. Drake, "Empire of the Seas" Ph.D. diss., Cornell University, 1970), 166.

17. Shufeldt to Commodore T. A. Jenkins, Chief Bureau of Navigation, in 1867 in Shufeldt papers at LC, box 24, and also Drake, *Empire*, 112.

18. Ibid., 125.

19. Ibid., 132. Also see letter from Mahan to Sam Ashe, 20 September 1870, Robert Seager and Doris Maguire, eds., *The Letters and Papers of Alfred Thayer Mahan*, v. 1 (Annapolis: Naval Institute Press, 1977) 356–58.

> I have had two offers of service—one to accompany a surveying expedition to Nicaragua, a propos of the ship canal business. . . . I have made one reply . . . that "I have strong personal reasons for desiring to remain in or near New York during the succeeding winter." I have determined to do my best to make friends in my own region of the country, that I may not find myself quite alone in my latter day; and shall, if persevering, at least have the opportunity of getting in love with usual consequences.

That winter Mahan met Ellen Lyle Evans, and married her in 1872.

That Mahan was still undecided as to the benefits of a canal is demonstrated in his unclear contemporary reference to it as "the canal business"; this indicates how ambivalent he was at this point concerning American control of the seas (Mahan, 356–58). As the next chapter will demonstrate, he remained equally ambivalent even during his last cruise before joining the Naval War College a dozen years later.

For those who would see greed motivating American expansion into the Pacific, both Shufeldt and Mahan are instructive: neither sought personal profit from the increased trade by buying shares in any Pacific trading company or in trans-isthmian project.

20. R. W. Shufeldt, *The Relation of the Navy to the Commerce of the United States* (Washington, DC: John L. Ginck, 1878), henceforth, Shufeldt, *1878*. The pamphlet opens with the claim, "No nation can be really great without an external commerce. China, for instance, with four hundred million people, has no status in the world as a nation" (1).

21. This was an idea widely accepted through the late nineteenth century. Shufeldt had also expounded it in his "Sargent Letter" in which he stated, "This seems to be the great law of movement to the human tide—from East to West" (*San Francisco Evening Bulletin*, 20 March 1882, 4; henceforth: Shufeldt, *1882*).

22. Shufeldt, *1878*, 1. See also Shufeldt in open letter to San Francisco *Sunday Chronicle*, "The American Navy, a Criticism of Our Naval Critics", 6 November 1887, in which he defended the types of ships that allowed the old navy its effectiveness. See also Shufeldt in *New York Herald*, "Are We Prepared for War?" 28 May 1858, for earlier effort at debunking the "big gun" myth. Clipping in Shufeldt collection at Library of Congress mss.

23. For an explication of the long-standing effort to secure such an engine, see James Chace and Caleb Carr, *America Invulnerable* (New York: Summit, 1989) and Robert O'Connell, *Of Arms and Men: A History of War, Weapons, and Aggression* (New York:

Oxford University Press, 1989). In a later chapter, "The Best Defense is a Defense," Shufeldt's preferred strategy would fall into the category of an offensive-defense, but of the first type, which would include commerce raiding, not battle fleets.

24. He called them *commerce savers* in peace and *commerce destroyers* in war. These ships might also serve as troop and supply transports in war. This commerce-raiding strategy represented the only naval philosophy through the 1870s. Reality showed that the navy was only just competent for its peacetime activities. Commerce raiding was not at all possible before the commission of the ABCs in the 1880s (Shufeldt, *1878*, 4–5).

25. For examples of earlier fulminations, see Shufeldt, *The American Navy and Liberia: An Address before the American Colonial Society, 18 January 1876* (Washington, DC: ACS, 1876). For quotations, see Drake, *Empire*, 167, and Shufeldt, *1878*, 1.

26. On Chinese navy, see Shufeldt, *1882*. For Li, see Shufeldt quoted in Drake, *Empire*, 262. He could also have noted Li's great military successes suppressing the Nien rebellion in 1868.

27. For authoritative history of Sino-American relations, see John King Fairbank, *The United States and China* (Cambridge: Harvard University Press, 1979); Akira Iriye, *Across the Pacific: An Inner History of America East-Asian Relations* (New York: Harbinger, 1967); or Jonathan Spence, *The Search for Modern China* (New York: W. W. Norton, 1990). And see Hagan, *American Gunboat*, 120–25; Shufeldt, *1882*.

28. Shufeldt, *1882*. Said wrote, "As a cultural apparatus Orientalism is all aggression, activity, judgement, will-to-truth, and knowledge" (204). Writing within this tradition, Shufeldt used many of these devices.

29. Said, *Orientalism*, 222; Shufeldt, *1882*, 1.

30. *New York Times*, 6 July 1882; see also the *San Francisco Chronicle*. In fact, the sentiments of this letter and the *Times* review can be found throughout the discourse of American writings on East Asia, but they only resurface as the predominant facet in the 1890s. Akira Iriye in *Across the Pacific*, 3–7, notes more generally that Americans found Asia to be "the opposite of one's image of America" (6). Iriye notes the impression of "oriental despotism" among Americans in general in the century 1780–1880, to which I would add that those Americans familiar with East Asia (particularly officers of the old navy) were less prone to, but not immune from, making these gross characterizations. Whatever truth may have been in Shufeldt's diatribe, it must be noted that his inability to understand the workings of Sino-Korean relations and his drastic change in attitudes, as well as the tremendous influence of his own personal goals in his efforts at objective writing, could easily condemn Shufeldt to the same list of epithets that he had ascribed to the empress, "ignorant, capricious, and immoral."

31. Drake best summarizes the intricate diplomacy of Korea's "opening" (*Empire*, 233–304). Long, *Gold Braid*, chapter 19, provides a more concise discussion.

32. Shufeldt Collection, LC, box 29.

33. Melville, although a product of the old navy, should be classified as a member of the new navy, for his steam engineering and progressive attitudes regarding naval administration. Indeed, he helped to lead the move to integrate the line-staff ranks, see Karsten,

Aristocracy, 67/ff. For quotations, see "Discussion of Polar Question. . . ." U.S. Naval Institute *Proceedings* 11, no. 4, whole no. 35 (1885): 687.

34. Jonathan Danenhower, "The Polar Question," U.S. Naval Institute *Proceedings* 11, no. 4, whole no. 35, (1885): 685. Danenhower had outranked Melville while serving on the *Jeannette* together, but a serious eye illness prevented him from commanding the whale boat that eventually brought the survivors back from the disaster. Melville commanded in his stead.

For the dozen years following the *Jeannette* expedition, the navy generally stayed out of the northern Pacific, until the Bering Sea Fleet assembled to contend with Canadian, Russian, and Japanese fleets by protecting pelagic seals in the early 1890s.

35. The island is now more properly called Pohnpei, but historical references are to Ponape, which I continue for the sake of consistency. I have not found books on the crisis of the 1890s, although two recent works discuss the history around it: David L. Hanlon, *Upon a Stone Altar: A History of the Island of Ponape from the Beginnings of Foreign Contact to 1890* (Honolulu: University of Hawaii Press, 1984), which became *Upon a Stone Altar: A History of the Island of Pohnpei to 1890* (Honolulu: University of Hawaii Press, 1988) and Paul Mark Erlich, "The Clothes of Men": Ponape Island and German Colonial Rule, 1899–1918" (Ph.D. diss., State University of New York at Stony Brook, 1978). Unfortunately, these works avoid the crucial years of the 1890s; see D. A. Ballendorf review of the Hanlon book in *American Historical Review* 95:1 (February 1990): 239-240.

36. Most of this chronology comes from the appendix to the report of the commander Henry Clay Taylor of the *Alliance* who visited Ponape in late October 1890, in NARA RG 45, box 683, folder 8. For quotation, see Rear Adm. Ralph Chandler to secretary of the navy, 20 June 1887, in NARA, RG 45, Old Subject File "OO" box 469, file 14/01. Mr. Doane was arrested on 14 April 1887, taken to Manila aboard *La Manila* in July, and returned to Ponape on 1 September, apparently acquitted. In all correspondence, he is referred to simply as "Mr. Doane."

37. Julius Voight (Manila) to John M. Birch (U.S. consul in Nagasaki) to be relayed to Admiral Chandler, letter of 23 September 1887 in NARA RG 45, box 683, File 8.

38. Voight asked Rear Admiral Chandler to send a good man, according to his letter of 10 October 1887 in NARA RG 45, box 683, folder 8. The quotation is from Chandler (in Nagasaki) to Secretary of the Navy William Whitney (at Navy Department), 17 October 1887, also in NARA RG 45, box 683, folder 8. Jewell had previously served on diplomatic duty in Korea. Chandler's experience in the Pacific was considerable; see his journal of 1849–51, which is item 1401 in Baker Library at Harvard.

39. Letter from Chandler to secretary of the navy (Whitney) dated 24 October 1887, in NARA RG 45, box 683, folder 8. In China in 1883, for instance, the navy protected all Americans, while in Chile in 1891, the United States consul negotiated for Americans' protection, while the navy stood by silently.

40. Commissioned in 1876, the *Essex* was carrying one 8-inch muzzle-loading rifle (a converted smooth bore), one 5.3-inch breech loading gun, and several other small breech loaders. See Roger Chesnau, ed., *Conway's All the World's Fighting Ships 1860–1905*

(London: Conway Maritime Press, 1979), 128. The synopsis was acquired for Jewell by Chandler from the Consul General C. R. Greathouse, according to the letter he sent the secretary of the navy on 17 October 1887, in NARA RG 45, box 683, file 8, appendix 13, "Chronological Table."

41. See Commander Henry Clay Taylor's report from the *Alliance,* which was sent in response to the burning (RG 45, box 683, file 8, appendices 12 and 13); also see excerpt of letter from Mrs. Frank Rand, a missionary, to her brother-in-law Herbert Rand, 13 December 1890, in NARA RG 59, T-90, roll 1.

42. Taylor to Belknap, 31 October 1890, Department of Navy NARA RG 45, box 683, file 8, and 25 June 1891, Department of State NARA RG 59, T-90, roll 1. Taylor acted diplomatically and with the intention on preserving America's amity with other powers. "I said to all around me that the United States was a friend of Spain and would so remain"; he is quoted by Karsten, *Naval Aristocracy,* 170.

43. Als Rand to State, 13 October, 12 November, and 21 November 1891, NARA RG 59, T-90, roll 1.

44. Daniel Ammen, *The Old Navy and the New* (Philadelphia: J. B. Lippincott, 1891). Slightly misleading, this title suggests ties to the new navy, whereas Ammen's perspectives distinctly reflect the old. Joining during the Civil War, Barker's ties to the new navy are closer, although he, too, reflected values and mind-set of the older generation.

45. Ammen, *Old Navy,* 29. How did Ammen know that the Fijians were planning to eat Underwood? For background on Wilkes's "Great United States Exploring Expedition," see William Goetzmann, *New Lands, New Men: America in the Second Great Age of Discovery* (New York: Penguin Books, 1986), chap. 7. Note which peoples' action is described as an "outrage": not the confessed burning of a village and mass murder of its people, but the alleged murder of an invading sailor.

The old navy had numerous incidents of this type of border-style violence, while the new navy considered itself too modern for it; only with the "Philippine Insurrection" would the new navy be reminded of its roles in the untidy corners of U.S. foreign policy.

46. Ammen, *Old Navy,* 125. Robert Shufeldt on the *Wachusett,* for example, had escorted opium into China as late as 1866, although he reported regret for having done so (Drake, *Empire,* 108–15). The "Opium War" of 1838–42 was fought by Britain on the pretense of recovering compensation for narcotics lost to the Chinese. In reality, they fought to drive a wedge of British rule into the Chinese marketplace: Britain needed the drug revenues to support its own addiction—Indian tea.

47. Ammen, *Old Navy,* 145, 313.

48. Thomas O. Selfridge, *Memoirs of Thomas O. Selfridge, Junior* (New York: G.P. Putnam's, 1924). The original navy was founded by Congress and President John Adams in 1798; T. O. Selfridge Sr. was among its first commanders.

49. Ibid., 245 and 13.

50. Ibid. 155. Secretary George Robeson to Selfridge.

51. S. R. Franklin, *Memoirs of a Rear Admiral* (New York: Harper & Brothers, 1898), 41 and 64.

52. Barker, *Everyday Life.*

53. Ibid., 79, 81, 87, 147, and 151.

54. Ibid., 174 and 184–85.
55. Ibid., 276.

———————— Chapter 5 ————————

THE NEW NAVY'S PACIFIC

1. This approach intends to amend the works of Samuel Huntington and Walter Millis, which appear to find relatively continuous attitudes among military men; even deeply ingrained attitudes can change dramatically over the course of a generation (Huntington, *Soldier and State* [Cambridge: Harvard University Press, 1957] and Millis, *Arms and Men: A Study of American Military History* [New York: Putnam, 1956]. See also Geoffrey Perret, *A Country Made By War* [New York, Random House, 1989]).

2. Peter Karsten, *Naval Aristocracy* (New York: Free Press, 1972), 214, 244. Note that his examples are taken from the writings of those whom I call officers of the new navy (most of whom Karsten calls "Young Turks"): Mahan, Washington I. Chambers, Richmond P. Hobson, Albert P. Niblack, and officers of the Great White Fleet.

Cynthia Eagle Russett, among others, questions Richard Hofstadter's thesis on the pervasiveness of Social Darwinism in America. Russett also notes that many of the statements that appear now to have been influenced by Charles Darwin, Herbert Spencer, Josiah Strong, and others were more likely to have grown out of larger, less-specific trends toward individualism and *laissez-faire* ideology, which had long run through the American intellectual climate (*Darwin in America: The Intellectual Response, 1865–1912* [San Francisco: W. H. Freeman & Co., 1976]).

3. Mahan, *Influence of Sea Power upon History 1660–1783* (Boston: Little, Brown, & Co., 1890) was first in a series, followed by *Influence of Sea Power upon the History of the French Revolution* (Boston: Little, Brown, & Co., 1893); *Sea Power in Its Relations to the War of 1812* (Boston: Little, Brown and Co., 1905) in two volumes; *Naval Strategy: Compared and Contrasted with the Principles and Practice of Military Operations on Land* (London: Sampson, Low, Marston & Co., 1911) and the collection of essays *Interest of America in Sea Power* (Boston: Little, Brown, & Co., 1897) as well as his numerous other books, articles, and published letters. For several useful analyses of Mahan and his works, see John B. Hattendorf, editor, *The Influence of History upon Mahan* (Newport: Naval War College Press, 1991) and see John B. Hattendorf and Lynn C. Hattendorf, compilers, *A Bibliography of the Works of Alfred Thayer Mahan* (Newport: Naval War College Press, 1986).

4. See Robert Seager, *Alfred Thayer Mahan: The Man and His Letters* (Annapolis: Naval Institute Press, 1977); Barry M. Gough, "The Influence of History on Mahan" and John B. Hattendorf, "Alfred Thayer Mahan and His Strategic Thought," in Hattendorf, *Influence of History;* Kenneth J. Hagan, *American Gunboat Diplomacy and the Old Navy, 1877–1889* (Westport, CT: Greenwood Press, 1973); Paul Kennedy, *The Rise and Fall of the Great Powers* (New York: Random House, 1987) and "Mahan *versus* Mackinder: Two Interpretations of British Sea Power" in *Strategy and Diplomacy, 1870–1945* (London: George Allen & Unwin, 1983).

5. For biographers, see Seager, *Mahan,* 146 and 200; Gough, "Influence"; and any of the early biographies: Charles C. Taylor, *The Life of Admiral Mahan* (New York: Doran, 1920); William D. Puleston, *The Life and Work of Captain Alfred Thayer Mahan, USN* (New Haven: Yale University Press, 1939); and William E. Livezey, *Mahan on Sea Power* (Norman: University of Oklahoma Press, 1947).

For historians, see Russett, *Darwin*; Karsten, *Naval Aristocracy;* Ronald Takaki, *Iron Cages: Race and Culture in Nineteenth-Century America* (New York: Oxford University Press, 1990); Robert L. O'Connell, *Sacred Vessels: The Cult of the Battleship and the Rise of the U.S. Navy* (Boulder, CO: Westview Press, 1991).

6. Lieutenant Commander Mahan served as executive officer on the *Iroquois* from 1867 to 1869 and then commanded the *Aroostook* through 1869. Commander Mahan was given the *Wachusett* in 1883.

7. Robert Seager and Doris Maguire, *The Letters and Papers of Alfred Thayer Mahan* (Annapolis: Naval Institute Press, 1975) in three volumes [henceforth *Letters*], A. T. Mahan diary, 116. Seager and Maguire estimates that they have 10 percent of Mahan's writings. They have scrupulously compiled not only many letters but also his very revealing diary from 1867 and 1869 while he was on the Asiatic Station.

For "Hakodate," see A. T. Mahan to Dennis Hart Mahan, 18 November 1868, *Letters,* 343–44. Compare this gloomy memory with the rhapsodic description of this visit in *From Sail to Steam: Recollections of Naval Life* (New York: Harper & Brothers, 1907), 259–61.

8. Mahan violated his vow on eight of eighteen days with entries in his incomplete diary for the month of January (A. T. Mahan diary, January 1869, *Letters,* 256 *et pass.*). For previous quotations, see Mahan diary, 9–14 May 1869 ("human regard") and 26 May 1869 ("more tendency"), *Letters,* 155–59, 313/ff.

9. Mahan, Yokohama, to Mary Helena Okill Mahan, 1 March 1868, *Letters,* 131–32.

10. Mahan was searching for a way to return to equanimity and composure after his frustrating, disturbing, and possibly homosexual affection for Woolverton. He later wrote of the Pacific that if the United States were to take control of the strategic points closest to it, stability would return. For, "whatever temporary aberration may occur, a return to mutual standards of right will follow" ("The United States Looking Outward," *Atlantic,* August 1890, 27, as reprinted in *The Interest of America in Sea Power Past and Present,* 3–27).

11. John Dixey was a seventeen-year-old Chinese landsman on the *Iroquois,* according to Seager's footnote (Mahan diary, 11 May 1868, *Letters,* 157). See also 10 May 1868, 20 May 1868, and elsewhere. Decades later Mahan spelled out his religious tenets as he saw them while again ill and uncomfortable, this time recovering from a prostatectomy in his 1909 *Harvest Within: Thoughts on the Life of a Christian* (Boston: Little, Brown & Co,. 1909). Of it, Seager writes with characteristic bluntness, "In the final analysis, the volume was a dull exercise in Mahan's post-surgery enthusiasm for Christ. True, the writing of it may have helped restore the author's faith. But from a theological stand-point, it was a traditional and unoriginal piece of nineteenth-century apologetics" (Seager, *Alfred Thayer Mahan,* 576). It must be said that Mahan made persistent efforts to live what he viewed as a Christian life.

12. A. T. Mahan letters to Jane Leigh Mahan, 13 and 16 January 1868, *Letters*, 122–25. Fifteen people died according to *Sail to Steam*, 238–42.

13. This effort correlates to the ordering of so many disciplines in the late nineteenth century, an effort stemming from the movement to professionalize through systematizing. See Robert Wiebe, *Search for Order* (New York: Hill and Wang, 1967).

14. A. T. Mahan to Jane Leigh Mahan, 16 January 1868, *Letters*, 124.

15. A. T. Mahan to Jane Leigh Mahan, 16 January 1868, *Letters*, 124–25.

16. For rue, Mahan letter to S. Ashe, 14 August 1883, *Letters*, 557. Missing Ellen, see Alfred Mahan to Ellen Mahan, 25 April 1884, *Letters*, 566. Mahan had been on station only nine months, but the secretary had recently issued strong orders that officers should serve full terms at sea and should not seek relief from their primary form of duty (*Annual Report of the Secretary of the Navy for the Year 1884* [Washington, DC: Government Printing Office, 1884], "General Recommendations" of the secretary, 41).

17. For collision, see A. T. Mahan to Secretary of the Navy, 5 April 1885, *Letters*, 598, and Hugh Rodman, *Yarns of a Kentucky Admiral* (Indianapolis: Bobbs-Merrill, 1928), 30, and Seager biography, *Alfred Thayer Mahan*, 140. There was insignificant damage to the ship from these incidents.

For "now arrested," see "Hawaii" in Mahan, *America*, 35–36. Writing in January 1893, Mahan anticipated Frederick Jackson Turner's frontier thesis—applying it to the Pacific before the Wisconsin historian had applied it to the continental borders.

18. Robert E. Johnson, *Thence Round Cape Horn: The Story of United States Naval Forces on Pacific Station, 1818–1923* (Annapolis: Naval Institute Press, 1963), 143.

19. His essay of 1890 "Outward" echoed the same desire to be able to control completely the Pacific, or at least, at this early stage, the eastern Pacific. He wrote, "it should be an inviolable resolution of our national policy, that no foreign state should henceforth acquire a coaling station within three thousand miles from San Francisco,—a distance which includes the Hawaiian and Galapagos Islands and the coast of Central America" (26).

20. See Karsten, *Naval Aristocracy*, 213–14; Russett, *Darwin*, 91. And see Richard Hofstadter, *Social Darwinism in American Thought* (New York: George Braziller, 1959), especially 48, 177–78.

21. On taking up writing: Mahan, "Outward." The reasons should also include the hope of staying on shore duty as well as any possible rewards of promotion or remuneration. The original publication dates were "Outward," August 1890; "Hawaii," January 1893; "Isthmus," June 1893; "Anglo-American," July 1894; "American Naval," June 1895; "Preparedness," December 1895; "Twentieth-Century," May 1897; "Mexico," June 1897. The three most important articles were written before the crash of 1893.

22. Compare Shufeldt, *Relationship of the Navy to the Commerce of the United States* (Washington, DC: John L. Ginck, 1878) and Mahan, "Outward," 4.

23. Mahan, "Outward," 4–8. Mahan's professional and personal life significantly improved when he moved to the Naval War College and helped to design and preside over the nation's first war games.

24. Mahan, "Hawaii," 41. He describes the sea surrounding Hawaii as such and the islands as the only choke points in the region from which a power could allegedly control the sea lanes of communication.

25. Dewey was born in 1837 and graduated from the academy in 1858. For Dewey, see *Autobiography of George Dewey, Admiral of the Navy* (New York, Charles Scribner and Sons, 1913); A. M. Dewey, *The Life and Letters of Admiral Dewey* (New York: Woodfall Co., 1899); and especially Ronald Spector, *Admiral of the New Empire: The Life and Career of George Dewey* (Baton Rouge: Louisiana State University Press, 1974).

26. In 1873, at the beginning of the first Cuban Revolution, the American-flagged *Virginius* was caught by the Spanish while running guns to the freedom fighters. After a *pro forma* trial, fifty-three of the officers and crew were shot (eight Americans), despite their having flown the Stars and Stripes. Secretary of State Hamilton Fish averted war by settling with Spain, which agreed to pay an indemnity. Neither government wanted nor could afford a war with the other—in 1873.

27. This text, although published in 1913, appears to come from diaries written at the time of the events, as these sections, at least, are written in the present tense. Of course, war was deferred for a quarter century, until the new navy philosophy was ascendent; at which time Dewey did take Manila. I find no evidence that the leaders of the navy planned an attack on Manila in 1873 (rather the entire fleet was stationed at Key West in an attempt to intimidate the Spanish in Cuba); Dewey was twenty-five years ahead of his time. "If war," Dewey, *Autobiography,* 145; "two years," 149.

28. W. S. Schley, *Forty-five Years under the Flag* (New York: D. Appleton, 1904). His Pacific duty included: Asiatic (1860–61), Pacific (1865–66), China (1866–70), Asiatic (1870–72), Pacific (1891–92), and Mare Island (1892–94). He called Batavia (Djakarta) "an ideal tropical city, where work and rest have been perfectly adjusted to suit the high temperatures" (*Forty-five Years,* 16). His time in Japan in 1866 allowed "a happy friendly visit to a land which had not seen but a few whites" (*Forty-five Years,* 19); for "Peru," 59–62; for Tientsin, 71; for Shanghai, 74; for Korea, 80, 96.

In 1871, the Asiatic Squadron under the command of John Rodgers bombarded Korea's premier port with heavy casualties to the Koreans, because the king refused to "open" his nation to trade and to sign a shipwreck treaty. After such treatment, it is no wonder that Bradley Fiske believed in 1897 that "the Koreans had the reputation of being the most abject cowards living" (Fiske, *From Midshipman to Rear Admiral* [New York: Century Co., 1919], 233).

29. Charles E. Clark, *My Fifty Years in the Navy,* (Boston: Little, Brown, 1917) 187.

30. Ibid., 216–17. See also Marilyn Young, *Rhetoric of Empire: American China Policy, 1895–1901* (Cambridge: Harvard University Press, 1968); Ronald Robinson, "Non-European Foundations of European Imperialism: Sketch for a Theory of Collaboration" in Roger Owen and Bob Sutcliffe, *Studies in the Theory of Imperialism* (London: Longman's, 1972).

31. Seaton Schroeder, born 1849, joined the service during the Civil War. See *A Half Century of Naval Service* (New York: D. Appleton, 1922); "It was important," 18, "prompt retribution," 19. Alaska became more like the Western frontier if and when the officers were able to view the peoples like the "indians" whom their fathers had self-righteously fought and displaced.

32. For Laning, see Harris Laning (edited with introduction by Mark Shulman), *An Admiral's Yarn* (Newport: Naval War College Press, forthcoming). All the following cita-

tions of *Yarn* come from the typescript of the autobiography composed in the late 1930s and available at the Naval War College Archives.

33. Ibid., 18, 30, and 32.

34. Ibid., 32–38. Compare his use of the term "islands" to describe the "will of the people" to the equally negating terms used by Mahan to describe the people of Hawaii in the above discussion.

35. Ibid., 72.

36. Ibid., 72–73.

37. That Leahy shared the ethnological perspectives of his peers, but more sympathetically, is demonstrated in Gerald E. Thomas, "William Leahy, The Imperial Years" (Ph.D. diss., Yale University, 1973). For "Tierra," see W. D. Leahy diary (1897–1931) in archives of State Historical Society of Madison, Wisconsin, 24.

38. Leahy diary, 24/ff.

39. Background for American-Chilean relations can be found in Stephen Dechman Brown, "The Power of Influence in United States-Chilean Relations" (Ph.D. diss., University of Wisconsin-Madison, 1983).

40. Secretary William Chandler to Rear Adm. George Balch, 22 April 1882. NARA Area file of Naval Records Collection, 1775–1910, microfilm m625, area 9, roll 290.

41. Chile had traditionally been considerably more stable than most nations of South and Central America; it had been the only independent, stable, white nation on the Pacific, aside from the United States. For more on the events in Chile and the relations of the United States to them, see Brown "Power," Joyce S. Goldberg, *The Baltimore Affair* (Lincoln: University of Nebraska Press, 1986), and R. D. Evans, *Sailor's Log* (New York: Appleton, 1901). For orders, see Commander, Pacific Squadron to Chief Bureau of Navigation, Office of Detail (John Grimes Walker), 28 February 1887 in NARA Area File, microfilm m625, roll 290.

42. For draft of Harrison speech, 25 January 1892, to Congress calling for an ultimatum see George Hedges, compiler, *The Speeches of Benjamin Harrison* (New York: United States Book Company, 1892), "The Chilean Message" (25 January 1892), 565. It would certainly have been interesting if China had taken the same position in 1883 during the anti-Chinese riots, which killed scores in California, let alone what was done to people of African descent in the United States throughout the years.

43. Hoar, like many mugwumps, eventually joined the anti-imperialists of 1898. At this point, he had not made up his mind about American expansion. Before the Spanish-American War, he could only judge attitudes; during and after the war, he had more blatant aggression against which to protest. See Robert Beisner, *Twelve Against Empire* (New York: McGraw Hill and Co., 1968).

G. F. Hoar [from United States Senate] to Charles F. Adams, 20 January 1896, regarding the speech of 25 January 1892. Microfilm of Als from Massachusetts Historical Society collection of C. F. Adams correspondence in Library of Congress, Manuscripts Division, C. F. Adams Collection, reel 18.

44. *"Errazuriz"* in Karsten, *Aristocracy,* 265; "Senior officer," in Evans, *Sailor's Log,* 287.

45. Ibid., 298 and 288. Here we find some of the first modern uses of the rhetoric of the American flag to mask intimidation and brute force.

46. According to Evans, the fleet was the second largest in the United States Navy (Evans, *Sailor's Log*, 305). He boasted that this was "quite a showing for a commander" (313).

47. Some Alaskans had already had the opportunity to experience American guns; in 1868 Seaton Schroeder had noted in his diary, "it was important to let the inhabitants of the few scattered villages see the American flag and learn what it meant. . . . and several times our little guns had to do more than send a warning that white traders must not be molested" (Schroeder, *Half Century*, 18). Charles H. Stockton, "Journal of the Cruise of the *Thetis* in Alaskan and Arctic Water, May 31st to. . . ." manuscript available in Naval War College Archives (Ms. Collection, 56, ms ac 81-4, box 2); "At Cape Prince," 21 July 1889; "What a pity," 15 September 1889.

48. J. R. Soley, "Address of the Honorable James R. Soley, Assistant Secretary of the Navy on the Occasion of the unveiling of the *Jeannette* Monument," U.S. Naval Institute *Proceedings*, 16, no. 4, whole no. 55 (1890), 569–82. Soley, among the first to rewrite the history of the War of 1812 for navalists' purposes, carefully rewrote the historical representation of the *Jeannette* expedition to reflect hope and glory, instead of the despair and loss that the navy had originally attributed to it. See James Thomas Gay, *American Fur Seal Diplomacy* (Washington, DC: Peter Long Publishing Co., 1987), and Samuel Flagg Bemis, 2d and 4th editions, *Diplomatic History of the United States* (New York: Holt, 1942, 1955).

49. Evans, *Sailor's Log*, 328. Clark, with his disaffection for the Alaskan people, later relieved Evans in command of the sealing fleet (Clark, *Fifty Years*, 254–56).

Chapter 6

THE BEST DEFENSE IS A DEFENSE

1. For "satirical semblance," see *Nation* (5 February 1880). For "good gracious," see *Frank Leslie's Illustrated Newspaper,* 17 April 1880, 112. Lance Buhl convincingly argued that this navy was sufficient for the needs of the nation. But by the 1880s, the perception of need had changed ("The Smooth Water Navy: American Naval Policy and Politics, 1865–1876" [Ph.D. diss., Harvard University, 1968] and "Maintaining 'An American Navy' 1865–1889," in Kenneth J. Hagan, ed., *In Peace and War* [Westport, CT: Greenwood Press, 1984]).

The standard works based primarily on government documents on the origins of the new navy include: Walter Herrick, *American Naval Revolution* (Baton Rouge: Louisiana State University Press, 1966); Benjamin F. Cooling, *Benjamin Franklin Tracy: Father of the Modern American Fighting Navy* (Hamden: Archon, 1973); Kenneth J. Hagan, *American Gunboat Diplomacy and the Old Navy, 1877–1889* (Westport, CT: Greenwood Press, 1973); and Ronald Spector, *Professors of War: The Naval War College and the Development of the Naval Profession* (Newport: Naval War College Press, 1977).

2. Generally, the greater the armor and speed, the less efficiency and distance. Also, since the size of ships was limited by these factors and also technological limitations (and the fear of putting all the eggs in one basket) armor came at the expense of guns. In the

1880s, no one ship could have everything to please everyone, so certain more popular features survived—foremost were the size of the ships and of the guns.

3. These coastal ships would possibly include fast torpedo (launching) boats and possibly rams—fast boats with reinforced bows to plow through an enemy's ship.

4. J. C. Soley, "On a Proposed Type of Cruiser for the United States Navy," U.S. Naval Institute *Proceedings,* 4, no. 2, whole no. 5: 127–40, especially 129. On 9 May 1878, Soley had delivered this paper before the Naval Institute with Cdr. Alfred Thayer Mahan (then vice president of the Naval Institute and head of the USNA Department of Ordnance and Gunnery) chairing the meeting. Soley was the son of James Russell Soley and, at the time, an instructor of gunnery under Mahan (United States Navy, *Register of the Commissioned, Warrant, and Volunteer Officers of the Navy of the United States . . . .* (Washington, DC: Government Printing Office, 1878), 86). For the Naval Institute, see chapter 2 above and Lawrence Allin, *The United States Naval Institute: Intellectual Forum of the New Navy, 1873–1889* (Manhattan, KS: MA/AH Publishing, 1978), which presents a solid summary of the role the *Proceedings* played as a springboard for the ideas of the new navy.

5. Benjamin H. Harris (R-MA), the House Committee on Naval Affairs, "House Report No. 169, 46th Cong., 2d session, printed as "valuable information" in Senate Report No. 653, 46th Cong., 2d session, 8 (serial volume no. 1898), ordered printed 21 May 1880. Harris chaired the committee between 1881 and 1883. Then he did not serve in the 48th Congress, when John D. Long (future secretary of the navy) ascended to his chair.

Here Harris presages the strategy propounded by the French "young school" under Admiral Aube, the major works of which were presented in the 1880s. For a brief history of the *jeune école,* see William R. Langer, *Diplomacy of Imperialism* (New York: A. Knopf, 1935), 420–21, or see Theodore Ropp, "Continental Doctrines of Sea Power," in Edward M. Earle, *Makers of Modern Strategy* (Princeton: Princeton University Press, 1943), chapter 18. Also see Ropp, *The Development of a Modern Navy: French Naval Policy, 1871–1904,* ed. S. S. Roberts (Annapolis: Naval Institute Press, 1987).

6. "The fixation with decisive battleship actions was simple-minded and distracted from seriously examining alternative uses of sea power that were appropriate to the geographical and strategic circumstances of the situation they faced," according to John Hattendorf, "The Anglo-American Way in Maritime Strategy," *Naval War College Review,* 42, no. 1, seq. 329 (1990): 96; see also Kenneth J. Hagan, *This People's Navy: The Making of American Sea Power* (New York: Free Press, 1991), introduction.

For foundation of Torpedo School, see John Hattendorf, et al., *Sailors and Scholars: The Centennial History of the U.S. Naval War College* (Newport: Naval War College Press, 1984), 6. See also Mahan, "The Necessities and Objects of a Naval War College," U.S. Naval Institute *Proceedings,* 14, no. 4, whole no. 47 (1888): 621–40, and "The Practical Character of the Naval War College" U.S. Naval Institute *Proceedings,* 19, no. 2, whole no. 66 (1893): 153–66.

7. James Chace and Caleb Carr, *America Invulnerable: The Quest for Absolute Security from 1812 to Star Wars* (New York: Summit, 1988), examine the long-standing tendency of America to struggle messianically against those who fail to believe in the great myth of invulnerability. In many ways, these people become the "evil empire" fifth colum-

nists in American politics, and even arch-villains in historiography. The monomyth of America's unique mission inevitably encounters the "other" and historians have too often failed to see beyond this other-ing in domestic political culture if the other is essentially from the same ethnocultural background. Those who opposed the offensive-defense in the late nineteenth century are still reviled by historians, perhaps because those historians use the words of the probattleship men to describe their opponents.

8. For useful revisions, see Michael Sherry, *Rise of American Air Power* (New Haven: Yale University Press, 1987).

9. Mahan quoted Ramsay in *From Sail to Steam: Recollections of a Naval Life* (New York: Harper and Brothers, 1907), 311. For Ramsay, see comment in Robert Seager, *Alfred Thayer Mahan: The Man and His Letters* (Annapolis: Naval Institute, 1977), 242 and especially footnote 22 on page 649.

10. See Peter Karsten, *Naval Aristocracy* (New York: Free Press, 1972), 344.

11. The fleet assembled in response to the capture of the *Virginius* late in 1873 and could cruise at a mere four and a half knots, the speed of its slowest vessel. While Parker maneuvered the navy at a cost of $5 million, in part to threaten Spanish authority in nearby Cuba, an $80,000 indemnity was being negotiated by Secretary of State Hamilton Fish. The embarrassing display at Key West reminded those who were listening of the decrepit state of the navy.

Foxhall A. Parker, "Our Fleet Manoeuvre in the Bay of Florida, and the Navy of the Future," U.S. Naval Institute *Proceedings*, 1, no. 8 (1874), paper delivered on 10 December 1874. He later produced *Fleet Tactics under Steam* (New York: Van Nostrand, 1877) based in part on this service. See also Buhl, "American Navy," 147–48.

12. Parker, "Our Fleet," 170–71.

13. Ibid., 174 (italics original). For an example of Mahan's dictums, see "In a sea war, as in all others, two things are from the first essential,—a suitable base upon the frontier . . . and an organized military force, in this case a fleet, of size and quality adequate to the proposed operations" *Influence of Sea Power upon History, 1660–1783* [New York: Hill and Wang, Inc., 1957 edition of 1890 Little, Brown & Co., original], 460). For "adaptation of military, . . ." see Parker, "Tactics," as cited in John Hayes and John Hattendorf, eds., *Writings of Stephen B. Luce* (Newport: Naval War College Press, 1975), introduction.

14. F. M. Barber, *Lecture on Submarine Boats and their Application to Torpedo Operations* (Newport: U.S. Torpedo Station, 1875) See also his *Lecture on Drifting and Automatic Moveable Torpedoes, Submarine Guns, and Rockets* of December 1874, and *Lecture on the Whitehead Torpedo* of 20 November 1874. For the early history of submarines, see Nicholas A. Lambert, "The Influence of the Submarine upon Naval Strategy, 1898–1914," (Ph.D. diss., Cambridge University, 1992), especially chapter 1, "Introduction to the Development of the Submarine."

15. Barber, *Lecture on Submarine . . .*, esp. pp. 5–6, and 27, and also Alex Roland, *Underwater Warfare in the Age of Sail* (Bloomington: University of Indiana Press, 1977).

16. Barber, "A Practical Method of Arriving at the Number, Size, Type, Rig, and Cost of the Vessels of which the United States Navy should Consist in time of Peace" U.S. Naval Institute *Proceedings*, 12, no. 3, whole no. 38 (1886): 421. Other works were appearing at the same time, pointing to the same conclusions; however, most of these works were be-

ing printed in European countries, which were constructing the coastal defense boats, as well as the battlefleets.

17. In 1893 Cdr. Charles Chabaud-Arnault, retired from the French navy, had changed his mind, claiming that commerce destroying had never won a war and that the primary object of a navy is to engage hostile fleets at sea, keep blockades, and cooperate with land forces. His change of mind, as published in the *Proceedings,* fits exactly the change of strategy that the navy effected in the intervening years, more about which see later. (C. C.-Arnault, "The Employment of Torpedoes in Steam Launches against Men of War," U.S. Naval Institute *Proceedings,* 6, no. 11 (1880), published originally in the *Revue Maritime et Coloniale,* 62, no. 214; Charles Chabaud-Arnault, "Warships and Naval Warfare," U.S. Naval Institute *Proceedings,* 19, no. 2, whole no. 66 (1893): 178 and 180/ff.

18. Rodgers's fifty-two years in the navy gained him both respect from most colleagues and a sense of tradition that might have shaped his board's traditionalist philosophy (*Annual Report of the Secretary of the Navy, 1881* (28 November 1881), Appendix Number 1, "The Advisory Board," 28, 37–48. 47th Cong., 1st sess., House Report No. 653, "Construction of Vessels of War for the Navy," xxiv. Also in *ARSN* 1881, 37.

    a. Two first-rate steel double-decked unarmored cruisers, at 5,873 tons, average sea speed of 15 knots with four 8-inch guns and 21 6-inch guns. Cost $3,560,000.

    b. Six first-rate steel, double-decked, unarmored cruisers, at 4,560 tons, average sea speed of 14 knots, with four 8-inch guns and fifteen 6-inch guns. Cost $8,532,000.

    c. Ten second-rate steel, single-decked, unarmored cruisers, at 3,043 tons, average sea speed of 10 knots, with twelve 6-inch guns. Cost $9,300,000.

    d. Twenty fourth-rate wooden cruisers, of 793 tons, average sea speed of 10 knots, and one 6-inch gun and two 60 pounders. Cost $4,360,000.

    e. Five steel rams of 2,000 tons with average sea speed of 13 knots. Cost $2,500,000.

    f. Five torpedo gunboats of 450 tons, maximum sea speed of not less than 13 knots and one heavily-powered rifled gun. $725,000.

    g. Ten cruising torpedo boats, 100 feet long with maximum speed of not less than 21 knots. Cost $380,000.

    h. Ten harbor torpedo boats, 70 feet long, maximum speed of not less than 17 knots. Cost $250,000.

19. The transcript of these hearings appears in 47th Cong., 1st sess., House Report No., 653, pp. 1–228 (serial set volume number 2066 [henceforth *House 653*]. Sicard answered in the affirmative a question on whether the five-thousand-ton ship ought to be built, and went on to say, "I think the torpedoes [i.e., self-propelled torpedoes] and guns go together; I don't think they can be worked effectively separately. The torpedoes must be covered by the artillery, or they are likely to be destroyed" (*House 653,* 19). Later Sicard was more clear: torpedo boats "are absolutely necessary to the national defense," he wrote the secretary on 13 March 1884 (*Congressional Record*—Senate, 8 April 1884, 2759) (*House 653,* 22).

The committee chair, Benjamin Harris, also believed strongly in the potential of moveable torpedoes; see his speech in *Congressional Record—appendix*, 20 January 1883. It includes, "the torpedo is the creation of American genius" (73).

20. *House 653*, 57.

21. This legislation marks the beginning of the new navy (Albion, *Makers*, 209).

22. The Appropriations Committee authorized the two ships but with funds insufficient even to lay down their keels. See *Congressional Record*, 24 January 1883, 1562–64.

23. Much of this work is a result of having read each article on the navy or navy-related topics that appeared in the *New York Times* index between 1882 and 1898, as well as pieces that did not appear in the index but were found by chance or outside citations. Needless to say, this comprises an extensive body of literature, which, with the navy, grew larger each year. Like most of the other journals and newspapers, the coverage also grew increasingly favorable between 1882 and 1898, and articles were increasingly based upon navy sources. While the *Times* was not yet the "paper of record," it does demonstrate a moderate Republican view of the events and times.

Congress took increasing interest in the decayed navy and asked for information on its condition. A detailed report on the condition of the navy was delivered by William H. Hunt in "Letter from the Secretary of the navy in further response to A resolution of the House of Representatives, transmitting certain information in reference to steamers in the United States Navy," written on 7 April 1882, addressed to J. W. Keifer, Speaker of the House, and published as 47th Cong., 1st session, House Exec. Doc. 30, part 3. See also 47th Cong., 1st sess., House Report No. 653, "Construction of Vessels of War for the Navy," 1–30, and appendix 1, 1–228.

24. *New York Times*, 9 January 1882, anonymous letter to the editor on page 3, column 5. At the time, the navy had actually one allegedly "first-rate" ship, the *Tennessee*, a wooden frigate of Civil War vintage.

25. *New York Times*, 8 March 1882, 2, c. 3. In 1882 the fifteen-knot ships meant an offensive strategy (*Times* quoting from 47th Cong., 1st session, House Report No. 653, xxv).

26. A. S. Hewitt, "Shall we have a Real Navy or a sham Navy?" Speech in House of Representatives, 29 June 1882 (Washington, DC: Government Printing Office, 1882), 6. I do not know if there was any relation between Hewitt's call for a new steel navy and his partnership in the Cooper & Hewitt iron works. Hewitt had served in the 44th and 45th Congresses, returning in 1881 to the 47th. He was serving only on the House Select Committee on "Laws respecting the election of President and Vice-President," according to the *Congressional Directory*, 1882, 91. By the 48th Congress, he had found a place on the powerful Ways and Means Committee.

Harris Laning was aboard the *Monadnock* as it was towed from San Francisco to Manila; he gives the clear impression of how poorly suited these ships were to high-seas travel and how desperate the navy was for the gunboats that would have better served its purposes during the insurrection. The navy eventually impressed several gunboats from the Spanish navy (Mark R. Shulman, ed., *An Admiral's Yarn* (Newport: Naval War College Press, forthcoming).

27. George Robeson in the *Congressional Record*, 24 January 1883, 1559.

28. It was not normal procedure for the *Times* to review articles instead of books, another indication of how exciting they found Gorringe's ideas to be (*New York Times*, 25 April 1882, 4, c. 5). Germany, Russia, and Japan had not secured serious battle-fleets, nor would they become potential naval threats until the 1890s. Lt. Cdr. Henry H. Gorringe was on leave of absence in 1882, having last been at sea in 1869, according to the U.S. Navy Department, *Register* (Washington, DC: Government Printing Office, 1882), 20–21. The relative strengths of the European fleets were made explicit in 47th Cong., 1st session, House Report No. 653, 1–30, including the detailed strengths of England, France, Russia, Germany, Holland, Italy, Spain, Austria, Turkey, Denmark, and Japan. My italics are to emphasize that these were not commerce-destroying cruisers of which he wrote.

29. *New York Times*, 25 April 1882. The CSS *Alabama* destroyed at least 100,000 tons and $15.5 million worth of U.S. shipping and drove hundreds to reflag or into harbors during the Civil War. Great Britain later repaid the Union for these losses, admitting violation of international law in building the *Alabama* and its sister ship the *Florida* for the Confederacy.

30. *New York Times*, 5 June 1882, in review of Theodore Roosevelt's *Naval War of 1812*.

31. *New York Times*, 8 April 1883, 4. The "torpedoes" referred to would be called "mines" today (they were Farragut's torpedoes at Mobile Bay).

Put another way, the *Times* calculated what would be the best defense for the United States, and in the early 1880s, that calculation led to a conclusion that was in accord with the feelings about defense that were then ascendant among citizens and even among the navalists. The *Times* opinion concurred with that of the public and of the navalists, because it included a place for the cruiser. For the paper, the cruisers made good sense. For the public, the cruisers were the most dramatic expression of American foreign policy potentially available. In the years following, however, the *Times* would be left behind, not particularly because of changes in the strategic reality, but because its link to the popular attitudes was broken. Battleships became a political and physical reality, and thereupon claimed the cultural appeal that the cruisers had formerly held.

32. The ram was simply a fast cruiser with a heavily reinforced bow, which would ram other ships amidships, much like the triremes of ancient days. William Gibbons, "The Marine Ram As Designed by Rear Admiral Daniel Ammen, U.S.N.," U.S. Naval Institute *Proceedings*, 8, no. 2, whole no. 20 (1882). Gibbons was president of a Wilmington ship-building concern.

The institute called for as much building as possible. Lt. Carlos G. Calkins won the Naval Institute Prize for best essay on the subject "How may the sphere of usefulness of Naval Officers be extended in time of Peace with Advantage to the Country and Naval Service?" with his essay, "Pour Encourager Les Autres," which appeared in U.S. Naval Institute *Proceedings*, 9, no. 24 (1883). The essay stated, "Two cruisers, with the possible addition of a few monitors unfit for sea-service, will hardly remove the disparity" between the United States and the European powers (155). The first-prize essay of this quasi-official publication could indicate a frustration among officers at the slow progress of naval appropriations.

Alarm was laid up in 1885; *Intrepid* in 1882 was converted to a gunboat (Roger Chesnau, ed., *Conway's All the World's Fighting Ships, 1865–1905* (London: Conway Maritime Press, 1979), 132).

33. Porter called for the construction of "twenty torpedo boats of not less than 100 tons each, with a speed of 20 knots" noting that Britain would be building 250 such craft at the same time. *Alarm,* a torpedo ram commissioned in 1874, never joined a fleet and was laid up in 1885. See also *New York Times,* 20 November 1884; *ARSN 1883,* no. 19, "Report of the Admiral of the Navy," 383/ff, especially 396–97, on the uses and strengths of the torpedo boat *Alarm; ARSN 1884,* no. 2, "Report of the Admiral of the Navy," 63. *New York Times,* 21 November 1883, 2, gives a long extract from the admiral's statement in *ARSN 1883.*

34. Secretary of Navy to J. Warren Keifer, Speaker of the House of Representatives, 2 January 1883, in 47 Cong. 2d sess., House Report No. 1862, 8–9. The large cruiser mentioned was to be 5,873 tons. See also *Congressional Record,* 24 January 1883, 1562–64. For Rodgers Board recommendations, see *ARSN 1881,* 37.

35. Chandler to Speaker, 47th Cong., 2d sess., H. Report 1862, 8–9. Chandler was saying that such large ships would not fit the defensive-defense strategy in which the Navy Department (if not Congress) still believed. See also *Congressional Record,* 22 May 1884, 4400, and 23 May 1884, 4416, for request of Secretary of Navy to Speaker and Senate president respectively for torpedo boats.

36. Atkins in *Congressional Record,* 24 January 1883, 1564. For others, see William Holman (D-IND), *Congressional Record,* 24 January 1883, 1567.

37. For Shufeldt's recommendations and quotations, see 48th Cong., 1st sess., Senate Report number 161, appendix 7, "Views submitted to the Committee on Naval Affairs," 21–22; *ARSN 1883,* "Additional Cruisers," 88; Drake, *Empire,* 316.

38. Whitthorne in *Congressional Record,* 24 January 1883, 1560.

39. *ARSN 1882,* Report of the "Bureau of Steam Engineering and Bureau of Construction and Repair" based upon reports of Engineer-in-Chief W. H. Shock and Chief Constructor T. D. Wilson, 23–25. For vote, see *Congressional Record,* 24 January 1883, 1562–65.

40. For debate, see *Congressional Record,* 24 January 1883, 1650–1657 for examples especially from Congressman William Holman. For vote, see "Naval Appropriation Act of 1884," 3 March 1883, in *United States Statutes,* 22, 477, of the 47th Congress, 2d sess.

41. For some adverse discussion, see George T. Davis, *A Navy Second to None* (New York: Harcourt Brace & Jovanovich, 1940; repr. Westport, CT: Greenwood, 1971), 41. For further debate on why these early ships of the new navy were fully or partially rigged, see William McBride, "The Rise and Fall of a Strategic Technology: The American Battleship From Santiago Bay to Pearl Harbor, 1898–1941" (Ph.D. diss., The Johns Hopkins University, 1989), which claims that the "pro-sail hierarchy used strategic discontinuity to justify the anti-technology policies of the period" (xii).

42. For Hale's proposal's, see 48th Cong., 1st sess., Senate Bill 698. See also President Arthur's letter to House and Senate in "House Executive Document 127," 26 March 1884, and *Congressional Record,* 1884, 2317, 2318. For more background, Davis, *Navy,* 41–42.

43. *New York Times*, 23 February 1884, 5. Robert Albion concurs, calling the *Dolphin* a public image machine (*Makers*, 164–65). Isherwood also noted that the *Chicago* was too weak and small to be useful as a cruiser and that its sails were insufficient for any practical voyage.

44. *Scientific American*, 2 July 1887, 2.

45. Gorringe had been detailed by the department to write this article and otherwise promote naval issues in the popular press. See Gorringe, "The Navy," *North American Review*, May 1882.

46. Named for William C. Endicott, its chair, the board encouraged the creation of a permanent Board of Ordnance and Fortification, which oversaw a coastal defense, not as a joint effort but as one in which the army manned the resuscitated forts. See Russell Weigley, *The American Way of War: A History of United States Military Strategy and Policy* (Bloomington: Indiana University Press, 1973). For *New York Times* citations, see 8 March 1884, 4, editorial, and 10 March 1884, 4, editorial.

47. S. S. Cox (D-NY), "On the Necessity for Defenses on coast and at sea," given before House of Representatives, 30 June 1884 (Washington, DC: Government Printing Office, 1884). Cox agreed with his colleague Hewitt, "Our opposition is not to a navy, but to a fraudulent navy, a sham navy, a navy that can not fight, that can not cruise, that can not cope even with a good merchant steamer of modern type" (15). Quotations are from 15, 4, and 16 in "Necessity." Cox was new to and chaired the Naval Affairs Committee as well as serving on the House Select Committee on reform in Civil Service, according to the *Congressional Directory*, 1884.

48. Mahan, *The Influence of Sea Power upon History, 1660–1783* (Boston: Little, Brown & Co., 1890; London: Methuen, 1965), 138.

49. *New York Times*, 8 October 1884, 4,4, editorial; see also the report of same day for circumstances. See also *Times*, 14 July 1884, cited in chapter 1, for reaction to *Ashulot* collision due to drunkenness of the captain.

50. For Porter's recommendations, see ARSN *1884*; *New York Times*, 20 November 1884; 6 December 1884.

51. *New York Times*, 11 April 1885; 16 April 1885 and 23 April 1885.

52. Published as "The Navy and Its Prospects of Rehabilitation" in U.S. Naval Institute *Proceedings* 12, no. 36 (1886), quotation from page 1426 and 1430. Simpson was the senior graduate of the Naval Academy, and accorded some respect on this count as well. Two years later, the navy did purchase the *Stiletto* as WTB1, the nation's first working torpedo boat (*Conway's*, 159).

53. 48th Cong., 2d sess., House Executive Document, No. 238, "Moveable Torpedoes."

——————————— Chapter 7 ———————————

THE BEST DEFENSE IS AN OFFENSE

1. Benjamin F. Cooling, *Benjamin Franklin Tracy: Father of the Modern American Fighting Navy* (Hamden: Archon, 1973); William Widenor, *Henry Cabot Lodge and the Search for an American Foreign Policy* (Berkeley: University of California Press, 1980);

Edmund Morris, *The Rise of Theodore Roosevelt* (New York: Ballantine Books, 1979); Richard Turk, *The Ambiguous Relationship: Theodore Roosevelt and Alfred Thayer Mahan* (Westport, CT: Greenwood Press, 1987); Jon T. Sumida, *In Defence of Naval Supremacy: Finance, Technology, and British Naval Policy, 1889–1914* (Boston: Unwin Hyman, 1989); and Paul Kennedy, *Rise and Fall of the Great Powers* (New York: Random House, 1987).

2. "Strategy" here signifies the planning that goes into wars: mostly in construction and deployment plans. "Tactics" where used here signifies the details of engaging in battle.

3. The *Olympia,* authorized 9 July 1888, laid down in 1891, launched in 1892, and commissioned on 11 May 1895 at 5,865 tons (full load at 6,558) carried four 8-inch guns and ten 5-inch guns. The *Olympia* made 21.68 knots in trials. It had protective armor which ranged from two inches on the decks to four and a half inches on the barbettes (Roger Chesnau, ed., *Conway's All the World's Fighting Ships, 1865–1905* (London: Conway Maritime Press, 1979), 152). For another extremely useful compendium of ships, see K. Jack Bauer and Stephen S. Roberts, *Register of Ships of the U.S. Navy, 1775–1990: Major Combatants* (Westport, CT: Greenwood Press, 1991).

4. The Democrats under Grover Cleveland held the Executive Mansion from 1885–1889 at which time Benjamin Harrison brought back the Republicans. Despite Republican hegemony in the executive branch, they had a majority in the House of Representatives only between 1889 and 1891.

5. "Increase of the Naval Establishment," House Report 993 (49-1), 1–23. The *New York Times* had expected that the committee would report a recommendation of eight to ten million dollars *(Times,* 24 February 1886). The *Times* editors received these actual reports gleefully, concluding, "this navy bill has points [i.e., battleships] too valuable to be sacrificed" (27 February 1886). The bulk of the text of the report appeared on 6 March 1886.

6. House Report 993. Each battleship would also have a "complete torpedo outfit" including two torpedo tubes, which were removed before the ships were commissioned. The *New York Times* quoted the *Times* of London saying that this class comprised, "the most perfect fighting ship afloat" (27 February 1886). Yet, 6,000 tons was still extremely light for a battleship.

Protected cruisers of 3,500 to 5,000 tons, at approximately $1.5 million and with partial rigging, had 1.5-inch plates, protecting them only against small caliber rifles. In reality, they were unprotected as if they were actually designed for commerce raiding.

These torpedo boats would cost $100,000 each. This torpedo cruiser was to have done twenty-two knots and cost $300,000.

7. House Report 993, 3 and 9. This torpedo cruiser meant moving the front, not just off America's coast and into the blue water, but right up to the enemy's coast. This type of forward maritime strategy was so far forward that even Mahan did not broach it.

8. House Report 993, 3 and also figures on page 5 noting the "value of destructible property subject to the fire of an enemy's guns" and listing each major port city and a dollar amount. Herbert expanded on these issues, especially the sin of unpreparedness in his speech before Congress opening the debate for the appropriation. He admonished con-

gressmen not to "shut their eyes upon the lessons of experience and philosophize themselves into the belief that war will never come again" (*Congressional Record*, 24 July 1886, 7475–76 and 7479). Charles Boutelle in his debate with Herbert attempted to seize the War of 1812 as a lesson in the sins of Democratic weakness (7483); it was then reclaimed by a Democrat, Curtin (7486).

9. House Report 993, 3 (italics in original) and 7. The report concluded with a survey of the naval powers, detailing their fleets and construction (14–23). Herbert included a list (of twenty-one powers with ships already built that could threaten America) in his speech before Congress (*Congressional Record*, 24 July 1886, 7476).

10. The scheduling was attempted through late May and June 1886 by 49-1 House Reports 2619 and 2648. Democratic leaders did not want to discuss the bill (see *Congressional Record*, 21 July 1886, 7275–76, and *Congressional Record*, 24 July 1886, 7481.

The *New York Times* published the changes under the heading "The New Navy" dated 21 July on 22 July (3–7) but does not give any explanation for these "retrenchments." In 1890, Herbert reminded Congress that it should appropriate slowly money for battleships as the nation had not yet paid for those ships already authorized; he neglected to mention that this was a direct result of his having postponed paying for the ships that his committee had authorized.

11. Boutelle, *Congressional Record*, 24 July 1886, 7481. The dynamite cruiser was offered in place of the torpedo cruiser. The *Times* approved of experiments in pneumatic guns; see editorial of 28 June 1886 and letter to the editor from Lt. E. L. Zalinsky (USA), "Pneumatic guns at War," 23 July 1886.

12. *Congressional Record*, 24 July 1886, 7474–75. The Democratic party, briefly in control of both Congress and the White House, appeared to understand that it needed to reformat the political discourse to return the Democratic heroes of history to their place as leaders, reclaiming the tradition from the Republicans who had vilified their predecessors in the decades since secession.

13. *Congressional Record*, 24 July 1886, 7475–79. Thomas ap Catesby Jones and Ralph Semmes had left their colleagues to fight for the Confederacy. Most bizarre to me is lumping together Ralph Semmes, the greatest naval hero of Herbert's own Alabama, with David G. Farragut who opened that state to Union conquest at the Battle of Mobile Bay. Congressman Boutelle did not let it go either, remarking on 2 August that he wondered if Herbert thought he were "addressing another Congress that once assembled in another place within the limits of his own State" (i.e., the Congress of the Confederacy, which temporarily met at Montgomery) (*Congressional Record*, 7856).

14. *Congressional Record*, 24 July 1886, 7481–83. The *New York Times* made no mention of Boutelle's accusations, noting only that the measure had passed (25 July 1886).

15. *Congressional Record*, 24 July 1886, 7483–86, 7494, 7496, 7497, and 7498. Boutelle, a Republican, spoke in the discourse of Democrats-as-secessionist villains. The *Times* put it this way,

When the House appropriations managers decided that the six millions and more asked for by this committee must be cut down to three and a half, it went to work instantly and presented a substitute of the required amount, which was carried through after less than a day's debate. . . . In cutting down the appropriation, the House committee took care to leave intact the most important feature—the construction of two sea-going armor-clads." (15 August 1886)

The *Times* approved of the cuts made by the committee "when reduction was imposed on it." The New Orleans *Daily Picayune* rued the cuts and called for greater authorizations (20 July 1886). The Chicago *Tribune* did likewise (21 July 1886).

16. *Congressional Record,* 24 July 1886, 7489.

17. *Congressional Record,* 26 July 1887, 7518, and 28 July 1886, 7628.

18. The only Republican to vote in favor of it was the young Robert M. LaFollette of Wisconsin.

19. The Democrats voting against the amendment included: three Brooklyn Democrats (F. Campbell, P. P. Mahoney, and A. M. Bliss) whose districts bordered the New York Navy Yard; H. B. Lovering, born in Portsmouth and representing Massachusetts's north coast; J. G. Kind, a West Pointer; E. J. Gay, the first president of the Louisiana Sugar Exchange; W. G. Stahlnecker, of the New York Produce Exchange; F. Lawler, former president of Ship-carpenters and Ship-builder's Association; J. V. L. Findlay of Baltimore; R. S. Green of Atlantic City; and several members from interior districts who may actually have opposed the increase because they opposed increasing the navy.

20. As it turned out, the new armored ships took ten years to complete. Probably in part because a naval buildup was good for Maine's economy, Reed, like his fellow Maine representative Boutelle, was devoutly pronavy, until the midnineties when he discovered the navy's potential for subverting the republican virtues. In the spring of 1898, as Speaker of the House, "Czar" Reed made Herculean efforts to keep the nation out of war with Spain. So Reed is another case of an anti-imperialist who failed to see where the new navy would take the nation until war was all but declared. See the case of Carl Schurz discussed in chapter 8, "Flapdoodle Pacifists" (*Congressional Record,* 30 July 1886, 7742–43; 4 August 1886, 7982; and 5 August 1886, 8040).

21. The *Maine* was not commissioned until ten years later, in 1895. Three years later, its loss precipitated the Spanish-American War. The *Texas,* although generally viewed as useless, lasted longer. The *Baltimore* was commissioned in 1890 and sailed the next year into Valparaiso Harbor and infamy. The *Vesuvius* was also commissioned in 1890 but like the *Texas* never really entered fleet service. The *Cushing* proved to have an equally unimportant position in the fleet, because torpedo boats had no role in the strategy of the day.

22. The Cruisers *Philadelphia* and *San Francisco* were laid down near their namesake cities in 1888 and commissioned in 1890. Gunboats *Concord* and *Bennington* were laid down in 1888 and commissioned in 1891.

23. For "The efficacy," see "The Coast Defenses of the United States," *Scientific American,* 12 February 1887, editorial, 96. The attack became more forceful in the following issues; see especially "Great War Ships and Forts" (19 February 1887), which answered "no" to the question, "Are armored ships and big guns and forts necessary to an effective defense?" (112). For "Here we have" see "Our Slow New Navy," *Scientific American,* 2 July 1887, editorial, 2.

24. "Coast Defense," *Scientific American,* 12 February 1887, 96. "Submarine Boats," *Scientific American,* 12 February 1887, 106, reprinted from *English Mechanic.* See also "Great War Ships and Forts," *Scientific American,* 19 February 1887, 112, and also "Effects of Torpedo Boat on an Ironclad," *Scientific American,* 26 February 1887, 136–37, and "Torpedo Boats and Pneumatic Dynamite Guns," 26 February 1887, 137. The efforts continued unabated through the spring of 1887; see editorials in *Scientific American:* "Sham Fighting Ships" and "The New guns for the Navy" (2 April 1887); "Berden Torpedo Boat" (21 May 1887); and especially "Our Slow New Navy" (2 July 1887), 2.

25. Change in early July 1887 from "Our Slow New Navy," *Scientific American,* 2 July 1887 to "Our New Navy," 16 July 1887. Quotation from "Our New Navy," 36.

26. If the imagery appears unsubtle, note the composition of the cover pictures of *Scientific American,* a weekly, for the year 1887. Photographs or engravings of: guns—4, navy guns or ships—13, other boats—10, telescopes—3, other—23. A quarter of the pictures were of navy guns and ships; more than half the pictures were of ships, guns, or telescopes. Those of the navy ships and guns started to appear in March.

27. "Our New Navy," *Scientific American,* 16 July 1887, 36; "Blockades under Existing Conditions of Warfare" dismissed Colomb's notion, claiming that torpedo boat destroyers would negate the effect of the torpedo boats: *Scientific American,* 30 July 1887, 64. And see P. H. Colomb, 2d ed. and 3d ed., *Naval Warfare: Its Principles and Practice Historically Treated* (London: W.H. Allen & Co., Ltd., 1895 & 1899). For more on Colomb, see Donald M. Schurman, *The Education of a Navy: Development of British Naval Strategic Thought 1867–1914* (Chicago: University of Chicago, 1965), 36–59, and Barry M. Gough, "The Influence of History On Mahan," in John B. Hattendorf, ed., *The Influence of History on Mahan* (Newport: Naval War College Press, 1991).

28. The "sea-going armored vessels" *Texas* and *Maine* suffered a confusing early history. The former was never really classified or numbered and was generally considered to be a failure. It was not an armored cruiser, mostly because it lumbered under its twelve-inch guns. The latter ship was originally numbered "Armored Cruiser 1" but was reclassified as a second-class battleship without a number. The *New York* was ambiguously named for a city (like a cruiser), which shares the name of its state (as a battleship would be named). The *New York* was authorized on 7 September 1888, laid down in 1890, and commissioned in 1893 (the year by which the new navy was in place).

29. Bernard Brodie referred to the armored cruisers as "too weak to make good battleships and too expensive as cruisers" (*A Guide to Naval Strategy,* 5th ed. [New York: Frederick A. Praeger, 1965], 28). The Sprouts describe these events: "legislation, in short, was outrunning theory" (H. Sprout and M. Sprout, *The Rise of American Naval Power,* 2d ed. [Princeton: Princeton University Press, 1943], 200). For costs, compare to the $1.5 million for the "protected cruiser" authorized two years before.

For specifications, see Ivan Musicant, *U.S. Armored Cruisers, A Design and Operational History* (Annapolis: Naval Institute Press, 1985), 20. Its armament included six eight-inch guns and twelve four-inch guns, as well as smaller rapid fire guns and three torpedo tubes. The "*sic*" refers to the fact that the ship actually displaced either 8,679 tons with full load (as Musicant later states) or 8,200/9,021 tons (empty/full load) according to *Conway's* (147).

To travel the 4,800 miles, the maximum steaming radius, the *New York* required its maximum load of coal, 1,279 (instead of the normal capacity of 750) tons, which required on-deck storage—far from optimal for fast steaming let alone fighting. Forty-one of its sixty-one bunkers were above decks (Musicant, *Armored*, 25).

The *New York* attained 21.09 knots at below-average displacement during trials using special coal from the Pocahontas seam in West Virginia—the quality of which it would not normally be able to match. See J. Murray Jordan, *Warships of the United States which make their Trial Tests with Pocahontas Coal* (Philadelphia: n.p., 1897). Furthermore, at high speeds, the bow torpedo tubes allowed water into the hull, flooding "several forward compartments, including the sick bay" (Musicant, *Armored*, 27).

30. All these specifications come from Musicant, *Armored*, 42–43. The armor for the *Texas, Maine,* and *New York* caused the department endless grief, as Bethlehem Steel was chronically behind in deliveries. See Cooling, *Tracy,* 84; Musicant, *Armored*, 23.

31. The Republicans controlled both the House and Senate for the first time since 1875.

32. National Archives Record Group 45, United States Navy, Old Subject File, Box 465, file 1, "OO" Operations of fleets, squadrons, flotillas, and Divisions, 13 March 1889, Chief of Bureau of Navigation to Secretary of Navy.

33. Cooling, *Tracy,* 99. Cooling appears to approve of this ruse because it advanced the cause of Tracy's heavy surface fleet. Cooling is correct to point out the fact that the battleship campaign was carried out with the help of the lay press as well. See Luce, "Our Future Navy," *North American Review,* July 1889, or U.S. Naval Institute *Proceedings,* 15 (December 1889): 541–49. See also, for example, a long article by C. Stanhope Bill, "Chasing Blockade Runner," *Youth's Companion,* 7 November 1889.

34. Robert Albion *Makers of Modern Naval Policy, 1798–1947,* Rowena Reed, ed., (Annapolis: Naval Institute Press, 1980), 210.

35. "Report of the Naval Policy Board," U.S. Naval Institute *Proceedings,* 16 (1890): 207–73. Cooling discusses the leak as catastrophic to the navalist cause. A rough estimate would put actual expenditures on this project at closer to $315 million based on the actual payments for the ships built by the navy at around the same time (Cooling, *Tracy,* 80–82).

As for ranking, Cooling says "second greatest," but given the strategic overstretch of the British Empire, this construction plan would have given the United States the most powerful fighting fleet in the world.

36. U.S. Congress, House Naval Affairs Committee, "Vessels of the New Navy: Hearing on the Subject of the Policy of Naval Reconstruction Before the Committee on Naval Affairs of the House of Representatives" (Washington, DC: Government Printing Office, 1890). Meetings were held: 15 January, 21 January, and 25 February 1890. Quotation is from Tracy's testimony on 15 January 1890, 3–4.

Tracy's first annual report offers a glimpse into his unrealistic goal for American invulnerability: "Nothing short of a force of battleships, numerous enough to be distributed in the separate fields of attack and able to concentrate on any threatened point within their own field, will prove a complete protection" (*Annual Report of the Secretary of the Navy, 1890* [Washington, DC: Government Printing Office, 1890], 40, and cited in Cooling, *Tracy,* 101).

37. "Vessels of the New Navy," 7. The new ships, in fact, were not very successful for the same old problem: "too much was attempted on a very limited displacement" according to *Conway's*, 140. For report, see U.S. Congress (51-1) House Report 1178, reported as House of Representatives Bill 8909, as introduced by Boutelle. Presumably Tracy had arrived at this number, one considerably below his initial pleas, in conference with Boutelle.

As for dissent, Herbert said, "My colleague and I agree perfectly as to policy of building some battle-ships. The point we differ upon is as to how many we shall build." Even this point was not highly contested, as demonstrated by the fact that only eighty-three representatives bothered to vote on Herbert's amendment to that effect; see Herbert in *Congressional Record*, 10 April 1890, 3256, 3261–62.

The shipbuilders favored building first-class battleships, and indeed they received the contracts to do so. Cramp built the *Indiana* and the *Massachusetts* while Union constructed the *Oregon*.

38. For introduction, see *Congressional Record*, 8 April 1890, 3163. Compare the description to that of the "sea-going double-bottomed armored vessels" authorized in 1886. Chandler's monitors were, by 1890, generally viewed as atavistic and disregarded, until they were needed for coastal defense and then for securing the Philippine Islands between 1898 and 1901.

39. Cooper represented a region of Indiana with many Quakers and very few naval contractors. Inexplicably, Cooper did not vote in favor of deleting the battleships when the opportunity arose a week later (*Congressional Record*, 8 April 1890, 3167; 15 April 1890, 3396).

For Wheeler, see *Congressional Record*, 10 April 1890, 3261. In the end, none of the three ships were built on the Gulf coast.

40. For Spinola, see *Congressional Record*, 10 April 1890, 3269. For Kerr, 10 April 1890, 3268, 3273. Kerr was obviously a small-government Democrat opposed to these evils of the GOP's excessive republicanism. He would have made a fine antinavalist, except that Iowans do not make their names on foreign policy.

41. Here republican signifies the ideology first propounded by Alexander Hamilton that called for a relatively strong central government, with economic and military powers of coercion. The democratic ideology, in contrast, originated under Jefferson and valued choice and classical liberty, over a freedom to thrive. Democratic ideology, in this sense, was more chaotic and unplanned, while the republican ideology encouraged more central planning and ordering. The War of 1812, in this paradigm, was commonly believed in the late nineteenth century, to represent the natural outcome of Jefferson's laissez-faire government.

McAdoo was a Democrat who believed in strong government. He was not satisfied having the Republican party take credit for the successes of 1815; they were, after all, achieved under the direction of a Democratic president (*Congressional Record*, 8 April 1890, 3168–69).

42. *Congressional Record*, 8 April 1890, 3170.

43. Ibid.

44. *Congressional Record*, 10 April 1890, 3269.

45. See Albion, *Makers*, 211. Of the debate process, Cooling remarks, "The whole episode merely confirmed the fact that while the secretary might submit estimates of actual navy needs and suggest a national defense program, this did not guarantee Congressional acceptance" (*Benjamin Franklin Tracy: Father of Modern American Fighting Navy*, 80). This statement exemplifies the extent to which navalist rhetoric still dominates naval history. The author appears to believe that the navy secretary has the constitutional mandate to define "national defense." Cooling also accepts Tracy's proposals as reflecting the "actual needs" of such a program, as if they were objectively definable. Did the navy "need" eight ten-thousand-ton battleships in 1890? The question is, at best, moot.

Votes to strike the battleships failed in the House and Senate between mid-April and late May, with twenty-five of the twenty-six House Democrats who supported the battleships coming from coastal states. Over two-thirds of the Senate Democrats supporting the battleships also came from coastal states.

46. Even two years later, the Democratic platform stood strongly against the actions of the 1890 Republican Congress, pledging itself to "relentless opposition to the Republican policy of profligate expenditure, which, in the short space of two years, has squandered an enormous surplus and emptied an overflowing Treasury, after piling new burdens of taxation upon the already over-taxed labor of the country." Also, for the first time since the beginning of the naval revival, the Democratic platform did not even mention the navy. See *National Party Platforms*, volume 1, edited by Donald Bruce Johnson (Urbana: University of Illinois Press, 1978), 86–89.

47. *Congressional Record*, 10 April 1890, 3273.

48. Quotations from "The Recent Election," *North American Review*, December 1890, 645–47, and "What Congress Has Done," *North American Review*, November 1890, 527–29.

49. For Boutelle's initial report, see House of Representatives, H.R. Report No. 3339 (51-2), 20 December 1890 on bill 12,782. For consecutive attacks, see (1) *Congressional Record*, 21 January 1891, 1777–79; (2) 24 January 1891, 1812; (3) 24 January 1891, 1812; (4) 24 January 1891, 1805. For final version, see *Congressional Record*, 23 January 1891, 1793–95 and 1798–1801.

50. See especially the statements of E. E. Hale and John McPherson, *Congressional Record*, 10 February 1891, 2428—29.

51. House of Representatives Bill (52-1), 7093, reported to House in H.R. Report 621, 10 March 1892.

52. *Congressional Record*, 13 April 1892, 3270, and 14 April 1892, 3362.

53. For Scott, see *Congressional Record*, 14 April 1892, 3329–30; for Watson, see 16 April 1892, 3360.

54. *Congressional Record*, 16 April 1892, 3360, and 18 April 1892, 3400.

55. For these quotations, see *Congressional Record*, 17 May 1892, 4312–35, and 18 May, 3258, 4325, 4354, and 4365–67.

56. *The World Crisis*, vol. 1 (New York: Charles Scribner's Sons, 1923), 37.

57. For Herbert's resolution, see *Congressional Record*, 9 July 1892, 5953. This is not to say that battleships were without support from outside the Naval Affairs Committees. See, for instance, John M. Ellicott, who published at approximately the same time: "There

are many indications that a general type of battle ship is again being attained, after which all nations may pattern, and feel at least that there be none better in the near future" ("The Limit in Battle Ships," *Atlantic Monthly*, April 1892, 501–5). The *Iowa's* initial authorization was for 9,000 tons and approximately $4 million, but completed with armor, it weighed 11,525 tons and cost approximately half again the initial price.

For the act's history, see *Congressional Record*, 16 July 1892, House 6312, Senate 6274. President Harrison signed it on 19 July as noted on 20 July 1892, 6469. The *Iowa* was 360 feet long, a dozen feet longer and more heavily armed than the *Indiana*-class ships authorized in 1890. The *Brooklyn* was also heavier, more heavily armed, and faster than its precursor, the *New York*.

58. Cooling, *Tracy*, 144, and *Annual Report of the Secretary of Navy, 1892*.

59. House of Representatives (52-2), House Report 2489, 13 February 1893, 4, 6–7, and 10. While Mahan's biographer claims that Herbert was convinced of the value of the war college when he read *The Influence of Sea Power upon French Empire* as secretary of the navy, Representative Herbert already subscribed to the essential tenets of navalism (Robert Seager, *Alfred Thayer Mahan: The Man and His Letters* [Annapolis: Naval Institute, 1977], 179–81 and 245–73).

60. *Congressional Record*, 20 February 1893, 1878–79; 28 February 1893, 2273; 3 March 1893, 2495.

——————————————— Chapter 8 ———————————————

THE WHOLE FLAPDOODLE PACIFIST AND
MOLLYCODDLER OUTFIT

1. Bruce Russett, "Peace Research, Complex Causation, and the Causes of War," in Peter Wallensteen, *Peace Research: Achievements and Challenges* (Boulder, CO: Westview, 1988), 59–60.

2. Russett, "Peace Research," 59.

3. Based on George Modelski and William R. Thompson, *Sea Power and Global Politics, 1494–1993* (Seattle: University of Washington Press, 1988), 340; my calculations. Using the figures of 1876–81 the numbers are even closer: $15.94 million and $15.04 million.

4. Modelski and Thompson, *Sea Power*, 344.

5. Total seven-year increase of 12.64 percent, or 1.8 percent average noncompounded annual increase.

6. Between 1887 and 1897, things came to cost 15.2 percent less, bringing the total sixteen-year increase in purchasing power up to 36.8 percent. In 1913, the pound was still the currency against which others would be compared. Figures again based on Modelski and Thompson, *Sea Power*, 81, 340, with my calculations.

7. The other powers, especially Britain and Germany, which were undergoing their own naval buildups, have been analyzed by, among others, Paul Kennedy, *The Rise of Anglo-German Antagonism* (Boston: George Allen & Unwin, 1980), *The Samoan Tangle* (St. Lucia: University of Queensland Press, 1974), and *The Rise and Fall of British Naval*

Mastery (London: Macmillan and Co., 1983) as well as Jonathan Steinberg, *Yesterday's Deterrent: Tirpitz and the Birth of the German Battle Fleet* (London: Macmillan, 1965); A. J. Marder, *From Dreadnought to Scapa Flow*, 2d ed. (New York: Oxford University Press, 1978) and *Anatomy of British Sea Power* (Hamden, CT: Archon Books, 1964); Jon T. Sumida, *In Defence of Naval Supremacy: Finance, Technology, and British Naval Policy, 1890–1914* (Boston: Unwin Hyman, 1989); W. Mark Hamilton, *The Nation and the Navy: Methods and Organization of British Navalist Propaganda, 1889–1914* (New York: Garland Publishing Co., 1986).

8. For some background on the APS see Merle Curti, *American Peace Crusade, 1815–1860* (Durham, NC: Duke University Press, 1929; New York: Octagon, 1965), 223 *et pass.* Curti, father of the Wisconsin revisionists, claims that the peace movement was destroyed by the economic changes of the late nineteenth century, while still seeing 1898 as an aberration in United States history. "Before the peace movement as a whole had recognized and grappled with the economic undertow that was almost imperceptibly pulling it further to sea, it was beset by a new war and an adventure in imperialism" (Curti, *War or Peace: The American Struggle, 1636–1936* [New York: W. W. Norton & Co., 1939], 166). For the Anti-Imperialist League, see Robert Beisner, *Twelve Against Empire: The Anti-Imperialists of 1898* (New York: McGraw-Hill, 1968). See also the following: David Sands Patterson, *Toward a Warless World: The Travail of the American Peace Movement 1887–1914*, (Bloomington: Indiana University Press, 1976); Christine Phelps, *Anglo-American Peace Movement in the Mid-Nineteenth Century* (New York: Columbia University Press, 1930; Peter Brock, *Pacifism in the United States* (Princeton: Princeton University Press, 1968); Roland Marchand, *The American Peace Movement* (Princeton: Princeton University Press, 1972), which noted of the APS in the 1870s and 1880s that "its energies had been largely absorbed in the effect simply to stay alive" (6). See also Edson L. Whitney, *The American Peace Society: A Centennial History* (Washington, DC: American Peace Society, 1929). Quotation from Patterson, *Toward*, viii.

9. Figure from estimate by Robert McMurdy, leader of the National Arbitration League, cited by Curti. See also *Annual Report of R. McMurdy D.D. LL.D.* (Washington, DC: American Arbitration League, 1886), which favored a torpedo-boat defense attributed to Admiral Aube. Curti points out that peace activists failed also to take successful advantage of book and newspaper publishing, public libraries, or even religious sermons to state their case (Curti, *War or Peace*, 81, 87, 104–10).

10. See *World Affairs*, February 1882, for a list of APS officers. The APS monthly changed names several times in the late nineteenth century. In the text, I will cite it by the name it was currently using, but in the notes, I will call it *World Affairs*, the name upon which it eventually settled and still uses today. The APS also published a children's magazine, the *Angel of Peace*, throughout this era.

11. Carnegie, one of the leading anti-imperialists of 1898, also headed the company that supplied the navy with the steel plates needed to armor its battleships. He personally worked to ensure that the navy contracts were fulfilled.

For Spencer, see Robert C. Bannister, *Social Darwinism: Science and Myth in Anglo-American Thought* (Bloomington: University of Indiana Press, 1974). Other speakers at the banquet included William Graham Sumner, John Fiske, Henry Ward Beecher, and Carl

Schurz, about whom see below. Richard Hofstadter, *Social Darwinism in American Thought* (New York: George Braziller, 1959), 48–53. Spencer himself stated that wars would have to give way to peaceful resolution of disputes and in 1882 was publicly in sympathy with the peace movement (Curti, *War or Peace,* 119).

12. *World Affairs,* March 1886, chastised Walker. See also August 1884 and May 1886 for similar words regarding the works of Joel T. Headly, which—like those of Walker—are mentioned in chapter 1, "Influence of History Upon Sea Power." And see Curti, *War or Peace,* 110. For Walker as a "reactionary Darwinian," see Bannister, *Social Darwinism,* 125. Like Hofstadter and Cynthia Russett, Bannister credits Social Darwinism with providing some of the rationale for the imperialist cause. The quotation is from Merle Curti, *Growth of American Thought,* 3d ed. (New York: Harper & Row, 1964), 479.

13. R. B. Howard, "Peace Arbitration Topic" (Washington, DC: APS, 1886). Even the educator John Dewey did not heed the call of pacifism until the First World War, according to Charles F. Howlett, *Troubled Philosopher: John Dewey and the Struggle for World Peace* (Port Washington, NY: Kennikat Press, 1977), 5/ff. Lucia True Ames Mead, "the best informed woman in the United States on subjects of peace and war" was by the 1880s already a lecturer and writer of some note who failed to speak out against the growth of the navy until the *Maine* crisis when she started to earn "a place 'in the front rank among women peace advocates'" (John M. Craig, "Lucia True Ames Mead: American Publicist for Peace and Internationalism," in Edward P. Crapol, ed., *Women and American Foreign Policy: Lobbyists, Critics, and Insiders* [Wilmington, DE: Scholarly Resources Inc., 1992], 67–72).

14. Note the patriotic addition of "American" to the magazine's title. For the sealing dispute, see chapters 3 and 7 of this volume, "Selling the Navy" and "Best Defense is an Offense," as well as James T. Gay, *American Fur Seal Diplomacy* (New York: Peter Long Publishing Co., 1987).

The Universal Peace Union (henceforth UPU) was founded from the splinters of the peace movement left by the Civil War, in 1866 in Providence, Rhode Island (Curti, *War or Peace,* 77 and 149). Despite the spiritual and organizational core provided by its Quaker long-time president Alfred Love (who served from 1866 until his death in 1913), it was a more aggressive but even more impotent group than APS. The UPU published a monthly, *The Peacemaker,* with a circulation of only a few hundred (Patterson, *Toward,* 8). Peter Brock called it a "rather moribund society" in *Pacifism,* 923. See coverage in *World Affairs,* September 1892, for the Sherman bill.

15. *World Affairs,* January 1891. Apparently, the APS leaned neither Republican nor Democratic, enjoying only gentlemen's differences over naval policy. For White, see *World Affairs,* June 1892 reprint of 18 April 1892 speech.

The change to oppose navalism may be due to the new secretary of the APS and editor of the *AAP&A* between 1892 and 1915, Benjamin F. Trueblood (1847–1916), who contributed many of these pieces himself. But, from 1890 to 1891, the year before Trueblood took over, the APS expenditures increased from $4,772 to $7,323.30 giving the organization greater stability and strength (E. L. Whitney, *American Peace Society,* 190. See also Brock, *Pacifism,* 90).

16. John L. Sullivan was the brawling, bare-knuckled, heavyweight boxing champion from 1882 to 1892. Sullivan, an Irish-American from Massachusetts, was particularly popular in Boston, where the APS was based (*World Affairs,* June 1892).

17. *World Affairs,* May 1893, September 1892.

18. The committees of correspondence were based in different cities and states across the United States: Baptists in Richmond; Catholics in Chicago; Congregationalists in Massachusetts; Disciples of Christ in St. Louis, Cincinnati, and Washington, D.C.; Episcopalians in Washington, D.C.; Friends in Philadelphia; German Evangelicals in Baltimore; Lutherans in Baltimore and Washington, D.C.; Methodists in Washington, D.C.; Presbyterians in New York; and the remainders also in New York; see *World Affairs,* January 1893.

These peace-oriented groups were: APS based in Boston; Universal Peace Society in Philadelphia; Christian Arbitration and Peace Society (which had originally been founded after the Civil War by Lucretia Mott [Curti, *War or Peace,* 80]) in Philadelphia; National Association for Promotion of Arbitration (founded in 1882) in Washington, D.C.; Peace Department of the WCTU in Winthrop Centre, Maine; Peace Association of Friends in America in Richmond, Indiana; South Carolina Peace Society in Columbia; Illinois Peace Society in Chicago; Pacific Arbitration Society in Monterey, CA; Connecticut Peace Society in Old Mystic; and the Rhode Island Peace Society in Providence. It should be noted that "some of the peace societies [existed] only on paper" (Patterson, *Toward,* 7; *World Affairs,* March 1893).

For arbitration movement, see 51st Congress (1), Senate Misc. Doc. 131, as an example of a petition presented by the Friends of southern and western Indiana and Illinois to John Sherman on peace and arbitration.

19. For petitions, see 51st Congress (1), Senate Misc. Doc 131. The members of the Universal Peace Society had a different solution for the nation's problems, as in 1889, three thousand of their "passive" supporters adopted Henry George's call for a single tax (Curti, *War or Peace,* 133). The petitions are listed in the index to the *Congressional Record* (51-1) but not in those indices preceding and following, suggesting a concerted effort to bring the question to the political forefront. *Congressional Record. Index* (51-1), 498, lists petitions by state: AR—1, CT—1, DE—8, FL—2, IL—4, IN—19, IA—32, KS—8, KY—1, ME—3, MD—1, MA—8, MI—4, MN—2, NE—1, NH—4, NJ—8, NY—17, NC—12, OH—25, OR—1, PA—11, RI—3, SD—6, TN—1, WI—2, and one from the citizens of the "United States."

In particular, see also same Congress, *Congressional Record,* (51-1), 1857; petition from Charleston, SC, Chamber of Commerce, 4578; from Chicago's Iroquois Club, 4882; and especially from Mayor and Common Council of Prairie du Chien, the Board of Trade of Lacrosse, WI, favoring the establishment of navy yards at Rockport, IL, and New Orleans, 1639 and 1713, respectively.

20. Others, of course, opposed the pace or direction of buildup, but the Quakers were the only group vocally opposing any new navy or construction. This sections relies heavily upon Patterson, *Toward,* 25.

21. "Carl Schurz," *Dictionary of American Biography* (New York: Charles Scribner's Sons, 1935), 469.

22. See Carl Schurz, "Manifest Destiny," in *Harper's Monthly* (October 1893), 737–46, reprinted in Frederick Bancroft, ed., *The Writings of Carl Schurz* (New York: G.P. Putnam's Sons, 1913), v. 5, 191–214. See also Schurz in *Harper's Weekly,* 20 July 1889, 22 April 1893, and 25 February 1893.

23. Schurz, "Manifest Destiny," 737–38, 740–42.

24. Ibid., 741. For Haushofer and his idea of "heartland," see Derwent Whittlesey, "Haushofer: The Geopoliticians," in Edward M. Earle, *Makers of Modern Strategy* (Princeton: Princeton University Press, 1943), 389–411.

25. Schurz, "Manifest Destiny," 744–45. Note that Schurz called for a torpedo-boat strategy similar to that recommended by the APS.

─────────────── Chapter 9 ───────────────

THE TRIUMPH OF NAVALISM

1. Of trusts, Alfred D. Chandler notes, "By the 1880s these federations had become part of the normal way of doing business in most American industries" (*The Visible Hand: The Managerial Revolution in American Business* [Cambridge: Harvard University Press, 1977], 316).

2. John T. Hanley, Jr., "On Wargaming: A Critique of Strategic Operational Gaming" (Ph.D. diss., Yale University, 1991), 45 and 101–16.

3. See Gaddis Smith, *Morality, Reason and Power: American Diplomacy in the Carter Years* (New York: Hill & Wang, 1986), 12–15.

4. *New York Times,* 24 September 1990. Kennedy echoes McGeorge Bundy's statement that "Pleikus are like streetcars."

─────────────── Postscript ───────────────

1. Stevens (Minister to Honolulu) to Secretary of State James G. Blaine, 8 March 1892, *Foreign Relations of the United States* (Washington, DC: Government Printing Office, 1895), appendix 2, no. 48, 182. The story of the Hawaiian revolution is told in: William Adam Russ, Jr., *The Hawaiian Revolution (1893–94),* (Selinsgrove, PA: Susquehana University Press, 1959); Albertine Loomis, *For Whom Are the Stars?* (Honolulu: The University of Hawaii Press, 1976); Helena G. Allen, *Sanford Ballard Dole: Hawaii's Only President, 1844–1926* (Glendale, CA: Arthur H. Clark Co., 1988); Thomas J. Osborne, *"Empire Can Wait": American Opposition to Hawaiian Annexation, 1893–1898* (Kent, OH: The Kent State University Press, 1981).

2. K. Jack Bauer and Stephen S. Roberts, *Register of Ships of the U.S. Navy, 1775–1990* (Westport, CT: Greenwood Press, 1991), 141.

3. *FRUS,* 208.

4. Wiltse to Secretary of Navy B. F. Tracy (18 January 1893), FRUS, 223, and report Commander in Chief, Pacific Fleet, 597.

5. Testimony of John Ross, ibid. (20 June 1893), 641–42. Ross refers to the hall as "Harmony" but everyone else called it "Arion."

6. Testimony of Charles Gulick (12 May 1893), ibid., 819.

7. Ibid.

Selected Bibliography

──────────── Bibliographies ────────────

These published bibliographies were most helpful, as was that in Peter Karsten, *Naval Aristocracy* (New York: Free Press, 1972). For further historiography and bibliography, see Kenneth J. Hagan and Mark R. Shulman, "Mahan Plus One Hundred: The Current State of American Naval History," in *Ubi Sumus: The State of Naval and Maritime History,* edited by John B. Hattendorf (Newport: Naval War College Press, 1994).

Albion, Robert. *Naval and Maritime History: An Annotated Bibliography,* 4th ed. Mystic, CT: Munson Institute of American Maritime History, 1974.

Allard, Dean C., Martha Crawley, and Mary Edmison. *U.S. Naval History Sources in the United States*. Washington, DC: Naval History Division, 1979.

Burns, Richard Dean, ed. *Guide to American Foreign Relations since 1700*. Santa Barbara, CA: ABC-CLIO, 1983.

Coletta, Paolo. *A Bibliography of American Naval History*. Annapolis: Naval Institute Press, 1981.

———. *A Selected and Annotated Bibliography of American Naval History*. Lanham, MD: University Press of America, 1988.

Fredricksen, John C. *Free Trade and Sailor's Rights: A Bibliography of the War of 1812*. Westport, CT: Greenwood Press, 1985.

Harbeck, Charles T. *A Contribution to the Bibliography of the History of the United States Navy*. Cambridge: Riverside Press, 1906.

Hattendorf, John, and Lynn Hattendorf, compilers. *A Bibliography of the Works of Alfred Thayer Mahan.* Newport: Naval War College Press, 1986.

Hayes, John, and John Hattendorf, eds. *The Writings of Stephen B. Luce.* Newport: Naval War College Press, 1975.

Higham, Robin, and Donald J. Mrozek, eds. *A Guide to the Sources of United States Military History: and Supplements I, II, & III.* Hamden, CT: Archon Books, 1975, 1981, 1986, 1993.

Labaree, Benjamin. *A Supplement (1971–1986) to Robert G. Albion's Naval and Maritime History. An Annotated Bibliography.* 4th ed. Mystic, CT: Mystic Seaport Museum, 1988.

Neeser, Robert. *Statistical and Chronological History of the United States Navy, 1775–1907.* 2 vols. New York: Macmillan, 1909.

Smith, Myron. *American Naval Bibliography.* 5 vols. Metuchen, NJ: Scarecrow Press, 1972–74.

———. *Battleships and Battle Cruisers, 1884–1984.* New York: Garland, 1985.

Trask, David F., et al. eds. *A Bibliography of United States Latin American Relations since 1810.* Lincoln: University of Nebraska Press, 1968.

——— Books and Pamphlets: Primary Sources ———

Adam, G. Mercer, ed. *Scenic Marvels of the New World. New York:* James Clarke, 1894.

Adams, Henry. *Education of Henry Adams.* Boston: Houghton Mifflin, 1927.

———. *The Formative Years.* London: Collins, 1948.

———. *History of the United States during the Administrations of Jefferson and Madison.* 6 vols. New York: Scribner's, 1886–1891.

———. *The Life of Albert Gallatin.* Philadelphia: Lippincott, 1880.

Allen, George. *The Pilgrimage of the Ticonderoga.* San Francisco: n.p., 1880.

Armstrong, G. E. *Torpedoes and Torpedo Boats.* London: George Bell and Sons, 1901.

Bainbridge-Hoff, William. *Modern Naval Tactics.* Washington, DC: Government Printing Office, 1884.

Barber, F. M. "Lecture on Submarine Boats and Their Application to Torpedo Operations." Newport: U.S. Torpedo Station, 1875.

———. "Lecture on Drifting and Automatic Moveable Torpedoes, Submarine Guns, and Rockets." Newport: U.S. Torpedo Station, 1874.

———. "Lecture on the Whitehead Torpedo." Newport: U.S. Torpedo Station, 1874.

Barker, Albert. *Everyday Life in the Navy.* Boston: R.G. Badger, 1928.

Barnes, James. *Naval Actions of the War of 1812.* New York: Harper and Brothers, 1896.

Bartlett, W. H., and B. B. Woodward. *History of the United States of North America.* New York: George Virtue and Co., n.d.

Baum, L. Frank. *The Navy Alphabet.* New York: George M. Hill Co., 1900.

Beach, Edward L. *Blue Jacket's Manual.* Annapolis: Naval Institute Press, 1903.

Bedford, F. G. D. *Sailors' Hand Book.* London: Griffen, 1890.

———. *Sailors' Pocket Book.* London: Griffen, 1894.

Bennett, Frank. *The Steam Navy of the United States.* 2 vols. Pittsburgh: Warren and Company, 1896.

Bergman, Albert. *The Eclipse Expedition to the West Coast of Africa.* New York: n.p., 1890.

Bertin, L. *La Marine des États Unis.* Paris: E. Bernard et Compagnie, 1896.

Bliss, Richard. *Our Last Explorers.* Hartford: American Publishing Co., 1882.

Bolton, Sarah K. *Famous Voyagers and Explorers.* New York: Crowell, 1893.

Bowen, Abel. *The Naval Monument.* Boston: George Clark, 1842.

Brackenridge, H. M. *History of the Late War.* Philadelphia: James Kay, jun. and Brother, 1836.

Cable, Frank T. *Birth and Development of the American Submarine.* New York: Harper, 1924.

Chiles, Rosa, ed. *The Letters of Alfred Thayer Mahan to Samuel A'Court Ashe.* Duke University Library Bulletin, No. 4, Durham, 1931.

Colomb, Philip H. *Naval Warfare: Its Principles and Practice Historically Treated.* 2d and 3d eds. London: W. H. Allen, 1895 and 1899.

"Constitution of the United States Naval Veterans Association." N.p., n.d.

Cooper, J. Fenimore. *A History of the Navy of the United States of America.* 3 vols. New York: G. Putnam, 1856.

Cowie, T. J. *Money for the Navy and How Obtained.* Newport: Naval War College Press, 1915.

Cox, Samuel S. "On the Necessity for Defenses on Coast and at Sea." Washington, DC: Government Printing Office, 1884.

Davenport, Charles. *Naval Officers, their Heredity and Development.* Washington, DC: Carnegie Institution, 1919.

Davis, Parris. *An Authentic History of the Late War.* New York: Ebenzer F. Baker, 1836.

Dubosiq, Andre. *Le Problem du Pacifique.* Paris: Libraries Delagrave, 1927.

Eoggeshall, George. *History of American Privateers.* New York: n.p., 1856.

Gibbs, George T. *Junk: Collection of Naval Songs and Poems by Cadets of the United States Naval Academy.* Washington, DC: Patentee, 1889.

Goodrich, Caspar. "In Memoriam: Stephen Bleecker Luce, rear admiral United States Navy." New York: Naval Historical Society, 1919.

Greely, A. W. *Lady Franklin Bay Expedition.* Washington, DC: Government Printing Office, 1885.

"Handbook of the Philadelphia Centennial Exposition." Philadelphia: n.p., 1876.

Hapgood, Norman. *The Stage in America, 1897–1900.* New York: Macmillan, 1901.

Harrison, Benjamin. *The Speeches of Benjamin Harrison.* Comp. by George Hedges. New York: United States Book Co., 1892.

Hewitt, Abram. "Shall we have a Real Navy or a sham Navy?" Washington, DC: Government Printing Office, 1882.

Hobson, Richmond P. *Buck Jones at the Annapolis.* New York: D. Appleton, 1907.

Hogg, John W. *Compilation of Laws Relating to the Navy, Marines etc.* Washington, DC: Government Printing Office, 1883.

Howard, R. B. "Peace Arbitration Topic." Washington, DC: American Peace Society, 1886.

Ingersoll, Charles. *Historical Sketch of the Second War Between the United States and Great Britain.* Philadelphia: Lea and Blanchard, 1845.

Isman, Felix. *Weber and Fields, a pictorial souvenir.* n.p., 1901.

Jane, Fred T. *Fighting Ships.* London: Jane's, 1898

————. *Heresies of Sea Power.* New York: Longman's, Green, 1906.

————. *Imperial Japanese Navy.* London: W. Thacker, 1904.

Jewell, Charles T. *Book of Naval Cadets of 1892.* Washington, DC: Carnahan Press, 1912.

Johnson, Rossiter. *A History of the War of 1812–1815.* New York: Dodd, Mead, 1882.

Jordan, J. Murray. *Warships of the United States Navy which made their Trial Trips with Pocahontas Coal.* Philadelphia: n.p., 1897.

Kelley, J. D. Jerrold. *Our New Navy: Its Growth and Achievements.* Hartford: American Publishing Company, 1897.

Kidd, Benjamin. *Social Evolution.* New York: Macmillan, 1895.

King, James W. *Warships and Navies of the World.* Boston: A. Williams and Company, 1881.

Lewis, John. *History of the Second War between the United States and Great Britain.* Philadelphia: Hogan and Thompson, 1848.

Lockroy, Edouard. *La Marine de Guerre.* Paris: Benger-Levrault, 1897.

Long, John D. *New American Navy.* New York: The Outlook Company, 1903.

Loomis, Eben Jenks. *An Eclipse Party in Africa.* Boston: Roberts Brothers, 1896.

Lossing, Benson J. *Our Country: A Household History for All Readers from the Discovery of America to the Present Time.* New York: Henry J. Johnson, 1877.

————. *Story of the United States Navy for Boys.* New York: Harper Brothers, 1880.

"Lucky Bag." Annapolis: n.p. 1887, 1894, 1895.

McCutcheon, J. T. *TR in Cartoon.* Chicago: A. C. McClurg, 1910.

McGinley, William A. *Reception of Lt. A. W. Greely. . . .* Washington, DC: Government Printing Office, 1884.

Mackinder, Halford John. *Democratic Ideals and Reality.* New York: H. Holt and Co., 1919.

————. *Scope and Methods in Geography and the Geographical Pivot.* London: Royal Geographical Society, 1904, repr. 1951.

Maclay, Edgar S. *History of the Navy,* 2d ed., 2 vols. New York: Appleton, 1901.

McMurdy, R. *The Annual Report of R. McMurdy D. D. LL. D.* Washington, DC: American Arbitration League, 1886.

Mahan, Alfred Thayer. *David Farragut.* New York: Appleton, 1911.

————. *Influence of Sea Power upon History, 1660–1783.* Boston: Little, Brown, 1890 and subsequent editions.

————. *Influence of Sea Power upon the French Revolution.* Boston: Little, Brown, 1893.

————. *Interest of America in Sea Power: Present and Future.* New York: Harper's, 1897.

————. *Naval Strategy: Compared and Contrasted with the Principles and Practice of Military Operations on Land.* London: Sampson Low, Marston, 1911.

————. *The Problem of Asia and Its Effects upon International Policies.* Boston: Little, Brown, 1900.

Makaroff, S. J. *Naval Tactics.* Trans. J. B. Bernadou. Washington, DC: Government Printing Office, 1898.

Mason, T. B. *The War on the Pacific Coast of South America.* Washington, DC: Government Printing Office, 1883.

Mayo, L. S. *America of Yesterday as Reflected in the Diary of John D. Long.* Boston: Little, Brown, 1903.

Montechant, Z., and H. Montechant. *Les Guerres de Demain.* Paris: n.p., 1892.

Morris, Charles. *The Nation's Navy.* Philadelphia: Lippincott, 1898.

Nelson, S. A. *How to Gain Admission to Annapolis. . . .* New York: n.p., 1898.

Newcomb, Simon. *Reflections of an Astronomer.* Boston: Little, Brown, 1903.

————. *Sidelights on Astronomy.* New York: Harper, 1906.

Palmer, John McAuley. *America in Arms: The Experience of the United States with Military Organization.* New Haven: Yale University Press, 1941.

Patton, J. H. *The History of the United States of America. . . .* New York: Appleton, 1859, 1862.

Peattie, Elia W. *The Story of America. . . .* Chicago: R. S. King, 1889.

Poundstone, Homer. *Catalogue of the Exhibit of the United States Navy Department at the World's Columbian Exposition.* Chicago: W.B. Conkey, 1893.

Ridpath, John Clark. *A Popular History of the United States of America from the Original Times to the Present Day.* New York: Phillips and Hunt, 1882.

Roosevelt, Theodore. *Naval War of 1812.* New York: G.P. Putnam, 1st ed., 1882; 3d. ed., 1889; 4th ed., 1894.

————, and Henry Cabot Lodge. *Hero Tales from American History.* New York: Century Co., 1895.

Scudder, Horace E. *A History of the United States of America . . . for the use of schools and academies.* New York: Sheldon and Co., 1884.

Senarens, Luis. *How to Become a Naval Cadet.* New York: Frank Tousey, 1891.

Shippen, Edward. *Naval Battles of the World and Our New Navy.* Philadelphia: P. W. Siegler, 1894.

Shufeldt, Robert W. *The Relation of the Navy to the Commerce of the United States: A Letter Written by Request to Hon. Leopold Morse, Member of Naval Committee, House of Representatives.* Washington, DC: n.p., 1878.

————. *The United States Navy in Connection with the Foundation, Growth, and Prosperity of the Republic of Liberia.* Washington, DC: G.L. Ginck, 1877.

Sleeman, C. W. *Torpedoes and Torpedo Warfare.* Portsmouth: Griffen, 1880.

"Society of Veterans of the Regular Army and Navy of the United States." *Handbook for 1888.* n.p., 1888.

Soley, James R. *The Boys of 1812 and Other Naval Heroes.* Boston: Little, Brown, 1887.

————. *The Sailor Boys of 1861.* Boston: Little, Brown, 1888.

Strong, Josiah. *New Era.* New York: Baker and Taylor, 1893.

————. *Our Country.* New York: Baker and Taylor, for American Home Missionary Society, 1885, 1891.

Sturgis, D. N. B. *The Naval Militia.* n.p., 1894.

Thomas, Allen C. *A History of the United States.* New York: D. C. Heath, 1893, 1897.

Thomson, John Lewis. *History of the Second War between the United States and Great Britain.* 2d ed. Philadelphia: Hogan and Thompson, 1848.

Todd, David Peck. *Stars and Telescopes.* Boston: Little, Brown, 1900.

Todd, Mabel Loomis. *Corona and Coronet.* Boston: Houghton Mifflin, 1898.

Trident Society. *Book of Navy Songs.* Garden City: Doubleday, Page, 1926.

Turner, Frederick Jackson. "Importance of the Frontier in American History." *Annual Report of the American Historical Association of 1893.* Washington, DC: American Historical Association, 1894.

Very, Edward W. *Navies of the World.* New York: John Wiley, 1880.

"Vessels of the New Navy: Hearing on the Subject of the Policy of Naval Reconstruction Before the Committee on Naval Affairs of the House of Representatives" Washington, DC: Government Printing Office, 1890.

Walker, Francis Amasa. *The Making of the Nation.* New York: Scribner's, 1895.

Warfield, Ethelbert Dudley. *Joseph Cabell Breckenridge, junior, ensign in the United States navy; a brief story of a short life.* New York: Knickerbocker Press, 1898.

Williams, John S. *History of the Invasion and Capture of Washington.* New York: Harper, 1857.

Willson, Marcus. *American History, Comprising. . . .* New York: Newman and Luison, 1853.

Windsor, Justin, ed. *Narrative and Critical History of America.* New York: Houghton Mifflin, 1888.

Zogbaum, Rufus Fairchild. *All Hands: Pictures of Life in the United States Navy.* New York: Harper, 1897.

—————————— Memoirs and Published Papers ——————————

These books were generally written from contemporary diaries, notes, or letters.

Ammen, Daniel. *Old Navy and New.* Philadelphia: Lippincott, 1891.

Barker, Albert S. *Everyday Life in the Navy.* Boston: R. Dedger, 1928.

Boutwell, George S. *Reminiscences of Sixty Years in Public Affairs.* New York: Phillips, 1902.

Brady, Cyrus T. *Under Tops'ls and Tents.* New York: Scribner's, 1901.

Buenzle, Frederick. *Blue Jacket.* New York: W.W. Norton, 1939.

Clark, Charles E. *My Fifty Years in the Navy.* Boston: Little, Brown and Co., 1917; repr. Annapolis: Naval Institute Press, 1984.

Denby, Charles. *China and Her People: Being the Observations, Reminiscences, and Conclusions of an American Diplomat.* 2 vols. Boston: Page, 1906.

Dewey, A. M. *The Life and Letters of Admiral Dewey.* New York: Woodfall, 1899.

Dewey, George, with Frederick Palmer. *Autobiography of George Dewey.* New York: Scribner's, 1913.

Evans, Robley D. *Admiral's Log.* New York: Appleton, 1908.

———. *Sailor's Log.* New York: Appleton, 1901.

Farragut, Loyall. *Life and Letters of Admiral Farragut, First Admiral of the United States Navy.* New York: Appleton, 1879.

Fiske, Bradley A. *From Midshipman to Rear Admiral.* New York: Century, 1919.

Franklin, S. R. *Memories of a Rear Admiral.* New York: Harper, 1898.

Gleaves, Albert. *Life and Letters of Stephen B. Luce*. New York: Putnam's, 1925.

———. *The Life of an American Sailor: Rear Admiral William Hemsley, United States Navy, from His Letters and Memoirs*. New York: George H. Doran Co., 1923.

Goode, William. *With Sampson through the War*. New York: Doubleday and McClure, 1899.

Laning, Harris. *An Admiral's Yarn: The Autobiography of Harris Laning*. Edited by Mark R. Shulman. Newport: Naval War College Press, forthcoming.

Lejeune, John A., *Reminiscences of a Marine*. Philadelphia: Dorrance, 1930.

Lodge, Henry Cabot. *Selections from the Correspondence of Theodore Roosevelt and Henry Cabot Lodge 1884–1918*. 2 vols. New York: Scribner's, 1925.

Luce, Stephen B. *The Writings of Stephen B. Luce*. Edited by John D. Hayes and John B. Hattendorf. Newport: Naval War College Press, 1975.

Maddix, Daniel P. *The Old Navy*. New York: Macmillan, 1983.

Mahan, Alfred Thayer. *From Sail to Steam*. New York: Harper, 1907.

———. *Letters and Papers of Alfred Thayer Mahan*. 3 vols. Edited by Robert Seager II and Doris Maguire. Annapolis: Naval Institute Press, 1975.

Parker, William H. *Recollections of a Naval Officer, 1841–1865*. New York: Scribner's, 1883.

Porter, David Dixon. *Memoir of Commodore David Porter, of the United States Navy*. Albany: J. Munsell, 1875.

Rodman, Hugh. *Yarns of a Kentucky Admiral*. Indianapolis: Bobbs-Merrill, 1928.

Roosevelt, Theodore. *The Letters of Theodore Roosevelt*. Edited by Elting Morison and John Blum. Cambridge: Harvard University Press, 1952.

———. *Theodore Roosevelt: Addresses and Papers*. Edited by Willis F. Johnson. New York: Sun Dial Classics, 1908.

Schley, Winfield Scott. *Forty-five Years under the Flag*. New York: Appleton, 1904.

———. *The Greely Relief Expedition*. Washington, DC: Government Printing Office, 1887.

Schroeder, Seaton. *My Half Century of Naval Service*. New York: Appleton, 1922.

Schurz, Carl. *Speeches, Correspondence and Political Papers of Carl Schurz*. Selected and edited by F. Bancroft. New York: Putnam's, 1913.

Selfridge, Thomas. *Memoirs of Thomas O. Selfridge, Jr.* Edited by Dudley Knox. New York: G.P. Putnam's, 1924.

Sousa, John P. *Marching Along*. Boston: Hale, Cushman, and Flint, 1928.

Steedman, Charles. *Memoir and Correspondence of Charles Steedman, Rear Admiral, United States Navy, with His Autobiography and Private Journals, 1811–1890*. Edited by Amos Lawrence Mason. Cambridge: Riverside Press, 1912.

——— Books and Articles as Secondary Sources ———

Abrams, Richard. *Burdens of Progress*. Glenview, IL: Scott, Foresman, 1978.

———. *Conservatism in the Progressive Era*. New York: Columbia University Press, 1964.

Albion, Robert. *Makers of Naval Policy 1798–1947*. Edited by Rowena Reed. Annapolis: Naval Institute Press, 1980.

Alden, John. *American Steel Navy.* Annapolis: Naval Institute Press, 1972.

Allen, Helena G. *Sanford Ballard Dole: Hawaii's Only President, 1844–1926.* Glendale, CA: Clark, 1988.

Allin, Lawrence Carroll. *United States Naval Institute: Intellectual Forum of the New Navy, 1873–1889.* Manhattan, KS: Military Affairs/Aerospace Historian Publishing, 1978.

Altschuler, Glenn C. *Andrew D. White: Educator, Historian, Diplomat.* Ithaca: Cornell University Press, 1979.

Armstrong, William. *E. L. Godkin and American Foreign Policy, 1865–1900* (New York: Bookmen, 1957).

Bannister, Robert C. *Social Darwinism: Science and Myth in Anglo-American Thought.* Bloomington: University of Indiana Press, 1974.

Barrows, Chester L. *William M. Evarts: Lawyer, Diplomat, Statesman.* Chapel Hill: University of North Carolina Press, 1941.

Beach, Edward L., II. *The United States Navy.* Boston: Houghton Mifflin, 1986.

Beale, Howard K. *Theodore Roosevelt and the Rise of America to World Power.* Baltimore: The Johns Hopkins University Press, 1956.

Beard, Charles Austin. *The Navy, Defense or Portent?* New York: Harper, 1932.

Beisner, Robert. *From Old Diplomacy to New.* New York: Crowell, 1975.

————. *Twelve Against Empire: The Anti-Imperialists of 1898.* New York: McGraw Hill, 1968.

Bemis, Samuel Flagg. *American Secretaries of State.* New York: Alfred Knopf, 1928.

————. *Diplomatic History of the United States.* New York: Holt, 2d ed., 1942; 4th ed., 1955.

Blouet, Brian W. *Sir Halford Mackinder.* College Station: Texas A&M University Press, 1987.

Blum, John M. *The Republican Roosevelt.* Cambridge: Harvard University Press, 1954.

Bourne, Kenneth. *Britain and the Balance of Power in North America, 1815–1908.* Berkeley: University of California Press, 1967.

Bradford, James C. *Captains of the Old Steam Navy: Makers of the American Naval Tradition.* Annapolis: Naval Institute Press, 1986.

Braisted, William R. *United States Navy in the Pacific, 1897–1909.* Austin: University of Texas Press, 1958.

————. *United States Navy in the Pacific, 1909–1922.* Austin: University of Texas Press, 1971.

Brock, Peter. *Pacifism in the United States from the Colonial Era to the First World War.* Princeton: Princeton University Press, 1968.

Brodie, Bernard. *A Guide to Naval Strategy.* 2d ed., Princeton: Princeton University Press, 1959.

————. *Sea Power in the Machine Age.* Princeton: Princeton University Press, 1943

Browning, Robert S. *Two If By Sea: The Development of American Coastal Defense Policy.* Westport, CT: Greenwood Press, 1983.

Bryan, Edwin Horace. *American Polynesia and the Hawaiian Chain.* Honolulu: Tongg, 1942.

Bryant, Samuel W. *The Sea and the States: A Maritime History of the American People.* New York: Crowell, 1947, 1967.

Bryson, Thomas A. *Tars, Turks and Tankers: The Role of the United States Navy in the Middle East 1800–1979.* Metuchen, NJ: Scarecrow Press, 1977.

Burton, David. *Theodore Roosevelt: Confident Imperialist.* Philadelphia: University of Pennsylvania Press, 1969.

Bywater, Hector. *Sea-Power in the Pacific: A Study of the American-Japanese Naval Problem.* New York: Arno Press, 1970; reprint of Boston: Houghton Mifflin, 1921.

Callahan, James M. *American Relations in the Pacific and Far East 1789–1900.* New York: Praeger, 1969.

Cashman, Sean. *American in the Gilded Age.* New York: New York University Press, 1988.

Caswell, John E. *Arctic Frontiers: U.S. Exploration in the Far North.* Norman: University of Oklahoma Press, 1956.

Chace, James, and Caleb Carr. *American Invulnerable: The Quest for Absolute Security from 1812 to Star Wars.* New York: Summit, 1988.

Challener, Richard D. *Admirals, Generals, and American Foreign Policy, 1898–1914.* Princeton: Princeton University Press, 1973.

Chisolm, Lawrence W. *Fenollosa: The Far East and American Culture.* New Haven: Yale University Press, 1963.

Clinard, Outten J. *Japan's Influence on American Naval Power, 1897–1917.* Berkeley: University of California Press, 1947.

Coles, Harry L. *The War of 1812.* Chicago: University of Chicago Press, 1965.

Coletta, Paolo E., ed. *American Secretaries of the Navy.* Annapolis: Naval Institute Press, 1980.

————. *The American Naval Heritage in Brief.* Lanham, MD: The University Press of America, 1980.

————, ed., and K. Jack Bauer, assoc. ed. *United States Navy and Marine Corps Bases.* 2 vols. Westport, CT: Greenwood Press, 1985.

Combs, Jerald. *American Diplomatic History, Two Centuries of Changing Interpretations.* Berkeley: University of California Press, 1983.

Conkin, Paul, and John Higham, eds. *New Directions in Intellectual History.* Baltimore: The Johns Hopkins University Press, 1979.

Conway's All the World's Fighting Ships, 1860–1905. Edited by Roger Chesneau. London: Conway Maritime Press, 1979.

Coogan, John W. *The End of Neutrality: The United States, Britain, and Maritime Rights, 1899–1915.* Ithaca: Cornell University Press, 1981.

Cooling, Benjamin Franklin, III. *Benjamin Franklin Tracy: Father of the Modern American Fighting Navy.* Hamden, CT: Archon, 1973.

————. *Gray Steel and Blue Water Navy: The Formative Years of America's Military Industrial Complex, 1881–1917.* Hamden, CT: Archon, 1979.

Curti, Merle. *The American Peace Crusade, 1815–1860.* New York: Octagon Books, 1929; reprint 1965.

————. *Growth of American Thought,* 3d ed. New York: Harper and Row, 1964.

————. *Peace or War: The American Struggle, 1636–1936.* New York: Norton, 1936.

Darby, Phillip. *Three Faces of Imperialism: British and American Approaches to Asia and Africa, 1870–1970.* New Haven: Yale University Press, 1987.

Davis, George T. *Navy Second to None: The Development of Modern American Naval Policy.* New York: Harcourt, Brace, 1940.

Debebrata, Sen. *Basic Principles of Geopolitics and History.* Delhi: Concept, 1975.

Dennett, Tyler. *Americans in Eastern Asia.* New York: Macmillan, 1922, 1979.

Devine, Michael J. *John W. Foster: Politics and Diplomacy in the Imperial Era, 1873–1917.* Athens: Ohio University Press, 1980.

Dobson, John A. *America's Ascent: The US becomes a Great Power 1880–1914.* DeKalb: Northern Illinois University Press, 1978.

Dorwart, Jeffrey. *Office of Naval Intelligence: The Birth of America's First Intelligence Agency, 1865–1918.* Annapolis: Naval Institute Press, 1979.

Drake, Frederick. *Empire of the Seas: A Biography of Rear Admiral Robert Wilson Shufeldt, U.S.N..* Honolulu: University of Hawaii Press, 1984.

Dupree, A. Hunter. *Science in the Federal Government: A History of Policies and Activities to 1940.* Cambridge: The Belknap Press of Harvard University Press, 1957.

Earle, Edward Mead, ed. *The Makers of Modern Strategy: Military Thought from Machiavelli to Hitler.* Princeton: Princeton University Press, 1943.

Eggert, Gerald G. *Richard Olney: Evolution of a Statesman.* University Park: Pennsylvania State University Press, 1974.

Elson, Ruth Miller. *Guardians of Tradition: American Schoolbooks in the Nineteenth Century.* Lincoln: University of Nebraska Press, 1964.

———. *Myths and Mores in American Best Sellers, 1865–1965.* New York: Garland, 1985.

Fairbank, John K. *The United States and China.* Cambridge: Harvard University Press, 1979.

Gardner, Lloyd C., Walter LaFeber, and Thomas J. McCormick. *Creation of the American Empire.* 2d ed. Chicago: Rand, McNally, 1976.

Gay, James Thomas. *American Fur Seal Diplomacy.* American University Studies, series 9, History, vol. 31. New York: Peter Long, 1987.

Goldberg, Joyce. *The Baltimore Affair.* Lincoln: University of Nebraska Press, 1986.

Goode, James M. *Outdoor Sculpture of Washington, D.C.* Washington, DC: Smithsonian Institution, 1974.

Graff, Henry F. *American Imperialism and the Philippine Insurrection.* Boston: Little, Brown, 1969.

Grenville, J. A. S., and George B. Young. *Politics, Strategy and American Diplomacy 1873–1917.* New Haven: Yale University Press, 1966.

Griswald, A. Whitney. *The Far Eastern Policy of the United States.* New York: Harcourt Brace and World, 1938.

Hagan, Kenneth J. *American Gunboat Diplomacy and the Old Navy, 1877–1889.* Westport, CT: Greenwood Press, 1973.

———. *In War and Peace: Interpretations of American Naval History, 1775–1978.* 2d ed. Westport, CT: Greenwood Press, 1984.

———. *This People's Navy: The Making of American Sea Power.* New York: Free Press, 1991.

Hamilton, Mark. *The Nation and the Navy: Methods and Organization of British Naval Propaganda, 1889–1914.* New York: Garland, 1986.

Hanlon, David L. *Upon a Stone Altar: A History of the Island of a Pohnpei to 1890.* Honolulu: University of Hawaii Press, 1988.

Harrington, Fred Harvey. *God, Mammon, and the Japanese: Dr. Horace Allen and Korean-American Relations, 1884–1945.* Madison: University of Wisconsin Press, 1961.

Harris, Brayton. *Age of the Batleship.* New York: Franklin Watts, 1965.

Harrod, Frederick S. *Manning the New Navy.* Westport, CT: Greenwood Press, 1978.

Hattendorf, John, and Robert S. Jordan, eds. *Maritime Strategy and the Balance of Power: Britain and America in the Twentieth Century.* New York: St. Martin's Press, 1989.

———, et al. *Sailors and Scholars: The Centennial History of the U.S. Naval War College.* Newport: Naval War College Press, 1984.

Hattendorf, John, editor. *The Influence of History on Mahan.* Newport: Naval War College Press, 1991.

Hayes, James G. *Robert E. Peary: A Record of His Explorations 1886–1909.* London: G. Richards and H. Toumin, 1929.

Healy, David. *US Expansionism: The Imperialist Urge of the 1890s.* Madison: University of Wisconsin Press, 1970.

Henson, Curtis T., Jr. *Commissioners and Commodores: The East India Squadron and American Diplomacy in China.* Tuscaloosa: University of Alabama Press, 1982.

Herrick, Walter. *American Naval Revolution.* Baton Rouge: Louisiana State University Press, 1966.

Higham, Robin, ed. *Intervention or Abstention: The Dilemma of American Foreign Policy.* Lexington: University of Kentucky Press, 1975.

Himmelfarb, Gertrude. *The New History and the Old.* Cambridge: Harvard University Press, 1987.

Hofstadter, Richard. *Social Darwinism in American Thought.* New York: George Braziller, 1959.

Hooper, Edwin. *United States Naval Power in a Changing World.* New York: Praeger, 1988.

Horsman, Reginald. *The War of 1812.* New York: Alfred Knopf, 1964.

Hovgaard, William. *Modern History of Warships: Comprising a Discussion of Present Standpoint and Recent War Experiences. . . .* New York: Spon and Chamberlain, 1920.

Howard, Michael. *The Lessons of History.* New Haven: Yale University Press, 1991.

———. *War in European History.* New York: Oxford University Press, 1976.

Howard, Michael, ed. *Restraints on War: Studies in the Limitation of Armed Conflict.* New York: Oxford University Press, 1979.

Howard, Michael, George Andreopoulos, and Mark Shulman, eds., *The Laws of War: Constraints on Warfare in the Western World.* New Haven: Yale University Press, 1994.

Hoyt, Edwin P. *The Lonely Ships: The Life and Death of the U.S. Asiatic Fleet.* New York: David McKay, 1976.

Hughes, Wayne P. *Fleet Tactics: Theory and Practice.* Annapolis: Naval Institute Press, 1986.

Hunt, Michael. *Ideology and US Foreign Policy.* New Haven: Yale University Press, 1987.

Hunt, Thomas *The Life of William H. Hunt.* Brattleboro: E. L. Hildreth, 1922.

Huntington, Samuel P. *The Soldier and the State.* Cambridge: Harvard University Press, 1957.

Huxley, T. H. *The Struggle for Existence in Human Society.* (1888) In *Mutual Aid,* edited by P. A. Kropotkin. Boston: Extending Horizons Books, 1955.

Hyatt, A. M. J. *Dreadnought to Polaris: Maritime Strategy Since Mahan.* Annapolis: Naval Institute Press, 1973.

Iriye, Akira. *Across the Pacific: An Inner History of American–East-Asian Relations.* New York: Harbinger, 1967.

———. *From Nationalism to Internationalism.* Boston: Routledge and Kegan Paul, 1972.

———. *Pacific Estrangement: Japanese and American Expansion, 1897–1911.* Cambridge: Harvard University Press, 1972.

———, ed. *Mutual Images.* Cambridge: Harvard University Press, 1975.

Ishii, Kikuro. *Diplomatic Commentaries.* Edited by William R. Langer. Baltimore: Johns Hopkins University Press, 1936.

Isaacs, Harold. *Scratches on Our Minds: American Images of China and India.* New York: J. Day, 1958.

Johnson, Robert E. *Far China Station: The U.S. Navy in Asian Waters 1800–1898.* Annapolis: Naval Institute Press, 1979.

———. *Thence Round Cape Horn: The Story of United States Naval Forces on Pacific Station, 1818–1923.* Annapolis: Naval Institute Press, 1963.

Juergens, George. *Joseph Pulitzer and the New York World.* Princeton: Princeton University Press, 1966.

Karsten, Peter. *Naval Aristocracy: The Golden Age of Annapolis and the Emergence of Modern American Navalism.* New York: Free Press, 1972.

Kaufmann, William W. *A Thoroughly Efficient Navy.* Washington, DC: Brookings Institution, 1987.

Kearns, Gerry. *Closed Space and Political Practice: Frederick Jackson Turner and Halford Mackinder.* Liverpool Papers in Human Geography. Working Paper 5. University of Liverpool, 1981.

Keegan, John. *Price of Admiralty.* New York: Viking Press, 1989.

Kennedy, Paul M., *Realities behind Diplomacy.* London: Allen and Unwin, 1981.

———. *Rise and Fall of British Naval Mastery.* 2d ed. London: Macmillan, 1983.

———. *Rise and Fall of the Great Powers.* New York: Random House, 1987.

———. *Rise of the Anglo-German Antagonism, 1860–1914.* Boston: Allen and Unwin, 1980.

———. *Samoan Tangle.* St. Lucia: University of Queensland Press, 1974.

———. *Strategy and Diplomacy 1870–1914.* London: Allen and Unwin, 1983.

———, ed. *Grand Strategies in War and Peace.* New Haven: Yale University Press, 1991.

———, ed. *War Plans of the Great Powers 1880–1914.* Boston: Allen and Unwin, 1979.

Knox, Dudley W. *Eclipse of American Naval Power.* New York: American Army and Navy Journal, 1922.

————. *A History of the United States Navy.* 2d ed. New York: Putnam's, 1948.

LaFeber, Walter. *American Age: The United States Foreign Relations at Home and Abroad since 1750.* New York: W. W. Norton, 1989.

————. *Inevitable Revolutions.* New York: W. W. Norton, 1985.

————. *The New Empire: An Interpretation of American Expansion: 1860–1898.* Ithaca: Cornell University Press, 1963.

Lancaster, Clay. *The Japanese Influence in American Architecture.* New York: Abbeville Press, 1983.

Langer, William. *Diplomacy of Imperialism.* New York: Knopf, 1935.

Langley, Harold. *Social Reform in the United Sates Navy, 1798–1865.* Champaign-Urbana: University of Illinois Press, 1967.

Leopold, Richard. *Elihu Root and the Conservative Tradition.* Boston: Little, Brown, 1954.

————. *Growth of American Foreign Policy.* New York: Knopf, 1962.

Livezey, William. *Mahan on Sea Power.* Norman: University of Oklahoma Press, 1947.

Long, David F. *Gold Braid and Foreign Relations: Diplomatic Activities of U.S. Naval Officers 1798–1883.* Annapolis: Naval Institute Press, 1988.

Loomis, Albertine. *For Whom Are the Stars?* Honolulu: University of Hawaii Press, 1976.

Louis, William R., ed. *Imperialism: The Robinson and Gallagher Controversey.* New York: New Viewpoints, 1976.

Love, Robert William, ed. *Changing Interpretations and New Sources in Naval History.* New York: Garland, 1980.

Lowe, James Y. *Geopolitics and War: Mackinder's Philosophy of Power.* Washington, DC: University Press of America, 1981.

Luttwak, Edward. *On the Meaning of Victory.* New York: Simon and Schuster, 1986.

McCormack, Thomas. *China Market: America's Quest for an Informal Empire 1893–1901.* Chicago: Quadrangle, 1967.

McCullough, David. *Path between the Seas.* New York: Simon and Schuster, 1977.

MacKenzie, John M. *Imperialism and Popular Culture.* London: Manchester University Press, 1986.

Marchand, Roland. *The American Peace Movement.* Princeton: Princeton University Press, 1972.

Marder, Arthur J. *Anatomy of British Sea Power: A History of British Naval Policy in the Pre-Dreadnought Era, 1880–1905.* New York: Knopf, 1940; repr. Hamden, CT: Archon Books, 1964.

————. *From the Dread Nought to Scapa Flow.* 2d ed. New York: Oxford University Press, 1978.

Masterson, Daniel M. *Naval History: The Sixth Symposium of the U.S. Naval Academy.* Wilmington: Scholarly Resources, 1987.

May, Ernest. *American Imperialism: A Speculative Essay.* New York: Atheneum Press, 1968.

————. *Imperial Democracy: The Emergence of America as a Great Power.* New York: Harper and Row, 1961.

Merrill, Horace. *Bourbon Leader: Grover Cleveland and the Democratic Party.* Boston: Little, Brown, 1957.

Miller, Nathan. *United States Navy: An Illustrated History.* New York: American Heritage, 1977.

Millett, Allen R. *Semper Fidelis: The History of the United States Marine Corps.* New York: Free Press, 1980.

————, and Peter Maslowski. *For the Common Defense.* New York: Free Press, 1984; 2d ed., 1994.

Millis, Walter. *Arms and Men: A Study in American Military History.* New Brunswick: Rutgers University Press, 1935, repr. 1984.

————. *The Martial Spirit: A Study of Our War with Spain.* New York: Houghton Mifflin, 1931; repr. New York: Arno Press, 1979.

Modelski, George. *Long Cycles in World Politics.* Seattle: University of Washington Press, 1987.

————, and William R. Thompson. *Seapower in Global Politics, 1494–1993.* Seattle: University of Washington Press, 1988.

Morgan, Howard Wayne. *America's Road to Empire: The War with Spain and Overseas Expansion.* New York: Wiley, 1965.

Morison, Elting E. *Admirals Sims and the Modern American Navy.* New York: Houghton Mifflin, 1942.

Morris, Edmund. *The Rise of Theodore Roosevelt.* New York: Ballantine, 1979.

Mott, Frank Luther. *History of American Magazines.* Cambridge: Harvard University Press, 1957.

Musicant, Ivan. *U.S. Armored Cruisers.* Annapolis: Naval Institute Press, 1985.

Neeser, Robert W. *American Naval Songs and Ballads.* New Haven: Yale University Press, 1938.

Nelson, Dennis Denmark. *Integration of the Negro into the U.S. Navy.* New York: Farrar, Straus and Young, 1951.

Neumann, William. *America Encounters Japan: From Perry to MacArthur.* Baltimore: The Johns Hopkins University Press, 1963.

Nevins, Allen. *Abram S. Hewitt, with some account of Peter Cooper.* New York: Harper and Brothers, 1935.

————. *Grover Cleveland: A Study in Courage.* New York: Dodd, Mead, 1958.

O'Connell, Robert. *Of Arms and Men: A History of War, Weapons, and Aggression.* New York: Oxford University Press, 1989.

————. *Sacred Vessels: The Cult of the Battleship and the Rise of the U.S. Navy.* Boulder: Westview Press, 1991.

O'Gara, Gordon C. *Theodore Roosevelt and the Rise of the American Navy.* Princeton: Princeton University Press, 1943.

Oliver, Roland, and Anthony Atmore. *Africa Since 1800.* Cambridge: Cambridge University Press, 1972.

Osborne, Thomas J. *"Empire Can Wait": American Opposition to Hawaiian Annexation, 1893–1898.* Kent: The Kent State University Press, 1981.

O'Toole, G. J. A. *The Spanish War: An American Epic.* New York: W. W. Norton, 1984.

Paret, Peter. *Makers of Modern Strategy: From Machiavelli to the Nuclear Age.* Princeton: Princeton University Press, 1986.

Patterson, David Sands. *Toward a Warless World: The Travail of the American Peace Movement 1887–1914.* Bloomington: University of Indiana Press, 1976.

Paullin, Charles O. *Diplomatic Negotiations of American Naval Officers 1778–1883.* Baltimore: The Johns Hopkins University Press, 1912, repr. 1967.

————. *Paullin's History of Naval Administration, 1775–1911.* Annapolis: Naval Institute Press, 1968.

Perkins, Dexter. *The Monroe Doctrine 1867–1907.* Cambridge: Harvard University Press, 1927.

Perret, Geoffrey. *A Country Made by War: From the Revolution to Vietnam—The Story of America's Rise to Power.* New York: Random House, 1989.

Pletcher, David M. *The Awkward Years.* Columbia: University of Missouri Press, 1961.

Pomeroy, Earl S. *Pacific Outpost: American Strategy in Guam and Micronesia.* Palo Alto: Stanford University Press, 1951.

Potter, E. B. and C. W. Nimitz. *Sea Power: A Naval History.* 2d ed. Annapolis: Naval Institute Press, 1981.

Pratt, Julius W. *Expansionists of 1898: The Acquisition of Hawaii and the Spanish Islands.* Baltimore: The Johns Hopkins University Press, 1936; Chicago: Quadrangle Reprint, 1964.

Preston, Richard, S. Wise, and A. Roland. *Men in Arms: A History of Warfare and Its Interrelationships with Western Society.* 5th ed. New York: Holt, Rinehart, and Winston, 1991.

Prosser, William Farrand. *History of Puget Sound Country.* New York: Lewis, 1903.

Pugh, Philip. *The Cost of Sea Power: The Influence of Money on Naval Affairs from 1815 to the Present Day.* London: Conway Maritime Press, 1986.

Puleston, William D. *Mahan: The Life and Work of Captain Alfred Thayer Mahan, USN.* New Haven: Yale University Press, 1939.

Rappaport, Armin. *The Navy League of the United States.* Detroit: Wayne State University Press, 1962.

Reilly, John, and Robert L. Scheina. *American Battleships, 1886–1923.* Annapolis: Naval Institute Press, 1973.

Richmond, Herbert. *Naval Strategy.* London: Ernst Benn, 1930.

Robb, Janet. *Primrose League 1883–1906.* New York: Columbia University Press, 1942.

Robinson, Ronald, Jack Gallagher, and Alice Denny. *Africa and the Victorians.* Cambridge: Cambridge University Press, 1961.

Roland, Alex. *Underwater Warfare in the Age of Sail.* Bloomington: Indiana University Press, 1977.

Ropp, Theodore. *The Making of A Modern Navy.* Edited by S. S. Roberts. Annapolis: Naval Institute Press, 1986.

Russ, William Adam, Jr. *The Hawaiian Revolution (1893–1894).* Selinsgrove, PA: The Susquehanna University Press, 1959.

Russett, Bruce. *Trends in World Politics.* New York: Macmillan, 1965.

Russett, Cynthia Eagle. *Darwin in America: The Intellectual Response, 1865–1912.* San Francisco: W. H. Freeman, 1976.

Rydell, Robert W. *All the World's a Fair.* Chicago: University of Chicago Press, 1984.

Said, Edward. *Orientalism.* New York: Pantheon Books, 1975.

Sater, William F. *Chile and the War of the Pacific.* Lincoln: University of Nebraska Press, 1986.

Schurman, Donald M. *The Education of a Navy: Development of British Naval Strategic Thought 1867–1914.* Chicago: University of Chicago Press, 1965.

Seager, Robert. *Alfred Thayer Mahan, The Man and His Letters.* Annapolis: Naval Institute Press, 1977.

Seawall, Molly Elliot. *Twelve Naval Captains: Being a Record of Certain Americans who made Themselves Immortal.* New York: Scribner's Son, 1897.

Semmel, Bernard. *Liberalism and Naval Strategy: Ideology, Interest, and Sea Power During Pax Britannica.* Boston: Allen and Unwin, 1986.

Sherry, Michael. *Rise of American Air Power: The Creation of Armageddon.* New Haven: Yale University Press, 1987.

Simonds, Frank H., and Brooks Emeny. *The Great Powers in World Politics: International Relations and Economic Nationalism.* New York: American Book Co., 1935, 1937.

Simpson, B. Mitchell. *War, Strategy, and Maritime Power.* New Brunswick: Rutgers University Press, 1977.

Smith, Henry Nash. *Democracy and the Novel.* New York: Oxford University Press, 1978.

Spector, Ronald. *Admiral of the New Empire.* Baton Rouge: Louisiana State University Press, 1974; repr. Columbia: University of South Carolina Press, 1988.

Spence, Jonathan. *To Change China: Western Advisors in China 1620–1960.* Boston: Little, Brown, 1969.

———. *The Search for Modern China.* New York: W. W. Norton, 1990.

Sprout, Harold, and Margaret Sprout. *The Rise of American Naval Power, 1776–1918.* Princeton: Princeton University Press, 1939, repr. 1966.

Spykeman, Nicholas. *America's Strategy in World Politics.* New York: Harcourt, Brace, 1942.

Steinberg, Jonathan. *Yesterday's Deterrent: Tirpitz and the Birth of the German Battle Fleet.* London: Macmillan, 1965.

Still, William N. *American Sea Power in the Old World: The United States Navy in European and Near Eastern Waters, 1865–1917.* Westport, CT: Greenwood, 1980.

Sullivan, Mark. *Our Times.* Vols. 1, 2, 3. New York: Scribner's, 1926–35.

Sumida, Jon T. *In Defence of Naval Supremacy: Finance, Technology, and British Naval Policy, 1889–1914.* Boston: Unwin Hyman, 1989.

Swann, Leonard Alexander. *John Roach: Maritime Entrepreneur.* Annapolis: Naval Institute Press, 1965.

Sweetman, Jack. *American Naval History.* Annapolis: Naval Institute Press, 1984.

Symonds, Craig L. *Navalists and Anti-Navalists: The Naval Policy Debate in the United States, 1785–1827.* Newark: University of Delaware Press, 1980.

———, ed. *New Aspects of Naval History.* Annapolis: Naval Institute Press, 1981.

Taylor, Charles Carlisle. *The Life of Admiral Mahan, Naval Philosopher, Rear-admiral United States Navy.* New York: George H. Doran Co., 1920.

Todd, Alden. *Abandoned: The Story of the Greely Expedition of 1881–1884.* New York: McGraw Hill, 1961.

Trask, David. *The War with Spain in 1898*. New York: Macmillan, 1981.

Trefouse, Hans Louis. *Carl Schurz, a Biography*. Knoxville: University of Tennessee Press, 1982.

Trueblood, Benjamin Franklin. *Studies in Quaker Pacifism*. Philadelphia: Friends Peace Committee, 1934.

Turk, Richard. *The Ambiguous Relationship: Theodore Roosevelt and Alfred Thayer Mahan*. Westport, CT: Greenwood Press, 1987.

Van Alstyne, Richard W. *The United States in East Asia*. New York: W. W. Norton, 1973.

Varg, Paul. *The Making of a Myth: The United States and China*. East Lansing: Michigan State University Press, 1968.

―――. *Missionaries, Chinese and Diplomats: The American Protest and Missionary Movement in China, 1890–1952*. Princeton: Princeton University Press, 1958.

―――. *Open Door Diplomat: The Life of W. W. Rockhill*. Urbana: University of Illinois Press, 1952.

Wallenstein, Peter. *Peace Research: Achievements and Challenges*. Boulder, CO: Westview Press, 1988.

Warren, Gordon H. *Fountain of Discontent: The Trent Affair and Freedom of the Seas*. Boston: Northeastern University Press, 1981.

Weigley, Russell. *American Way of War*. Bloomington: Indiana University Press, 1977.

Weinberg, Albert K. *Manifest Destiny: A Study of Nationalist Expansion in American History*. Baltimore: The Johns Hopkins University Press, 1935.

Welch, Richard E., Jr. *George Frisbie Hoar and the Half-Breed Republicans*. Cambridge: Harvard University Press, 1971.

West, Richard Sedgewick. *Admirals of the American Empire*. Westport, CT: Greenwood Press, 1971.

Westerfield, H. Bradford. *Instruments of America's Foreign Policy*. New York: Crowell, 1963.

White, William C. *A History of Military Music in America*. New York: Exposition Press, 1944.

Whitney, Edson L. *The American Peace Society: A Centennial History*. Washington, DC: American Peace Society, 1929.

Widenor, William C. *Henry Cabot Lodge and the Search for an American Foreign Policy*. Berkeley: University of California Press, 1980.

Wiebe, Robert. *Search for Order, 1877–1920*. New York: Hill and Wang, 1967.

Wilkins, Myra. *The Emergence of Multinational Enterprise: American Business Abroad from the Colonial Era to 1914*. Cambridge: Harvard University Press, 1970.

Williams, William Appleman. *Contours in American History*. Cleveland: World Publishing Co., 1961; repr. Chicago: Quadrangle Press, 1966.

―――. *The Roots of the Modern American Empire*. New York: Random House, 1969.

―――. *Tragedy of American Diplomacy*. New York: Dell, 1962.

Woodruff, William. *America's Impact on the World*. London: Macmillan, 1975.

Young, Marilyn. *Rhetoric of Empire: American China Policy, 1895–1901*. Cambridge: Harvard University Press, 1968.

Zogbaum, Rufus Fairchild, II. *From Sail to Saratoga*. Rome: n.p., 1961.

―――――――――― Selected Theses and Dissertations ――――――――――

Allard, Dean. "The Influence of the U.S. Navy upon the American Steel Industry." MA thesis, Georgetown University, 1959.

Brandt, Walter. "Steel and the New Navy, 1882–1895." Ph.D. diss., University of Wisconsin, 1920.

Brown, Stephen Dechman. "The Power of Influence in United States-Chilean Relations." Ph.D. diss., University of Wisconsin-Madison, 1983.

Buhl, Lance. "The Smooth Water Navy: American Naval Policy and Politics, 1865–1877." Ph.D. diss., Harvard University, 1968.

Drake, Frederick. "'The Empire of the Seas': A Biography of Robert W. Shufeldt." Ph.D. diss., Cornell University, 1970.

Erlich, Paul Mark. "The Clothes of Men: Ponape Island and German Colonial Rule, 1899–1918." Ph.D. diss., State University of New York at Stony Brook, 1978.

Hanley, John Thomas. "On Wargaming: A Critique of Strategic Operational Gaming." Ph.D. diss., Yale University, Department of Operations Research/Management Science, 1991.

Lambert, Nicholas A. "The Influence of the Submarine upon Naval Strategy, 1898–1914." D.Phil. diss., University of Cambridge, 1992.

McBride, William M. "The Rise and Fall of Strategic Technology: The American Battleship from Santiago Bay to Pearl Harbor, 1898–1941." Ph.D. diss., The Johns Hopkins University, 1989.

Prefer, Nathan. "Uncertain Mission: The Role of the United States Marine Corps in National Defense." Ph.D. diss., City University of New York, 1983.

Shulman, Mark Russell. "The Emergence of American Sea Power: Politics and the Creation of U.S. Naval Strategy, 1882–1893." Ph.D. diss., University of California, Berkeley, 1990.

Spector, Ronald. "Professors at War: The U.S. Naval War College and the Modern American Navy." Ph.D. diss., Yale University, 1967.

Thomas, Gerald. "William Leahy: The Imperial Years." Ph.D. diss., Yale University, 1973.

Turk, Richard. "Strategy and Foreign Policy: The United States Navy in the Caribbean, 1865–1913." MA thesis, Tufts University, 1968.

Wicks, Daniel Howard. "New Navy and New Empire: The Life and Times of John Grimes Walker." Ph.D. diss., University of California, Berkeley, 1979.

―――――――――― Selected Articles and Chapters ――――――――――

Abrams, Richard M. "United States Intervention Abroad: The First Quarter Century." *American Historical Review,* 79, no.1 (February 1974): 72–102.

Albion, Robert G. "The Naval Affairs Committees, 1816–1947." U.S. Naval Institute *Proceedings,* 78, no. 11 (1952): 1226–37.

Campbell, C. S., Jr. "The Anglo-American Crisis in the Bering Sea 1890–1891." *Mississippi Valley Historical Review [Journal of American History]* 48 (December 1961): 393–414.

Goodrich, Caspar F. "In Memoriam: Stephen Bleecker Luce, Rear Admiral United States Navy." New York: Naval History Society, 1919.

Grenville, J. A. S. "American Naval Preparations for War with Spain, 1896–1898." *Journal of American Studies,* 2 (April 1968): 33–47.

———. "Diplomacy and War Plans in the United States, 1890–1917." In *The War Plans of the Great Powers, 1880–1914,* edited by Paul M. Kennedy. Boston: Allen and Unwin, 1979.

Hagan, Kenneth, and Mark R. Shulman. "Mahan Plus One Hundred: The Current State of American Naval History." In *Ubi Sumus: The State of Naval and Maritime History,* edited by John B. Hattendorf. Newport: Naval War College Press, 1994.

Hart, Kevin R. "Towards a Citizen Sailor: The History of the Naval Militia Movement, 1888–1898." *The American Neptune,* 33 (October 1973).

Hattendorf, John. "Alfred Thayer Mahan and his Strategic Thought." In *Maritime Strategy and the Balance of Power,* edited by Hattendorf and Robert S. Jordan. New York: St. Martin's Press, 1989.

———. "The Anglo-American Way in Maritime Strategy." *Naval War College Review,* 43, no. 1, seq. 329 (1990): 90–99.

Karsten, Peter. "The Nature of 'Influence': Roosevelt, Mahan and the Concept of Sea Power." *American Quarterly,* 23, no. 4 (1971): 585–600.

LaFeber, Walter. "A Note on the 'Mercantilist Imperialism' of Alfred Thayer Mahan." *Mississippi Valley Historical Review* [*Journal of American History*], 48, no. 4 (1962): 674–85.

Roberts, Stephen S. "An Indicator of Informal Empire: Patterns of U.S. Navy Cruising on Overseas Stations, 1869–1897." In *New Aspects in Naval History,* edited by Craig L. Symonds. Annapolis: Naval Institute Press, 1981.

Russett, Bruce. "Peace Research, Complex Causation, and the Causes of War." In *Peace Research: Achievements and Challenges,* edited by Peter Wallensteen. Boulder: Westview, 1988.

Seager, Robert. "Ten Years before Mahan: The Unofficial Case for the New Navy." *Mississippi Valley Historical Review* [*Journal of American History*], 40, no. 3 (1953): 491–512.

Shulman, Mark R. "The Influence of History upon Sea Power: The Navalist Reinterpretation of the War of 1812." *Journal of Military History,* 56, no. 2 (1992): 183–205.

———. "The Influence of Mahan upon Sea Power." *Reviews in American History,* December 1991, 522–27.

———. "The Rise and Fall of American Naval Intelligence, 1882–1917." *Intelligence and National Security,* 8, no. 2 (1993): 214–26.

———, and George Miles. "With Perry at Sea: The United States Navy and American Expansion." New Haven: Yale University Library, 1993.

Spector, Ronald. "The Triumph of Professional Ideology: The U.S. Navy in the 1890s." In *In War and Peace,* edited by K. J. Hagan. Wesport: Greenwood, 1984.

Winks, Robin W. "The American Struggle with 'Imperialism': How Words Frighten." In *The American Identity: Fusion and Fragmentation,* edited by Robert Kroes. Amsterdam: Amerika Instituut, 1980.

———————————— Manuscript Collections ————————————

Citations below and in the text are from the following libraries and archives: Library of Congress Manuscripts Division (LC), Naval War College Archives (NWC), Yale University Manuscripts and Archives (Yale M. and A.) and Beinecke Rare Books, University of California at Berkeley (UCB), Wisconsin State Historical Center at Madison (WSHC), Harvard University Houghton Manuscript Library and Baker Library at Harvard Business School, New York Public Library Manuscripts Division at Main Branch (NYPL), and the Naval Historical Center. A listing of the major collections cited follows:

Adams, Charles Francis junior, at LC; Arthur, Chester Alan, at LC; Belknap, Charles, at NWC; Caldwell, Harry H., at NWC; Campbell-Smith, Roy, at NWC; Chandler, Ralph, at Harvard Baker Library; Chandler, William E., at LC; Cleveland, Grover, at LC; Laning, Harris B., at NWC; Leahy, William, at WSHC; Little, McCarthy, at NWC; Lowe, John, at LC; Luce, Stephen B., at NWC and LC; Mahan, Alfred Thayer, at NWC, Harvard Houghton, LC, Yale Beinecke; Neeser, Robert Wilden, at Yale M. and A.; Peabody, Endicott, at Harvard Houghton; Porter, David Dixon, at LC; Pratt, William V., at NWC; Remey, George C., at NWC; Rodgers, John, at LC; Roosevelt, Theodore, at LC; Schurz, Carl, at LC; Shufeldt, Robert Wilson, at LC, Harvard Houghton, NYPL; Sims, William Sowden, at NWC; Smith, Roy Campbell, at NWC; Stockton, Charles H., at NWC; Taylor, Henry Clay, at NWC; Todd, David Peck, at Yale M. and A.; Tracy, Benjamin Franklin, at NWC; Whitney, William C., at LC.

———————————— Government Papers ————————————

CONGRESSIONAL PUBLICATIONS

Individual citations appear in end notes; the following is a general guide to the most useful Congressional papers.

Congressional Record, 1880–1898.
Historical Statistics of the United States. Washington, DC: Government Printing Office, 1975.
Statutes at Large, 1787–1898.

DEPARTMENT OF THE NAVY PUBLICATIONS

The National Archives and Records Administration houses most of the official records of the navy. The relevant sources are in Record Groups 38 and 45, the following department publications are cited. In addition to the papers in those archives (as cited in notes) and the government publications not ascribed to particular departments or branches (as cited in notes and in the above primary source lists), the following Navy Department publications have been cited.

Annual Register of the Commissioned, Warrant, and Volunteer Officers of the Navy of the United States. Washington, DC: Government Printing Office, 1882–1898.

Annual Report of the Secretary of the Navy. Washington, DC: Government Printing Office, 1882–1898.

Compilation of Laws Relating to the Navy. Washington, DC: Government Printing Office, 1883.

General Orders. Washington, DC: Government Printing Office.

"International Columbian Naval Rendez-Vous and Review of 1893 and Naval Maneuvers of 1892." Washington, DC: Government Printing Office, 1893. Original in NARA, RG 38, item 141, appendix 7, volume 12.

Recent Naval Progress, Information from Abroad. War and Information Series. Washington, DC: Government Printing Office, 1882–1898.

Register of the U.S. Naval Academy. Washington, DC: Government Printing Office, 1882–1898.

Periodicals

For each of these periodicals, I have examined each available issue or its index for the time in which its publication overlapped with the period under examination, 1882–1893. Newspapers are the exception; I have examined some of them only on dates that were particularly relevant, such as during or directly after an appropriations debate.

American Neptune; Angel of Peace; Army and Navy Journal; Atlantic Monthly; Century; Chicago *Daily Tribune; Comfort;* Dawson (GA) *News; Frank Leslie's Illustrated Newspaper; Harper's Weekly* and *Monthly; Journal of the American Society of Naval Engineers; Ladies Home Journal;* Laramie (WY) *Boomerang; Naval War College Review;* New Haven *Evening Register;* New Orleans *Daily Picayune;* New York *Herald; New York Times;* New York *World; North American Review; Proceedings of the United States Naval Institute; Public Service Review; Puck;* San Francisco *Chronicle; Scientific American; United Service Review;* Virginia City (NV) *Territorial Enterprise; World Affairs; Youth's Companion.*

Index

233

About
—*the*—
Author

Mark Russell Shulman is a fellow at the National Strategy Information Center (NSIC) and of Georgetown University's Foreign Affairs Research Program. A graduate of Yale (B.A.), Oxford (M.St.), and the University of California–Berkeley (Ph.D.), he taught military history and strategy at Yale for several years before joining NSIC. He has been a research associate of the Naval War College's Advanced Research Department since 1989 and is also a consultant for the Department of Defense.

Dr. Shulman's articles on naval and strategic history have appeared in the *Journal of Military History, Intelligence and National Security,* and *MHQ: The Quarterly Journal of Military History.* He has contributed chapters to volumes on the state and future of naval and maritime history. With Sir Michael Howard and George Andreopoulos, he was coeditor of *The Laws of War: Constraints on Warfare in the West.* He also edited the forthcoming volume *An Admiral's Yarn: The Autobiography of Harris Laning.* He is currently writing a history of American national security policy. A resident of Washington, D.C., Dr. Shulman is an avid runner and hiker.